TRUST AND TRUSTWORT

TRUST AND TRUSTWORTHINESS

RUSSELL HARDIN

VOLUME IV IN THE RUSSELL SAGE FOUNDATION SERIES ON TRUST

Russell Sage Foundation • New York

The Russell Sage Foundation

The Russell Sage Foundation, one of the oldest of America's general purpose foundations, was established in 1907 by Mrs. Margaret Olivia Sage for "the improvement of social and living conditions in the United States." The Foundation seeks to fulfill this mandate by fostering the development and dissemination of knowledge about the country's political, social, and economic problems. While the Foundation endeavors to assure the accuracy and objectivity of each book it publishes, the conclusions and interpretations in Russell Sage Foundation publications are those of the authors and not of the Foundation, its Trustees, or its staff. Publication by Russell Sage, therefore, does not imply Foundation endorsement.

Library of Congress Cataloging-in-Publication Data

Hardin, Russell, 1940–
    Trust and trustworthiness / Russell Hardin.
      p. cm. — (The Russell Sage Foundation series on trust)
    Includes bibliographical references and index.
    ISBN 0-87154-342-7
    1. Trust.   2. Reliability.   3. Interpersonal relations.   I. Title.   II. Series.

BJ1500.T78 H37 2002
179'.9—dc21   2001040817

RUSSELL SAGE FOUNDATION
112 East 64th Street, New York, New York 10021
10 9 8 7 6 5 4 3 2 1

*For Robert Bonazzi and, in memoriam,
Elizabeth Griffin-Bonazzi*

The Russell Sage Foundation
Series on Trust

T HE RUSSELL SAGE Foundation Series on Trust examines the conceptual structure and the empirical basis of claims concerning the role of trust and trustworthiness in establishing and maintaining cooperative behavior in a wide variety of social, economic, and political contexts. The focus is on concepts, methods, and findings that will enrich social science and inform public policy.

The books in the series raise questions about how trust can be distinguished from other means of promoting cooperation and explore those analytic and empirical issues that advance our comprehension of the roles and limits of trust in social, political, and economic life. Because trust is at the core of understandings of social order from varied disciplinary perspectives, the series offers the best work of scholars from diverse backgrounds and, through the edited volumes, encourages engagement across disciplines and orientations. The goal of the series is to improve the current state of trust research by providing a clear theoretical account of the causal role of trust within given institutional, organizational, and interpersonal situations, developing sound measures of trust to test theoretical claims within relevant settings, and establishing some common ground among concerned scholars and policymakers.

Karen S. Cook
Russell Hardin
Margaret Levi

SERIES EDITORS

Previous Volumes in the Series

Contents

About the Author

Russell Hardin is professor of politics at New York University and professor of political science at Stanford University.

Acknowledgments

I wish to thank many people—friends, relatives, colleagues, and new, often one-time acquaintances—for discussions of trust. Included in this large crowd are Richard Arneson, David Blau, Karen Cook, Sven Feldmann, Claire Finckelstein, Joan Rothchild Hardin, Josh Hardin, Daniel Kahneman, Margaret Levi, Bernard Manin, Howard Margolis, Sue Martinelli-Fernandez, Victor Nee, John Orbell, Pasquale Pasquino, Susan Pharr, Alejandro Portes, Adam Przeworski, Robert Putnam, Jonathan Riley, Sarah Rosenfield, Andrei Shleifer, Duncan Snidal, Fritz Stern, Edna Ullmann-Margalit, Eric Wanner, Toshio Yamagishi, Richard Zeckhauser, dozens of participants in more than a dozen workshops and conferences sponsored by the Russell Sage Foundation, and dozens more in various seminars to which I presented parts of the project. My most provocative discussant over the years of working on the project has been Robert Merton, who questioned and elaborated many of my arguments and who supplied me with a steady stream of references and examples on varied topics. I presented a telescoped version of the entire project to the Rationality on Friday seminar of the Center for Rationality and Interactive Decision Making at the Hebrew University in Jerusalem (May 2000). I thank Maya Bar-Hillel and Edna Ullmann-Margalit for arranging that session and the spectacular collection of scholars from many disciplines who engaged in intensive discussion.

For extensive commentary on much or all of the manuscript, I thank Nomy Arpaly, Jonathan Baron, Paul Bullen, Karen Cook, Avon Leong, Margaret Levi, Kristen Monroe, Jay Patel, Ines Patricio, Robert Putnam, Bo Rothstein, Thomas Schelling, Barry Weingast, Alan Wertheimer, and three anonymous reviewers for the Russell Sage Foundation. I also thank a seminar full of students for their debates on trust during a course at the University of Chicago in 1992 and participants in the informal Tuesday evening seminar on contemporary moral and social theory at the University of Chicago for their

cogent comments on earlier drafts of parts of the book. All of these
people raised far more questions than I have answered.

For financial and organizational support of much of this work, I
wish to thank the Center for Advanced Study in the Behavioral Sciences in Stanford, California, the National Science Foundation (grant
number SBR-9022192), the Guggenheim Foundation, the Andrew
Mellon Foundation, the Rockefeller Foundation, the Russell Sage
Foundation, the University of Chicago, New York University, and
Stanford University.

Finally, I have benefited from the research assistance of Paul
Bullen, Larisa Satara, Melissa Schwartzberg, Huan Wang, and the research staff of the Russell Sage Foundation, especially Pauline Rothstein and Camille Yezzi.

The material in this book has appeared elsewhere, in slightly different
versions. Chapter 1 was originally written for a Festschrift in honor of
Thomas Schelling, whose published view of trust seems to be similar
to mine. An earlier version of this chapter was published as "Trusting
Persons, Trusting Institutions," in *The Strategy of Choice*, edited by
Richard J. Zeckhauser (Cambridge, Mass.: MIT Press, 1991). I wish to
thank Richard Zeckhauser for causing the original paper to be written, for using its topic to cajole me into meeting deadline promises,
and for lively discussions and commentaries on the topic and earlier
drafts of the paper. I also wish to thank participants in his Harvard
seminar on the papers of the Schelling Festschrift.

Chapter 2 was initially written for presentation to a conference on
trust at the Institute of Cognitive and Decision Sciences, University of
Oregon, in November 1994. I thank the organizers of that conference
for the occasion and the participants for comments on the paper. An
earlier version was published as "Trustworthiness," *Ethics* 107 (October 1996).

Chapter 3 was presented at the conference on trust at the New
York University School of Law, February 1995, jointly sponsored by
New York University and the Russell Sage Foundation. A variant of
this chapter has appeared as part of "Conceptions and Explanations
of Trust," in *Trust in Society*, edited by Karen S. Cook (New York:
Russell Sage Foundation, 2001).

Chapter 4 was, intellectually, commanded by Robert Merton in a
private discussion and in a letter (4 May 1995). He noted, rightly, that
attention to trust requires attention to its correlative, distrust. The
chapter was written for presentation to the Russell Sage Foundation
conference on distrust, held under the auspices of the Rockefeller
Foundation at its splendid conference center, the Villa Serbelloni, Bellagio, Italy, October 13 to 17, 1997. I thank the participants in that

lovely conference for their comments—and for their spirited participation on the bocce court. I also wish to thank numerous commentators for their reactions to my arguments, including those in seminars
at the Institute for Social Research, University of Michigan, October
23, 1997; the Department of Sociology, Cornell University, October 31,
1997; the seminar conducted by John Ferejohn and Lewis Kornhauser
at the New York University School of Law, September 23, 1997; and
participants, especially Thomas Schelling, in the Trust Relationships
conference at the Boston University School of Law, September 22 and
23, 2000. An earlier version of the chapter appeared as "Distrust" in
the *Boston University Law Review* 81 (April–June 2001).

Chapter 5 was originally written for a pair of special issues of the
journal *Analyse und Kritik*, which constituted a Festschrift dedicated to
James Coleman and his work. It appeared as "The Street-Level Epistemology of Trust," *Analyse und Kritik* 14 (December 1992) and in *Politics and Society* 21 (December 1993).

Chapter 6 was presented to the fellows' seminar at the Russell Sage
Foundation. I thank Tom Tyler for organizing that session and the
many fellows, Robert Solow, Eric Wanner, and other staff members
for critical discussion at that session and the lunch that followed.

Chapter 7 appeared in an earlier version in *Trust and Governance*,
edited by Valerie Braithwaite and Margaret Levi (New York: Russell
Sage Foundation, 1998). Versions of this chapter were presented at the
meeting of the Pacific Division of the American Philosophical Association, San Francisco, April 1, 1995, and at the conference, Trust in
Government, held on February 2 and 3, 1996, at the Australian National University, Canberra, and cosponsored by the Russell Sage
Foundation and Australian National University. The chapter has benefited from commentary at these sessions and, especially, from extensive written commentary by Margaret Levi and two anonymous reviewers. I am grateful to these colleagues and others for their
comments. These comments included occasional looks of disbelief
from those who finally came to believe the argument was intended.

Chapter 8 was originally written for a Festschrift in honor of Albert
Breton, *Competition and Structure: The Political Economy of Collective Decisions: Essays in Honor of Albert Breton*, edited by Gianluigi Galeotti,
Pierre Salmon, and Ronald Wintrobe (Cambridge: Cambridge University Press, 2000). I thank the editors of this volume and numerous
commentators for their reactions to its arguments. I especially wish to
thank the participants in the Russell Sage Foundation–New York University conference, Behavioral Evidence on Trust, held on November
15 and 16, 1997.

I thank the editors and publishers of all these works for permission
to use them here in substantially revised form.

Preface

This book presents an account of a particular but important class
of trust relations: trust as encapsulated interest, in which the
truster's expectations of the trusted's behavior depend on assessments of certain motivations of the trusted. I trust you because
your interests encapsulate mine to some extent—in particular, because you want our relationship to continue. This is a workable notion that can be used to cover much of our experience of relying on
others, and it can be used to help explain variations in our behavior
from our beliefs about the reliability of others, including collective
others. My central concern is such explanation. I argue (in chapter 3)
that certain alternative, strongly asserted individual-level accounts are
implausible as general accounts of trust. They might fit some of the
apparent trusting relations we see, but they do not fit many trusting
relations.

I discuss trust as an individual-level problem, as in my trusting or
distrusting you, and then as an individual-institution problem, as in
my trust or distrust of our government. As it happens, the literature
on trust is richest in sociological accounts, such as Bernard Barber's
(1983) *The Logic and Limits of Trust*. Philosophers, economists, psychologists, and political theorists, especially those in the tradition of John
Locke, have addressed trust and have given interesting insights; but
there is surprisingly little in all of these disciplines. Discussions of
trust are almost entirely missing from moral philosophy, where trust
may be most often invoked in discussions of Kantian proscriptions on
lying, as in Sissela Bok's (1978) *Lying: Moral Choice in Public and Private Life*. In law, trust is often defined by a social norm or practice.
Certain actions legally justify trust, so that one who relies on such
trust can call on the law to enforce the entrusted action if necessary.

People regularly say, roughly, "when we say trust, what we mean
is X." Unfortunately, X is a variable with radically different meanings
for different people. Ordinary language analysis can exclude some

meanings, perhaps, but it cannot promote one meaning above all other contenders. In the vernacular, trust is, not surprisingly, a messy, even confused notion. Quarrels about what it "really" means sound like the worst of Platonic debates about the "true" meaning of something. No matter how enticing it may sometimes seem to be, to engage in that debate is foolish. I do not put forward the "true" meaning of trust. There is no Platonically essential notion of trust.[1] Ordinary-language usages of the term trust are manifold and ill articulated. Most such concepts have, in their vernacular applications, many and varied meanings. Looking up the meaning of such a term in a dictionary should dispirit any essentialist.

The point of the account in this book is to understand implications of trust in many contexts and to explain some behaviors. I therefore offer an account of trust that handles modal behavior across a wide array of contexts. There is remarkably wide disagreement over just what trust "really" is even among those who have given the topic a lot of careful thought. Arguably, much of the disagreement results from a mistaken focus of the inquiry on trust when what must first be understood is why another might be trustworthy in a particular relationship and context. Trust is a three-part relation that is grounded in the truster's assessment of the intentions of the trusted with respect to some action. Typically, the intentions of the trusted will be based in self-interest (as in the account of encapsulated interest), moral commitment, or idiosyncratic character. Other views, that trust is an attitude of ungrounded faith or belief or that it is inherently moral, are not convincing as general accounts of trust.

Writing parts of this book was made much easier by the fact that literature and opera seem more often to be about trust and its violation than about anything else other than love and its violation (an intimately related theme). Writers on trust therefore have available constant sources of examples of almost every nuance one might wish to explain, although such examples cannot be used to prove very much. One reader challenged me with the Yiddish quip that "'for example' is not proof." In fact, of course, it can be proof—of existence. If you have seen one example of the black swans in Taiwan, you cannot any longer truthfully say that all swans are white. At most, my examples from fictional accounts establish conceptual possibilities, which is a bit short of proving existence. It is in this spirit only that I invoke them. I do so because I think it is often important to reify any conceptual claim by giving an example of it.

Philosophers often use examples in a more limited way simply to elucidate a concept or a possibility. For this purpose they often prefer artificial examples that include none of the complicating features of real life. For the understanding of trust relationships, however, it is fundamentally important to keep real-world complications in view because they are the stuff of relationships, and trust is inherently relational. Examples taken from literature in its various forms commonly are relational and rich enough to keep real-world complications in view.

Very briefly, here is the plan of this book. The first four chapters are primarily about conceptual issues. In the last four chapters, which focus primarily on issues in explanation, I use the encapsulated-interest conception of trust presented in chapter 1 to explain a wide array of trust phenomena from individual level to societal level. The balance is odd. One should expect the bulk of the account to focus on explanation. Unfortunately, conceptual issues in the understanding of trust are far messier and more complicated than one might hope. Clearing up these issues turns out to be a major task.

Chapter 1

Trust

U SUALLY, to say that I trust you in some context simply means
that I think you will be trustworthy toward me in that context. Hence to ask any question about trust is implicitly to ask
about the reasons for thinking the relevant party to be trustworthy. In
chapter 2, I canvass some of the potentially many reasons for thinking
someone trustworthy. One of the most important and commonplace is
trust as encapsulated interest, which I discuss in this chapter. On this
account, I trust you because I think it is in your interest to take my
interests in the relevant matter seriously in the following sense: You
value the continuation of our relationship, and you therefore have
your own interests in taking my interests into account. That is, you
encapsulate my interests in your own interests. My interests might
come into conflict with other interests you have and that trump mine,
and you might therefore not actually act in ways that fit my interests.
Nevertheless, you at least have some interest in doing so.

There are two compelling reasons for taking up trust as encapsulated interest. First, such trust fits a centrally important class of all
trust relationships. Second, it allows us to draw systematic implications for trust relationships across varied contexts, as subsequent
chapters should make clear.

To begin, consider an example of trust from Dostoyevsky's *The
Brothers Karamazov*. The example is instructive because it involves
minimal conditions for trust as encapsulated interest: the only reason
for trustworthiness is the incentive to sustain the relationship—in this
instance, purely for its profitable character and not for any richer reasons. For many trust relationships there are additional considerations
beyond monetary benefits. For example, I value my relationship with
you in many ways, including for the favors we do each other, for the
pleasures of talking and being with you, and for the mutual supports
we give each other.

In *The Brothers Karamazov*, Dmitry Karamazov tells the story of a lieutenant colonel who, as commander of a unit far from Moscow, has managed substantial sums of money on behalf of the army. Immediately after each periodic audit of his books, he takes the available funds to the merchant Trifonov, who soon returns them with a gift. In effect, both the lieutenant colonel and Trifonov have benefited from funds that would otherwise have lain idle, producing no benefit for anyone. Because it was highly irregular, theirs was a secret exchange that depended wholly on personal trustworthiness not backed by the law of contracts. When the day comes that the lieutenant colonel is abruptly to be replaced in his command, he asks Trifonov to return the last sum, 4,500 rubles, loaned to him.

Trifonov replies, "I've never received any money from you, and couldn't possibly have received any" (Dostoyevsky 1982 [1880], 129). Trifonov's "couldn't possibly" is an elegant touch because it drives home in a subtle way that the entire series of transactions has been criminal. The lieutenant colonel could not have wanted any of it to become public—not even at the cost of the final 4,500 rubles to keep it secret. Had it become public, he most likely would have gone to jail, and his daughter's marriage prospects would have been ruined. Unlike many of our important relationships, this one was partially abstracted from social context rather than being heavily embedded in a context that could govern the interaction and enforce trustworthiness. Trifonov's misappropriated rubles thereafter thread their complex way through Dostoyevsky's entire novel, wrecking lives while motivating the plot.

While their relationship was ongoing, Trifonov and the lieutenant colonel could each end their cooperation at any moment. Trifonov could have cheated at any time along the way, but then he might have lost more on forgone future interactions than he would have gained on his single, cheating defection, and he would have cheated a very powerful man. This was true so long as the interaction was expected to continue indefinitely. Once the interaction was to end, however, the incentive to the next mover was clearly to withdraw from the cooperation. It was the lieutenant colonel's misfortune that Trifonov was the next mover at the end and, at that time, the lieutenant colonel had lost his power.

Dmitry Karamazov says that the lieutenant colonel implicitly trusted Trifonov. After his sad day of reckoning, the lieutenant colonel would presumably have said that Trifonov was not trustworthy. Unfortunately, Trifonov was trustworthy just so long as there was some longer-run incentive for him to be reliable in their mutually beneficial relationship. The moment there ceased to be any expectation of further gains from his relationship with the lieutenant colonel, Trifonov had no incentive to be trustworthy in this highly irregular commercial dealing between de facto crooks. Not surprisingly, he ceased to be trustworthy. The lieutenant colonel might have held the contradictory hope that Trifonov the crook was a man of honor who was, in that sense, trustworthy. If so, then he clearly misjudged his man.

Ordinary trust between individuals often fits the tale of Dostoyevsky's 4,500 rubles as a minimal condition and, more generally, the encapsulated-interest model as defined in this chapter. Understanding that model of trust can help us to understand many other issues. The encapsulated-interest conception fits three distinct categories of interaction: interactions that fit the model of the iterated one-way trust game, iterated exchange interactions as modeled by the prisoner's dilemma, and interactions in thick relationships. These categories of trust relations represent increasing complexity of the interactions. In all of these interactions, *trust is relational*. That is to say, my trust of you depends on our relationship, either directly through our own ongoing interaction or indirectly through intermediaries and reputational effects. If we have no or only a passing relationship, we are not in a trusting relationship.

Trust as Encapsulated Interest

It is compelling to see many interactions of trust and trustworthiness as similar to the interaction between Trifonov and the lieutenant colonel while it was ongoing. The trusted party has incentive to be trustworthy, incentive that is grounded in the value of maintaining the relationship into the future. That is, I trust you because your interest encapsulates mine, which is to say that you have an interest in fulfilling my trust. It is this fact that makes my trust more than merely expectations about your behavior. Any expectations I have are grounded in an understanding (perhaps mistaken) of your interests specifically with respect to me. The relationship of Trifonov and the lieutenant colonel exemplifies a minimal core part of a remarkable array of trust relationships. That minimal core is that there is a clear, fairly well defined interest at stake in the continuation of the relationship.

More generally, it is principally those with whom we have ongoing relationships that we trust. In addition, the richer an ongoing relationship and the more valuable it is to us, the more trusting and trustworthy we are likely to be in that relationship. When asked whom they trust in various ways, people typically name certain relatives, friends, and close associates. The relationship between Trifonov and the lieutenant colonel was a minimal instance of trust in that it was grounded merely in the interest in the ongoing material benefits from the interaction. The lieutenant colonel valued his relationship with Trifonov only for that material benefit. It was specifically his relationship with

Trifonov that mattered to him, however, because this relationship was beneficial to him. His interests and those of Trifonov were causally connected so long as their relationship continued.

While one might object superficially to bringing interests into trusting relationships, such as one's relationship with a close relative or friend, they are clearly there much, and perhaps most, of the time. For many other trusting relationships, the whole point is likely to be interests. For example, I have an ongoing commercial relationship with a local merchant that becomes a trust relationship. For many common trust relationships there is a far richer range of benefits from the relationship than the material interests that motivated Trifonov and the lieutenant colonel, two partners in crime. I enjoy the presence of many people in my life, and I want to maintain my relationships with them. Therefore, they can trust me in various ways. There might even be relationships that I value in themselves and not primarily because they are causally connected to certain other benefits that I get from them. For example, I love certain people and have rich friendships with others. Such relationships are at one extreme of the range of encapsulated interest, and the relationship between Trifonov and the lieutenant colonel is at the other, minimal, extreme. Many of our relationships with others develop from relatively minor exchange interactions and become much richer relationships of fairly broad reciprocity.

Both the relatively limited relationship between Trifonov and the lieutenant colonel and the relatively rich relationship you might have with a friend involve trust as encapsulated interest, which we may characterize as follows: I trust you because I think it is in your interest to attend to my interests in the relevant matter. This is not merely to say that you and I have the same interests. Rather, it is to say that you have an interest in attending to *my* interests because, typically, you want our relationship to continue. At a minimum, you may want our relationship to continue because it is economically beneficial to you, as in the case of Trifonov's relationship with the lieutenant colonel. In richer cases, you may want our relationship to continue and not to be damaged by your failure to fulfill my trust because you value the relationship for many reasons, including nonmaterial reasons. For example, you may enjoy doing various things with me, or you might value my friendship or my love, and your desire to keep my friendship or love will motivate you to be careful of my trust.

Note that *our merely having the same interests with respect to some matter does not meet the condition of trust as encapsulated interest*, although it can often give me reason to expect you to do what I would want you to do or what would serve my interests (because it simultaneously serves yours). The encapsulated-interest account does entail that the truster and the trusted have compatible interests over at least some matters, but such incentive compatibility, while necessary, is not sufficient for that account, which further requires that the trusted values the continuation of the relationship with the truster and has compatible interests at least in part for this reason. Other drivers on a highway and I enjoy incentive compatibility, and therefore each of us can be expected to try to drive on the appropriate side of the road to avoid accidents with one another. Generally, however, there is no sense in which the other drivers want me to be in the relationship of driving on the same road with them, and therefore I am not in a relationship of trust as encapsulated interest with them.

One could assert a definition of trust that is nothing more than incentive compatibility or rational expectations of the behavior of the trusted. The word trust would be otiose in such a theory, however, because it would add nothing to the somewhat simpler assumption of compatible interests in explaining behavior. The massive literature on trust has not been stimulated by any such simplistic conception of trust. Much of that literature seems to suppose, for example, that there are important normative issues in the seeming fact of declining trust, and much of it supposes that trust is a complex and important matter in its own right. Indeed, Niklas Luhmann (1980, 22, 30) supposes that institutional devices that arrange for merely stable expectations have, of necessity, been substituted for relationships of trust in our complex modern times.

A fully rational analysis of trust would depend not solely on the rational expectations of the truster but also on the *commitments*, not merely the regularity, of the trusted. How can one secure commitments from someone whose love or benevolence does not guarantee good will toward oneself? The most common way is to structure incentives to match the desired commitment. You can more confidently trust me if you know that my own interest will induce me to live up to your expectations. Your trust is your expectation that my interests encapsulate yours. On this view, as Thomas Schelling (1960, 134–35) notes, "trust is often achieved simply by the continuity of the relation between parties and the recognition by each that what he might gain by cheating in a given instance is outweighed by the value of the tradition of trust that makes possible a long sequence of future agreement."

Continuity of the relationship is not enough, of course, because the commitments matter. In a favorite philosopher's example, Immanuel Kant's neighbors may have relied on his punctuality in his morning walk to set their own schedules. To trust him, however, would require more: that they rely on his having their interests at heart in deciding when to take his walk. If they could not think he did, they could not be said to trust him in the strong sense of the encapsulated-interest account (Baier 1986, 234).

Writings on trust often take the view that it involves something beyond merely reasonable expectations based in self-interest.[1] In particular, some writers suppose trust is an inherently normative notion (Elster 1979, 146; Hertzberg 1988). We can make some sense of such claims by supposing they are really misplaced claims about trustworthiness rather than about trust. You might be trustworthy in the strong sense that you would reciprocate even when it was against your interest to do so, as Trifonov might have returned the final 4,500 rubles.

Various social scientific accounts of trust take for granted that trust is rational in the sense of being based on empirically grounded expectations of another person's (or an institution's) behavior (Barber 1983; Luhmann 1980). Trust can lead to intentional or motivational moves by the trusted as well as by the truster. A rational analysis of trust of another intentional being, as opposed to "trust" of a force of nature (our "trust" that it will not rain on a July day in Palo Alto), must take account of the rationality of both intentional parties. Indeed, in a trust relationship, I must think strategically, because my purposes are served by the interaction between what I do and what another does (or others do). My outcome is the joint outcome of both our actions. In this sense, mere expectation accounts are only half strategic, and they therefore fail to address the central nature of trust relationships. They have a liability not unlike that of the similarly half-strategic Cournot theory of market behavior. In the Cournot theory, actors assume regularity of behavior on the part of others in the market in order better to decide how to act themselves; but, although they are strategic in responding to others' actions, they suppose that others are not strategic in responding to them. Hence they fail to take account of second-order effects of others' responses to their actions. Cournot actors are somewhat smart but they think others are dumb.

Many writings on trust convey a vague sense that trust always requires more than rational expectations grounded in the likely interests of the trusted. If this sense is correct, then we are at a very early stage in the development of any theory to account for trust or even to characterize it in many contexts. If an account from interests is largely correct for a large and important fraction of our trusting relationships, however, we already have the elements of a theory of trust that merely wants careful articulation and application. In what follows, I give an account of trust as essentially rational expectations about the self-interested behavior of the trusted. The effort to construct such an account forces attention to varieties of interaction in which trust might arise and hence to differences in the plausible explanations of trust. The sense that trust inherently requires more than reliance on the self-interest of the trusted may depend on particular kinds of interaction that, while interesting and even important, are not always of greatest import in social theory or social life—although some of them are, as is the trust a child can have in a parent.

Elements of Trust as Encapsulated Interest

The encapsulated-interest view of trust includes several elements, some of which are common to other accounts of trust. First, trust is generally a three-part relation that restricts any claim of trust to particular parties and to particular matters. Second, trust is a cognitive notion, in the family of such notions as knowledge, belief, and the kind of judgment that might be called assessment. All of these are cognitive in that they are grounded in some sense of what is true. These cognitive notions—and trust, in particular—are not a matter of choosing: we do not choose what is to count as true, rather we discover it or are somehow convinced of it. Hence we do not trust in order to accomplish anything, although our trust might encourage us to enter beneficial interactions. (We may well choose to be trustworthy in order to encourage others to cooperate with us.) Generally, we wish to explain cooperation or its failure by reference to trust. To make the cooperation itself a matter of trust would make the thing we want to explain the explanation of it. Thus we wish to keep trusting and acting from trust cleanly separated. Finally, acting on trust typically involves risk.

Other issues of trust need be only mentioned, not discussed at length here. First, trust involves expectations of behavior from another, but not just any expectations. The expectations must be grounded in the trusted's concern with the truster's interests. Second, trust and trustworthiness are subject to the larger context. Your encapsulation of my interest in making your own choices may not be sufficient to get you to fulfill my trust because other considerations may trump. For example, two people might trust you with respect to different things, and in fulfilling one of those trusts you might violate the other. Taken out of context, your trustworthiness in each of these relationships might be in your interest. But when they come into conflict in the context of your wider life, one interest might trump the other.

Many writers take issue with one or another of these elements of trust. Some of the criticisms appear to be matters that are normative, as in some of the views canvassed in chapter 3, where I take up alternative conceptions of trust. Some of the disagreements, however, are genuinely conceptual. The view for which I argue here seems to fit modal cases of actual trusting, in which the trusting makes a real difference to how people then behave. It also seems to yield or fit with an explanation for both the trusting and the behavior that follows from it.

One other element of trust is shared in virtually all views: competence to do what one is trusted to do. You should not trust me to get you safely to the top of Mount Everest and back, even if I convince you that I have the best will in the world to do so. I usually assume throughout this book that competence is not at issue in the trust relationships under discussion. The point of this is not to dismiss the problems of competence and of judging someone's competence—such problems are often severe and de facto insurmountable barriers to trust—but merely to concentrate on motivational issues. There are, of course, many contexts in which competence is a major issue as well as many in which the problem of knowing how competent someone is can be very difficult. A substantial book could be written on these issues, but this is not that book.

Competence is a major issue in many contexts in which specialized abilities are at issue, as is typically true of professional services as well as ordinary individual interactions. You would probably have less confidence in the competence of a young and inexperienced teenager as a baby-sitter than in that of an older and experienced person. In such a case, you might know enough to judge the relative competence of these two people. In other contexts, however, the issue is how to judge someone's competence. We commonly prefer to call on people whom we know to be competent and avoid relying on those about whom we know too little to judge them.

My competence in getting up Mount Everest is, of course, a fairly fixed characteristic that is not specifically mobilized to answer to your potential trust in me. If I have not already developed such a capacity, you should not want to rely on my somehow developing it while leading you up that mountain. Most of the motivational issues in trust—for the encapsulated-interest account as well as for most others—are much more clearly specific to the particular relationship at issue. Again, therefore, the focus of this book is on motivations, which are far less well understood in the trust literature than is the problem of competence.

Certain institutional arrangements convert our particular personal judgment problems into problems of generalized assessments. For example, we have agencies that assess the competence of such professionals as doctors, lawyers, and even mountain-climbing guides. These agencies also commonly oversee motivational commitments of the professionals—for example, they attempt to regulate conflicts of interests. Testing and certification of competence is, however, a major part of their task. Such agencies convert our relations with professionals into something different from the kind of trust relationship I might have with you personally. Indeed, they arguably eliminate much of the trust we might otherwise have developed, so that our dealings with professionals have more the character of assessing and acting on mere expectations. Similar devices of third-party "certification"—as by a mutual friend or a Chinese guanxi mediator—also often stand in for direct assessments of those we must rely on for ordinary personal relations.

Trust as a Three-Part Relation

A characteristic of trusting relationships, one that is not uniquely relevant to the encapsulated-interest view, is that trust is generally a three-part relation: A trusts B to do X (Baier 1986; Luhmann 1980, 27).[2] Even then, the trust depends on the context. For example, I might ordinarily trust you with even the most damaging gossip but not with the price of today's lunch (you always—conveniently?—forget such debts), while I would trust another with the price of lunch but not with any gossip. I might trust you with respect to X but not with respect to ten times X. Some few people I might trust with almost anything, many others with almost nothing. But in a radically different context, such as when you are under great duress and my piece of gossip would help you out of a bad situation, I might no longer trust you with it.

To say "I trust you" seems almost always to be elliptical, as though we can assume some such phrase as "to do X" or "in matters Y."[3] Only a small child, a lover, Abraham speaking to his god, or a rabid follower of a charismatic leader might be able to say "I trust you" without implicit modifier. Even in their cases we are apt to think they mistake both themselves and the objects of their trust. Many of us, of course, might start by taking a risk on newly encountered people or people in newly undertaken areas, but we would prefer not to take such a risk in important matters without a substantial prior history of trustworthiness and a strong sense that the trusted will have incentive to follow through.

Those who see trust as normative or otherwise extrarational argue that it is more richly a two-part or even one-part relation than this view implies. It is a one-part relation if I trust out of a pure disposition to trust anyone and everyone with respect to anything and everything, in which case I am the only variable part. There may be people, especially children, naïve enough to have such a disposition, but most of us clearly do not have it. There is a fairly extensive literature on so-called generalized trust, which is trust in the general other person whom we might encounter, perhaps with some restrictions on what matters would come under that trust. Conceptual issues in survey research on generalized or social trust are discussed in chapter 3 (also see the appendix) and the implications of the results of such research in chapters 7 (trust in government) and 8 (trust and society). But here note that this category has two odd features. First, it sounds more nearly like a simple expectations account than a richer trust account. In this account, I supposedly think everyone is reliable up to some degree independently of who they are or what relationship I have with them. I think this of them the way I might think the typical person would behave in certain ways in various contexts.

Second, when survey respondents say they trust most people most of the time, this is almost surely an elliptical claim. They do not mean that, if a random stranger on the street were to ask for a loan of, say, a hundred dollars, they would trust that person to repay and would therefore make the loan. This ellipsis might be covered by the phrase "most of the time." Hence even this open-ended answer to a badly framed, vague question is almost certainly just a loose way of saying they would trust most people within somewhat narrow limits. Moreover, it is also elliptical in its reference to "most people." Few of the respondents would genuinely trust just anyone much at all.

Trust and Cooperation

Trust is in the cognitive category with knowledge and belief. To say I trust you in some way is to say nothing more than that I know or believe certain things about you—generally things about your incentives or other reasons to live up to my trust, to be trustworthy to me. My assessment of your trustworthiness in a particular context is simply my trust of you. The declarations "I believe you are trustworthy" and "I trust you" are equivalent. If it is cognitive, it follows that trust is not purposive (Baier 1986, 235). I do not trust you in order to gain from interacting with you. Rather, because I do trust you, I can expect to gain from interacting with you if a relevant opportunity arises. Moreover, if trust is cognitive, it is not behavioral. I may act from my trust, and my action may give evidence of my trust, but my action is not itself the trust, although it may be compelling evidence of my trust.[4] If I trust you, I trust you right now and not only in some moment in which I act on my trust by taking a risk on you.[5]

Suppose my trusting you in some matter is rational in the sense of being well grounded. What follows? Perhaps nothing. That I trust you does not entail that I should act on the trust. There might be other things I would rather do at the moment or other people whom I similarly trust for the matter at hand. Therefore, I face a choice of what to do even though it is incoherent to say I choose to trust you. If I trust you, I will think it not very risky to rely on you in some matter. (I return to this issue in chapter 3.)

I can, however, also choose to take the risk of cooperating with you on some matter even if I do not trust you. While he was the prime minister of Israel, Ehud Barak, when asked if he trusted Yassir Arafat, said, "I don't know what it means to trust. He is the Palestinian leader, not the Israeli leader, and he is determined to do whatever he can to achieve Palestinian objectives. The real question is not whether we trust him. The question is whether there is a potential agreement that could be better overall for both sides, a win-win, not a zero-sum game" (quoted in Goldberg 2001, 66). Cooperation or coordination is the general goal, but there are many ways to achieve it, some of which do not depend on trust. Hence my actions are not simply determined by the degree of my trust, although they are often likely to be influenced by my trust or distrust.

In the encapsulated-interest account of trust, the knowledge that makes my beliefs about you a matter of trust rather than of mere expectations is my beliefs about your incentives toward me in particular. These are not merely bald, unarticulated expectations about your behavior. I have bald expectations that the sun will rise tomorrow, and I might not be able to give any account of why I think that, other than induction from the past. (As a physicist, you might be able to give a very good account, so that your expectation of the sun's rising is theoretically grounded.) What matters for trust is not merely my expectation that you will act in certain ways but also my belief that you have the relevant motivations to act in those ways, that you deliberately take my interests into account because they are mine.

It is common in the vernacular to say I "trust" you to do such things as, for example, defend yourself if attacked by a dog, in which case your motivations are not at all like those of the encapsulated-interest account of trust. You defend yourself, as most of us would, for your own direct interest. If trust reduces to such bald expectations of behavior, there is little point in using the loaded term "trust." My "trust" would be useless in helping us explain your self-defense, which is not motivated by your concern with my interests (or any other commitments you might have to me specifically). Moreover, my trust—as my assessment of your encapsulation of my interests in your own interests—will commonly help explain relevant actions of mine, specifically my choosing to rely on you to do something on my behalf, whereas my "trust" that you would defend yourself when attacked by a dog would explain none of my behavior.

Acting on Trust as Involving Risk

As virtually all writers on trust agree, acting on a trust involves giving discretion to another to affect one's interests. This move is inherently subject to the risk that the other will abuse the power of discretion. As David Hume (1978 [1739–40], 3.2.2: 497) observes, "'Tis impossible to separate the chance of good from the risk of ill." Hence to act on trust is to take a risk, although trust is not itself a matter of deliberately taking a risk because it is not a matter of making a choice.

As an objection to the encapsulated-interest account, one might suppose it perverse to say I trust you to do X when it is in your interest to do X. For example, consider an extreme case: I am confident that you will do what I want only because a gun is pointed at your head. (I have grasped the wisdom of Al Capone, who is supposed to have said, "You can get so much farther with a kind word and a gun than with a kind word alone" [McKean 1975, 42n]).

My coercing you to do what I "trust" you to do violates the sense that trust has no meaning in a fully deterministic setting. I do not trust the sun to rise each day, at least not in any meaningful sense beyond merely having great confidence that it will do so. Similarly, I would not, in our usual sense, trust a fully programmed automaton, even if it were programmed to discover and attempt to serve my interests—although I might come to rely heavily on it. Many writers therefore suppose that trust is inherently embedded in uncertainty. "For trust to be relevant," Diego Gambetta (1988, 218–19) says, "there must be the possibility of exit, betrayal, defection" by the trusted (see also Yamagishi and Yamagishi 1994, 133; Luhmann 1980, 24). More generally, one might say trust is embedded in the capacity or even need for choice on the part of the trusted. Giving people very strong incentives seems to move them toward being deterministic actors with respect to the matters at stake. At the other extreme, leaving them with no imputable reasons for action generally makes it impossible to trust them. Trust and trustworthiness (and choice and rationality) are at issue just because we are in the murky in-between land that is neither deterministic nor fully indeterminate. Yet it still can make sense to say of someone, such as your mother, that you trust her virtually beyond doubt with respect to very many things. Such people, however, are rare in our lives. Trust is a problem of often great interest just because so few of our relationships are like that one.

Part of the issue in the gun case is that your compliance with my request is not motivated by your concern with my interest at all. It is motivated purely by your concern with your own interests. Hence the gun case fails to fit the encapsulated-interest account of trust, which would require your concern with my interests. Luhmann (1980, 42; see also Hertzberg 1988) seemingly opposes the encapsulated-interest account because it turns on the interests of the trusted. "It must not be that the trusted will toe the line on her own account, in the light of her interests," he writes. This unexplicated obiter dictum runs counter to his own general account, according to which the overriding consideration is that the two parties in a trust relation are typically going to meet again (Luhmann 1980, 37)—presumably in an iterated or ongoing exchange relationship in which a strong reason for trustworthiness is one's interest in keeping the relationship and its exchanges going. His claim, however, might be the misstated observation that trust must not be a matter of the trusted's acting only on his or her own account without reference to the interests of the truster.

The Rationality of Trust

At the individual level, my trust of you must be grounded in expectations that are particular to you, not merely in generalized expectations. If I always trust everyone or if I always act from generalized expectations, then I do not meaningfully trust anyone. Trust is therefore in part inherently a rational assessment. My expectations about your behavior may be grounded in my belief in your morality or reciprocity or self-interest. With no prior knowledge of you, I may initially risk treating you as though I trust you, but our relationship can eventually be one of trust only if there are expectations that ground the trust. As Karamazov's lieutenant colonel learned, expectations that are well grounded in one context may not be reliable for new contexts, such as his sudden loss of status as base commander.

That trust is essentially rational is a common view. For example, James Coleman (1990, chapter 5; also see several contributions to Gambetta 1988) bases his account of trust on complex rational expectations. There are two central elements in applying a rational-choice account of trust: incentives of the trusted to fulfill the trust and knowledge to allow the truster to trust. The knowledge at issue, of course, is that of the potential truster, not that of the theorist or social scientist who observes or analyzes trust. Hence we require an account of the epistemology of individual knowledge or belief, of street-level epistemology, to complete the rational theory of trust (see chapter 5).

A full statement of the rational theory, including the incentive and knowledge effects, is as stated earlier: Your trust turns not directly on your own interests but rather on whether these are encapsulated in the interests of the trusted. You trust someone if you believe it will be in her interest to be trustworthy in the relevant way at the relevant time, and it will be in her interest because she wishes to maintain her relationship with you. Some accounts of trust do not specifically include reference to the trusted's interest in being trustworthy toward the truster but merely require an expectation that the trusted will fulfill the trust (Barber 1983; Gambetta 1988, 217–18; Dasgupta 1988). Adequate reason for such an expectation, however, will typically turn on an assessment of likely future incentives.[6]

The encapsulated-interest account backs up a step from a simpler expectations account to inquire into the reasons for the relevant expectations—in particular, the interests of the trusted in fulfilling the trust. The typical reason for the expectations is that the relations are ongoing in some important sense. There are two especially important contexts for trust: ongoing dyadic relationships and ongoing—or thick—group or societal relationships. The two classes are closely related, and both are subsumed in the encapsulated-interest account of trust. The first class is divisible into one-way and mutual trust relations, both of which are grounded in ongoing dyadic interactions. Such interactions pose incentives to the trusted that are of increasing severity. The sanction that compels the trusted party in a one-way trust game and both of the trusted parties in the mutual trust exchange interaction is withdrawal by the other party and therefore the loss of future benefits from the interaction. The sanction in thick relationships can go beyond such withdrawal to include shunning from the whole community of those who share in the thick relationships. Let us consider each of these in turn.

One-Way Trust

The interaction of Trifonov and the lieutenant colonel was, the first time they dealt with each other, an instance of what we may call the one-way trust game. This standard game has been widely used for the experimental study of trust for about a decade (Kreps 1990; McCabe and Smith in press; Hardin in press a). (Variants of this game with other payoffs are strategically identical in the sense that the orders of the payoffs are the same.) The lieutenant colonel must act as though he trusts Trifonov in order to gain from their interaction, whereas Trifonov need only act in his own interest. The game illustrates one-way trust because it is only the lieutenant colonel whose actions might depend on his trusting. The lieutenant colonel can never cheat Trifonov. In the game, the lieutenant colonel makes the first move of lending or not lending the rubles. If he does not lend, the game ends with payoffs of nothing to both parties. If he lends, then there follows a next stage in which Trifonov chooses whether to repay fully with an additional personal gift or not to repay. The play of the game ends with his choice.

If the game is played only once, clearly Trifonov's interest is to defect, and therefore the lieutenant colonel's interest is not to make the initial loan. In many experiments using variants of this game, the first mover (the lieutenant colonel here) often risks cooperation and the second mover often reciprocates, even when the game is to be played only once (which appears to be the most common way to use the game experimentally). If the experiments were run with payoffs on the scale of what the lieutenant colonel and Trifonov faced, we might expect almost no cooperative plays in games played only once. If, however, the players were like the lieutenant colonel and Trifonov and were able to play the game repeatedly over the years, their interests might change dramatically, because both could do very well over many plays of the game.

Let us suppose that after every audit, there will be about 4,500 rubles to play with and that Trifonov makes a generous profit from his investments, enough to yield 2,000 rubles to himself and a gift of 300 rubles to the lieutenant colonel. The payoff structure of a single play of their game will then be as in game 1 (figure 1.1). Moves are sequential. First, the lieutenant colonel must choose either to defect or to cooperate. If he chooses to cooperate, then Trifonov must decide whether he will defect or cooperate. If Trifonov gets the loan three times and successfully invests it and repays it, he makes a clear profit (1,500 rubles) in comparison with cheating already on the first loan of 4,500 rubles. If he carries it off often for several years, he makes a very large profit that swamps the initial 4,500 ruble loan. Repayment, with the small gift, is therefore clearly in Trifonov's long-run interest. Presumably Trifonov can cheat the lieutenant colonel only once, and while the lieutenant colonel is powerful, Trifonov might suffer reprisals if he cheats. Hence so long as he can foresee two more plays of the game beyond the current play, it always serves his interest to repay the money. Once the relationship is clearly over, however, and there is no longer any chance of reprisal, there is only a short-run gain from a single final loan, and that is substantially trumped by the gain from cheating and keeping the 4,500 rubles (plus any profit he has made from them).

The game as represented might not include all the relevant payoffs. For example, so long as he has the resources of his power over the military base and his standing in the local community, the lieutenant colonel has power to take vengeance on Trifonov if Trifonov cheats. When he was embarrassed by an unannounced audit and discovered that he would be replaced in office, however, he lost that power. If the initial loan had been a personal loan from the lieutenant colonel's own funds, it could have been governed by a legally enforceable contract, so that trust need have played little or no role in the lieutenant colonel's expectation of getting full repayment with a bit of interest.

Note, incidentally, that the one-way trust game of game 1 is a three-part relation. The lieutenant colonel trusts Trifonov with respect to about 4,500 rubles. This is true for the general trust game no matter who the parties are or what the stakes are. In addition, it would, of course, be plausible for the lieutenant colonel not to trust Trifonov in

Figure 1.1   Game 1: One-Way Trust

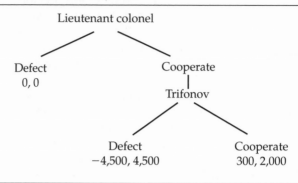

Source: Author's configuration.

a one-way trust game with radically higher stakes even though he did trust him with the stakes at 4,500 rubles.

It is a great strength of the experimental protocol for the trust game that it virtually forces us to be clear on at least some of what is at issue. It is difficult to imagine a reduced analog of the one-way trust game that would represent only a two-part relation unless it allowed the payoffs to be merely ordinal and completely open-ended. In that case, however, the relevant player would be unable to choose to cooperate at the first move because the loss, if the other party chose to take the noncooperative payoff, could be catastrophic. Players who understood such a game could not, if their own resources were at stake, seriously claim to think it smart to cooperate at the first move. Unlike the findings of experiments using these games, survey results on so-called generalized trust can be based on questions that are vague and even glib and can therefore confuse what is at issue (see the discussion in chapter 3 and the typical survey questions presented in the appendix).

As the example of Trifonov and the lieutenant colonel shows, even when it is played once only, the one-way trust game represents real choice problems. The choices precede any trust relation, however; hence calling it a trust game is misleading if the game is not iterated. The example is also in a sense only half of commonplace trust relations, in which both parties are at risk, both might trust or not trust, and both might be trustworthy or not trustworthy. For example, in an ongoing mutual exchange relationship, you and I might both be in a position on occasion to cheat each other. Neither of us would have the restricted role of the lieutenant colonel, who can trust or not trust but cannot act on the misplaced trust of Trifonov, because Trifonov need not trust. Let us turn to this slightly more complex case of mutual trust, in which the two parties are in a symmetric relationship.

Mutual Trust

Iterated one-way trust relationships are of great analytical interest because of their simplicity, although they are arguably somewhat unusual in the mass of all trust relationships. One can imagine that some parent-child relationships are virtually one-way relationships, as are many others in which the parties are not equal or are not in symmetric roles. For good reason, the more stable and compelling trust relationships are likely to be mutual and ongoing. Why is this so? Because a good way to get me to be trustworthy in my dealings with you, when you risk acting on your trust of me, is to make me reciprocally depend on your trustworthiness. A reciprocal trusting relationship is mutually reinforcing for each truster, because each person then has built-in incentive to be trustworthy (Coleman 1990, 77). I trust you because it is in your interest to do what I trust you to do, and you trust me for the reciprocal reason. If, as subjectively seems to be true, trust relationships are typically reciprocal, we have reason to suppose they are not typically grounded in particular characteristics of the trusted. They are relational because they are grounded in incentives for trustworthiness, as in the encapsulated-interest account.

The prototypical case of mutual trust at the individual level involves an interaction that is part of a long sequence of exchanges between the same parties. Each exchange is simply the resolution of a prisoner's dilemma (Hardin 1982b). A sequence of exchanges is therefore an iterated prisoner's dilemma with, perhaps, some variation in the stakes at each exchange. Hence the main incentive that one faces in a particular exchange in which one is trusted by the other is the potential benefit from continuing the series of interactions. The sanction each of us has against the other is to withdraw from further interaction.

The model of mutual trust as trust from iterated exchange is not a definition of trust in certain relationships, but it is an explanation of much of the trust we experience or see, much of which is reciprocal and is grounded in ongoing relationships. As discussed further in chapter 3, trust is typically reducible to other terms. We can determine what some of these other terms are from the iterated exchange model, which is an explanatory theory of trust. Ongoing dyadic relationships of trust typically involve mutual trust.[7]

Ordinary exchange can be represented as a prisoner's dilemma game, as in figure 1.2 (see Hardin 1982b). In this game, the payoffs to each player are strictly ordinal. They bear no relation to dollars or

Figure 1.2   Game 2: Prisoner's Dilemma or Exchange

		Column Player	
		Cooperates	Does not cooperate
	Cooperates	2, 2	4, 1
Row Player			
	Does not cooperate	1, 4	3, 3

Source: Author's configuration.
(x,y)
x = row player
y = column player
Note: In each cell, the first payoff is the row player's, the second the column player's.

utiles. They merely indicate the order of optimal benefit for each player from each possible interaction. The first cell, for example, indicates that the cooperation of both parties yields the second-best payoff for each of the players. The outcome with a payoff of 1 is the player's first choice, or most preferred outcome, that with a payoff of 2 is the player's second choice, and so forth. There is therefore no sense in which we can add, say, the payoffs that are ranked 1 and 4; nor can we say that Row's 1 is comparable in magnitude to Column's 1. In each cell of the matrix, the first payoff goes to the row player and the second to the column player (in the mnemonic Roman Catholic convention). Hence the top left cell of the game gives both players their second-best outcomes, which are an improvement over their status quo third-best outcomes that result from joint failure to cooperate with each other. (Such games are more commonly presented with cardinal payoffs in money rather than with merely ordinally ranked outcomes.)[8]

If we play the prisoner's dilemma once only with no expectation of encountering each other again in an exchange relation and without the benefit of any external agency to compel us to cooperate, it is in our interest individually not to cooperate. If we play the game repeatedly, however, we have strong incentive to cooperate, if we can get each other to recognize this fact. Therefore, the once-only interaction has none of the force of the encapsulated-interest account to get us to trust each other, but an iterated, ongoing interaction does have that force (Hardin 1982a, chapters 9 to 14). Some game theorists argue that iteration cannot generate incentives to cooperate in ongoing interactions in the ordinary prisoner's dilemma. I briefly address their objection later in this chapter.

Several types of behavior often identified as moral can be clearly understood as self-interested in many contexts. Promise keeping, honesty, and fidelity to others often make sense without any presupposition of a distinctively moral commitment beyond interest. Consider promise keeping, which has been the subject of hundreds of articles and books in moral theory during the past century.[9] In the eighteenth century, David Hume (1978 [1739–40], 3.2.5: 523) said, without seeming to think the statement required much defense, that the first obligation to keep a promise is interest. The claim is obviously true for typical promises between close associates who have an ongoing relationship that they want to maintain. If I promise to return your book, I will be encouraged to do so by frequent contact with you and frequent desire to make other exchanges with you. If I generally fail to keep such promises, I can probably expect not to enjoy as many exchanges and reciprocal favors. Promising relationships typically are those in which exchanges are reciprocated over time. Because exchanges are resolutions of prisoner's dilemma problems, promising relationships involving exchange have the incentive structure of iterated plays of the prisoner's dilemma.[10] Prima facie, it is in one's interest to keep such a promise, although that interest might be trumped by some other (see further Hardin 1988b, 41–44, 59–65). (I discuss the relationship between promise keeping and trust in chapter 3.)

A strong external force generally backs promises: the loss of credibility that follows from breaking them. Without credibility, one loses the possibility of making promises. Why should anyone want the power to make promises? All I really want in my own interest is the power to receive them. And there's the rub, because promises are generally part of a reciprocal exchange. The real penalty here is not that others will no longer rely on me but that they will not let me rely on them. As is commonly true also of trust relationships, promising typically involves intentions on the parts of two people. As with promising, future expectations, generally based in ongoing experience, contribute much of the force that binds in a trusting relationship. Trifonov and the lieutenant colonel could trust each other so long as future expectations of their relationship were motivating.

When it is repeated, the one-way trust game has some of the quality of the iterated prisoner's dilemma and therefore of mutual trust. It is not a prisoner's dilemma, however, *because there is no outcome that is best for the lieutenant colonel that is simultaneously worst for Trifonov.* When played once, the prisoner's dilemma of game 2 (figure 1.2) has four outcomes, whose orderings of payoffs define the prisoner's dilemma, while the one-way trust game has only three outcomes. The worst outcome for Trifonov in any given play of the one-way trust game is analogous to the noncooperation, or status quo, outcome (3,

3) in the prisoner's dilemma. If Trifonov is the column player in game 2, the outcome in which the lieutenant colonel's payoff is 1 and Trifonov's 4 is not possible; hence a two-by-two matrix representation of the one-way trust game has an empty cell. Still, there must be some degree of mutual trust if they are to continue playing because each time he returns the 4,500 rubles Trifonov must take a risk that the lieutenant colonel will not continue the arrangement after the next and other future audits.

In mutual trust, again, the interaction is a finitely iterated exchange or prisoner's dilemma. According to a standard argument in game theory, one should not cooperate in such a game. The argument begins with the premise that one should treat the final play of a finite series of plays of the game as a one-shot game, in which one should defect. If one should defect on the final play, however, then the penultimate play is de facto a final play in the sense that it can have no effect on anything thereafter, and so one should defect on the penultimate play as well. By tedious induction backward, one should defect already on the first play in the series.

If the backward induction argument is compelling, it is hard to see how rational individuals could ever enter into normal relationships of trust and exchange. All such relationships would have to be grounded in something extrarational, perhaps in normative commitments to be altruistic or more decent than is rational. On this view, the fact that there is apparently a great deal of trust in our lives suggests that we are not rational. I think, on the contrary, that trust is eminently rational and that the backward induction argument is flawed. In brief, the flaw is this: Suppose I know that you are eminently rational and that you believe the backward induction argument. I also know that we could gain substantially from entering a series of exchanges that must terminate, perhaps unhappily, at some distant future point. I can now wreck your backward induction by simply cooperating at our first encounter. You may now suppose I am irrational, or you may reconsider your induction. Either way, you may now decide it is in your interest to reciprocate my cooperation, so that we both gain far more than we would have from continuous mutual defection. Indeed, I think you must reconsider your induction because if I, by acting cooperatively, can get you to cooperate, you should realize that you could do as well with others in such an interaction. That is to say, you must agree that it would be sensible for you to cooperate initially rather than to defect.[11]

Moreover, and more to the point here, if you think cooperation in finitely iterated prisoner's dilemma interactions is irrational, you must wonder at your own tendency initially to take risks of cooperating with those whom you do not yet know well. All our relationships with people are of perhaps ill-defined but necessarily finite duration. The backward induction argument recommends initial distrust and, furthermore, continued distrust. This is a recommendation for slow death by abnegation in mimicry of Herman Melville's (1984) Bartleby, the scrivener, who became so asocial that he died of starvation and whose response to every entreaty was, "I would prefer not to." Whatever the apparent force of the backward induction argument for rarefied game theorists, it appears that actual people in living societies, including the game theorists who preach against the rationality of doing so, regularly take the risk of initially cooperating to upset that argument. Only for that reason do we have living societies.

The analysis here of the iterated prisoner's dilemma applies as well to an iterated one-way trust game, such as that between the lieutenant colonel and Trifonov. When that game is iterated, Trifonov has reason to cooperate in order to induce the lieutenant colonel to continue to loan him the loose cash after each periodic audit.

Thick Relationships

Now turn to trust that is grounded in a complex of overlapping iterated interactions over broad ranges of matters. In a small, close community, each of us can have ongoing relationships with every other one of us. Such overlapping relationships typically generate a lot of knowledge relevant to trusting any particular person, and they generate incentives not only between two partners in trust but also between each of them and others in the thick community. Even outside such a close community, I may belong to a subcommunity of similarly overlapping relationships with a close circle of relatives and friends and a small number of others with whom I regularly deal. In our subcommunity we may all know one another well enough to know the limits of one another's trustworthiness and to rely on each member's being responsible not merely to a particular truster but to the entire group of us. Those with whom we deal have not only the incentive of loss of our relationship but also that of loss of reputation and the possibility of shunning by others if they cheat us on a deal. Among these people we therefore know whom we can trust for what (Williams 1988). We may say that trust in these contexts of a close community or subcommunity builds on thick relationships.

Bernard Williams (1988) explicitly and some others implicitly define trust as a function of thick relationships. Williams supposes that therefore trust is not possible in many contexts in which we do not have such relationships. For example, he views the issue of my trusting political leaders as though it were an exact analog of the more familiar problem of my trusting a close associate. Because I am not involved in many overlapping interactions with the typical political leader, then, on the thick-relationship theory I cannot trust him or her; hence trust cannot handle this relationship in general (Luhmann 1980).

Williams, Luhmann at times, perhaps the anthropologist F. G. Bailey (1988), and others seem to see thick relationships as virtually definitive of trust. The correct way to see the role of thick relationships, however, is as one possible source of knowledge for the truster about the trustworthiness of another and one possible source of incentives to the trusted to be trustworthy. The first of these is essentially an epistemological role. Obviously, however, thick relationships yield only a part of the knowledge we have of others. Our understanding should not stop with only the thick-relationship class of epistemological considerations. In practice, this class may often have priority among our sources in our face-to-face interactions, but this descriptive fact does not give it conceptual or theoretical priority. A fully articulated theory will include this class as a part, not as the whole story, of the epistemology of trust. There is unlikely to be any quarrel with the view that knowledge of another's trustworthiness can come from many sources other than thick relationships.

Similarly, a thick relationship with another is only one of many possible ways to give that other the incentive to be trustworthy. A thick relationship with the truster commonly gives the trusted such incentives not only through the workings of an iterated prisoner's dilemma of reciprocal cooperation but also through reputational effects on others in the thick community. Such reputational effects must have a substantial effect on trustworthiness among familiar relations. Reputational effects give me an incentive to take your interests into account even if I do not value my relationship with you merely in its own right. They do this indirectly because I value relationships with others who might react negatively to my violation of your trust. Because my reputation is valuable to me in my further relationships, I encapsulate your interests in my own to some extent. The thick-relationship theory is therefore merely a special case of the encapsulated-interest theory of trust. It is a partial theory that does not generalize to many contexts. In any theory of trust, the restriction to small-scale thick relationships must follow from other principles. Going back to those principles is a first step in generalizing the theory.

It is a merit of the thick-relationship theory of trust that it blocks the quick blurring of individual and institutional problems, which is one of the most common mistakes in writings on trust. Writers in all disciplines occasionally succumb to the easy analogy from individual to institutional issues that abstracts from the differences in individual-

level and institutional-level constraints and possibilities. For some explanatory theories of trust and how it can work, Williams's conclusion that trust cannot be generalized beyond the small scale may well
follow. For other theories, it might be easy to see how individual-level
and institutional-level trust are conceptually related even though different kinds of data or evidence are commonly relevant at different
levels. I address this issue further in chapter 7.

From Interests to Well-Being

Framing an account of trust as encapsulated interest may provoke an
unfortunate misunderstanding. Sometimes interests are the whole
story of a person's motivations in a particular context. Typically, however, I have an interest in having more resources, such as money, only
because they enable me to consume or experience various things.
These consumptions constitute my welfare. The whole story is one of
well-being through the use of resources. Interests are merely a proxy
for this whole story. It would be a mistake, however, to suppose that
interests translate smoothly into well-being or even consumptions.
Consumptions generally trade off against one another (and against
interests), because if I use my resources for one consumption I may
have none for other consumptions.

It is also a mistake to suppose that my well-being is merely selfish.
Among the things that make me enjoy life are the enjoyments of certain others. I might enjoy a lovely dinner, but I might enjoy it even
more with you. Or I might want my son to enjoy the evening and
might use some of my resources to make that possible. My well-being
will often depend on my sharing intentions with you to do things
with or for you.

It is common to say that people are rational in some contexts and
not in others. One might be seemingly rational in choosing between
two jobs but not in choosing a spouse. It is even supposed that some
whole cultures are less rational than others. James Scott (1976) has
argued that the peasants of Southeast Asia, for example, are driven
by a "moral economy." What he means is that they do not maximize
their production of rice. Rather than adopting seed grains that would
have large average annual yields, they stick with grains that will almost always produce enough to keep them from starving but much
less on average than the most productive seeds.

Scott says that these peasants have "preferences which do not
make sense in terms of income alone" (Scott 1976, 35). But preferences
make sense only over whole states of affairs, in which income is only
part of what matters. The peasants are like anyone else; they want
income only for what it will buy for them. If in a bad year with the

higher-yielding grain they starve, their income will have done little for them. As is presumably true of Scott and virtually everyone else as well, I also do not have an unrestricted preference for higher income. If higher income entails giving up my academic life or more of my leisure time, I may not prefer it to my present income with my present lifestyle and consumption pattern. There are *no preferences* that "make sense in terms of income alone." Income is just a proxy for what we really want. And interest in the encapsulated-interest model of my trust of you is merely a proxy for all that you might take into account on my behalf.[12]

Concluding Remarks

The encapsulated-interest account of trust holds that the trusted encapsulates the interest of the truster and therefore has incentive to be trustworthy in fulfilling the truster's trust. The encapsulation happens through causal interactions in the iterated one-way trust game, iterated exchange (or prisoner's dilemma), and thick relationships. None of these, however, is itself definitive of the trust relation. They are all merely ways to give the trusted incentive to take the interests of the truster into account. This might be done in other ways as well. For example, we might suppose that a near variant of the iterated exchange relationship is reputational effects on my incentives (as discussed further in chapter 6). If I fulfill your trust, that action might help me in other relationships that I value or would value, and if I fail your trust, that action might jeopardize other relationships I might have.

Consider another class of ways I might come to take your interest into account. If I love you, or am your close friend, or am altruistic toward you, I might directly count your interest to some extent as my own. In economists' jargon, I might partially include your utility in mine. Hence you can trust me to some extent just because the effect of our interaction on your welfare will matter to me. We commonly trust our parents, siblings, close friends, spouses, and others who are close to us in this way within varying limits. One might wish to call these normative instances of trust. But the actual trusting is not different from the purely interested cases under the trust game or iterated exchange. If there is a normative quality to these instances from love and so forth, it is in the fact of the love or friendship and the caring for another that follows from these.

It might also happen that what affects your welfare similarly affects mine, so that I should act de facto in your interest just because the same action would be in my interest. Here, however, we would not want to count me as someone you could trust so much as merely someone from whom you can expect beneficial actions. For example, in the important coordination of traffic, as noted earlier, with everyone driving on the right (or everyone on the left), we share an interest to such an extent that our welfares are causally interdependent even though we need not care at all about one another. My driving on the right is not an instance of my having a positive causal interest in your actions in the sense that I actually want you to interact with me, as I do want you to interact with me in a beneficial exchange and as the lieutenant colonel wanted Trifonov to interact with him. It is, rather, a case in which I would actively prefer that you and I were not even interacting—I would be safer if you were off the road. If your interest is to do what you do independently of my presence, your interest does not meaningfully encapsulate mine.

If we consider all the trust relations we experience, we find that a large fraction of them fall into three categories: relationships or interactions that are iterated, those that are backed up by institutions, and those that are mediated by other (noninstitutional) third parties. This chapter has focused on the first of these categories. Chapter 4, on distrust, suggests that such interactions are inadequate to secure cooperative behavior in many contexts. Chapter 6 considers mediation by third parties (often institutional third parties), and chapters 7 and 8 consider social and institutional devices for mobilizing cooperation where trust might be lacking or inadequate to secure cooperation. All of these categories can be understood easily without any supposed residue beyond rational expectations grounded in the motivations or interests of the cooperating parties because each of them builds in the incentives necessary to induce trustworthy behavior—although, of course, these incentives can be and sometimes are trumped by others. The first category—iterated interactions—seems to be far and away the largest in ordinary interpersonal life. That is because much of our lives is spent in ongoing relationships, such relationships constitute much of what is most valuable to us, and we make substantial commitments to one another in such relationships.

Some of the alternative visions of trust (canvassed in chapter 3) are plausible accounts of some instances of trust. I might trust you with respect to certain things because your moral commitments make you reliable or because your character virtually ensures your relevant action. In such cases, my trust is grounded in an account of your trustworthiness. Such accounts differ significantly from the model of trust as encapsulated interest, and they often have different implications in various social contexts. Consider two examples.

I once had an acquaintance of whom many people said, with genuine force, that he was a person you could trust. Alas, that depended on who "you" were. Many people did not trust him at all because they thought him deceitful and manipulative. The latter group included people whose interests often conflicted with his and whose future value to him he had seemingly written off. He could be richly and deeply trusted by those who shared enough of his interests, not at all by those who did not. He was almost mythical in his capacity to put people into two distinct classes. On a cynical reading, he was not trustworthy on the encapsulated-interest account. He was merely reliable to those whose interests he happened to share.

For the second example, one might note that a member of some ethnic or other group is extremely reliable within that group but is capable of viciousness and deceit outside it. Within the group, I might be considered wonderfully trustworthy, but outside the group I might be thought utterly reprehensible in my abuse of any opportunity to exploit or harm certain others.

Ethnic bigots and my acquaintance of the past, if viewed strictly in the contexts of their own groups, might seem generally to be acting from trustworthy character or moral commitments. Seen in a different or much broader context they might seem to be not trustworthy either in character or moral commitments. On the account of trust as encapsulated interest, however, their actions might readily fit their own interests both within and outside their groups. We should therefore be clear which of these conceptions we are using when we attempt an explanation of some behavior.

If trust is grounded in encapsulated interest, then clearly it is, as noted earlier, relational. It is not merely a reflection of my character or yours. Little of the systematic empirical work on trust allows us to assess any relational elements. Much of the psychological work is on high and low trusters. Most of the survey work is on relatively loose claims of how much subjects "trust" most people or government. The game theoretic work often deliberately excludes any possibility that the players will have any broader relationship—often, for example, the adversary-partner of a player is unknown and will not be met again after a single, initial interaction. Claims from these bodies of empirical research therefore can tell us virtually nothing about trust as encapsulated interest or any other relational conception of trust. (I address many of the empirical studies later in relevant contexts.) Typically, the most we can get from this research is some insight into the readiness of people initially to take risks of cooperation with unknown others—usually very small risks. Because trust in our lives is generally relational and is commonly to be explained by relational considerations, one may hope that empirical studies will begin to take relational elements into account.

The discussion in this chapter is of trust between individuals. Later, in chapters 7 and 8, I take up generalizations from trusting individuals to trusting groups or institutions. The goal in these chapters is to make sense of trusting groups or institutions in terms analogous to those of trusting individuals. When people say, in ordinary language, that they trust the government, *they do not mean anything closely analogous to what they typically mean when they say they trust another person*. That can become clear, however, only if we first unpack what ordinary individual-level trust is about in common instances.

Chapter 2

Trustworthiness

T HE GREAT importance of trust in ordinary life can be read in the massive role it plays in great literature—or, rather, the role that betrayal of trust plays. Trust may be second only to love as a plot line and motivator, and even half of the power of love as a plot line is in the eventual betrayal of it. Betrayal is, of course, not a failure of trust but a failure of trustworthiness. It is odd therefore that in academic writings—both philosophical and social scientific—the focus is heavily on trust rather than on trustworthiness (but see Shklar 1984). Poets, playwrights, and novelists get the issue right, but academics often miss it. Indeed, throughout academic writings on trust there seems to be a tendency to say things that would make easy sense if applied to trustworthiness but make less sense when applied to trust. They make sense for trust, if at all, only indirectly through the causal connection that trustworthiness begets trust.

If my trust in you is well placed, that is because you are likely to have the motivation to do what I trust you to do. That is to say, you are likely to be trustworthy. In the encapsulated-interest account, trustworthiness is just the capacity to judge one's interests as dependent on doing what one is trusted to do. In virtually all accounts, the central problem in your trustworthiness is your commitment to fulfill another's trust in you. We commonly assert commitments, but those who are to rely on us must want not merely the assertion of a commitment now but some hope that the commitment will actually motivate relevant actions in a future moment. How do we make a present commitment work into the future? There are three general categories of reasons for fulfilling such commitments. First, there are internal inducements. We might simply have or somehow adopt a relevant disposition. We can do this by bootstrapping a bald commitment, from moral compunction, or out of character or habit.

Second, we can subject ourselves to external inducements. We can try to arrange matters so that our interests will be aligned with our commitment when the time for acting on that commitment comes. We can do this by setting up ad hoc personal devices or by relying on societal and institutional devices. An individual cannot do much about the availability of societal and institutional arrangements—they either exist or they do not. But if they do, I can hope and often even contrive that they will help me rely on you. Legal and other institutional constraints can give us strong incentives to be trustworthy.

Third, we can subject ourselves to a mixture of internal and external inducements. We can be induced by norms that motivate and even sanction behavior. Norms can evidently be internalized, so that we simply act from them without need of sanction. I have little to say here about this possibility, on which even the best arguments for how it works are not very compelling, although the claim that it works seems clearly to be correct. Instead, I discuss norms primarily in their external role, in which their effectiveness depends on the success of sanctions from others.

The encapsulated-interest account of trust is grounded in the partial alignment of the interests of the trusted with those of the truster, and it comes primarily under the second of these categories. Because many norms and social conventions are backed by sanctions, it is commonly in our interest to follow them. Hence it will often be in our interest to be trustworthy even though it would sometimes be wrong to say that this is because our interests encapsulate the interests of someone who might trust us. If you are driven by institutional constraints or societal conventions, then you have a strong incentive that does not depend on me or any ongoing relationship with me. In such a case, we can have merely congruent or compatible interests without having the least concern for each other.

These three general forms of inducement—internal, external, and mixed inducements—to be trustworthy in some future moment determine the range of forms that commitments must take in the three cases. After discussing the sometimes mistaken tendency to speak of trust when the issue is trustworthiness, I discuss the internal inducements of dispositions for trustworthiness, beginning with a case of a bald disposition that is simply and deliberately adopted—the case of Richard Wagner's Alberich, the Nibelung. I then discuss other internal dispositional accounts of trustworthiness, accounts based on external interest, and, finally, the mixed-motive account from norms.

Trust and Trustworthiness

Surprisingly, much of the literature on trust hardly mentions trustworthiness, even though implicitly much of it is primarily about trustworthiness, not about trust. Consider four striking cases. First, under the guise of discussing trust, the philosopher Bernard Williams (1988) gives an account of the possibilities of general trustworthiness, from which trust is merely inferred. Second, the economist Roland McKean (1975) ostensibly addresses the economics of trust, but his actual problem is that of trustworthiness. It is not trust itself that is the collective good in his account but trustworthiness. Creating institutions that help secure trustworthiness thus helps to support or induce trust.

Third, Bernard Barber (1983, 170) says that "we need to discover . . . how to foster trust and make it more effective." His concern is with general social relations. Surely, what we need for making these go better is trustworthiness. This is the inference to be drawn from Barber's study of professionalism and the problems of getting professionals to behave well on behalf of their clients, clients who need professional help because they do not know enough to handle their own problems of health care, legal advocacy, and so forth. Resolving this problem is, in Barber's account, what the creation of professional norms is about. Their point is to make doctors, lawyers, and other professionals trustworthy. Teaching potential patients merely to trust their doctors would be perverse if the doctors are not trustworthy.

The fourth case is more complicated. The sociologist Niklas Luhmann (1980, 8) says trust constitutes a more effective form of complexity reduction. This is a very elliptical claim. Clearly, where there is trust that is justified there are increased possibilities for beneficial experience and action. Trust by itself, however, constitutes nothing. Presumably Luhmann is saying that we cannot handle enormous complexity without having others act de facto on our behalf. If we cannot count on their acting in our interests, however, we may be reluctant to empower them or to follow their advice. Hence whatever can secure their trustworthiness enough for us to trust them will help us manage complexity. That is to say, again, the focal problem is trustworthiness, not trust.[1] Elsewhere, Luhmann (1988, 95) says he is concerned with social mechanisms that generate trust. Once again, he has substituted concern with trust for concern with trustworthiness. Commonly, the best device for creating trust is to establish and support trustworthiness.[2] As before, acting on trust without the latter can bring harm.

Linger with this issue for a moment. In *The Remains of the Day*, Kazuo Ishiguro portrays Mr. Stevens, an aging butler rethinking his life with his late master. In an imagined debate with another servant, Stevens says, "the likes of you and I will never be in a position to comprehend the great affairs of today's world, and our best course will always be to put our trust in an employer we judge to be wise and honourable, and to devote our energies to the task of serving him to the best of our ability" (Ishiguro 1990, 201). He slowly revalues his master from the point of view of others, who detested the master's reprehensible and foolish politics. "At least [his lordship] had the privilege of being able to say at the end of his life that he made his own mistakes," Stevens reflects. "I cannot even claim that. You see, I *trusted*. I trusted in his lordship's wisdom. All those years I served him, I trusted I was doing something worthwhile. I can't even say I made my own mistakes. Really—one has to ask oneself—what dignity is there in that?" (Ishiguro 1990, 243). Stevens recognizes that trust can finally be stupid and, when it seemingly justifies action or inaction, even culpable.

Hence merely trusting in itself obviously need not help in managing complexity well—it could lead to dismal results, including quick destruction. Again, the core of Luhmann's account of the role of trust must be an account of the importance of trustworthiness. If his account really commends trust in its own right, it elevates Stevens's culpable stupidity. Trust has led Stevens not to manage complexity so much as to fall victim to it.

In general, the complexity of the problem of trust derives primarily from the complexity of the problem of trustworthiness. As this chapter demonstrates, the motivations for being trustworthy are manifold. In a sense, trusting someone in some context is simply to be explained as merely the expectation that the person will most likely be trustworthy. Trust is little more than knowledge; trustworthiness is a motivation or a set of motivations for acting. Motivationally, there is much to be explained about why someone acts as though with trust when there is little ground to believe that the other is trustworthy, so that, in fact, there is little or no trust. The explanation of your actually trusting in some context will be simply an epistemological, evidentiary matter—not a motivational problem. The explanation of your trustworthiness can be either simple or complicated, and it will depend on motivation.

In the discussions of several conceptions of trust in chapter 3, the slippage from trust to trustworthiness becomes evident. This is true of the moralized accounts, with the possible exception of that of Lars Hertzberg (1988), who seems genuinely to insist that it is trust that is morally demanded of us. It is also true of both the genetic and the social evolutionary explanations for the rise of trust, which actually make sense rather of the rise of trustworthiness. The misconception infects the discussion of trust as a commodity and, perhaps, of trust as social capital. It might even infect functional accounts, such as Barber's (1983) and, less clearly, Luhmann's (1980; on functional accounts of trustworthiness, see further chapter 6).

Perhaps the most compelling reason for the frequent slippage, or at least for why it is not recognized immediately as such, is that trustworthiness commonly begets trust, because my trustworthiness will potentially reward your trusting me (if you act on your trust of me). Hence if something conceptually entails or causes trustworthiness, then indirectly it might entail or cause trust.

Dispositions of Trustworthiness

Much of the literature on trust seems to be grounded in dispositional assumptions, although these are often not articulated. I therefore discuss the plausible role of dispositions in establishing trustworthiness. A dispositional account of trustworthiness must be highly relational, because we cannot sensibly hope to assess others' dispositions unless we know them well either directly or by reputation. Dispositional accounts in psychology are often about the disposition of the truster rather than of the trusted. For example, people are assumed to be either high trusters or low trusters. Often the disposition is simply posited and left unexplained. In chapter 5, I treat the disposition to trust as essentially a problem in learning to judge trustworthiness.

Alternatively, we might suppose that the trusted acts from a disposition to be trustworthy. This is a somewhat peculiar disposition that might not ever have occurred to most people, other than perhaps in contexts of promising. Although a simple disposition to be trustworthy might be a real disposition for some people, we might sooner suppose that the issue is having a disposition to keep promises, to reciprocate, or to be cooperative with others who are cooperative. Following such dispositions would make one act in trustworthy ways in various contexts.

The ability to make commitments for future actions is of much more general interest than merely for the establishment of trustworthiness, and we can approach the more specific problem from the more general. An instructive way to characterize the problem of commitment is through the problem of "trusting" oneself. Can one depend on oneself? (see further Dasgupta 1988, 54). Again, as with ordinary trust of another, this is not a singular question. It involves at least three parts. What can *I* depend on myself to do? What can I depend on *myself* to do? *What* can I depend on myself to do? I may be morally certain that I will live up to some commitments and much less confident that I will live up to others. I may know very well that, under the influence of camaraderie and drink at a party, I will suffer weakness of will and will stay too late and will therefore fail to meet some commitment I have made for tomorrow. You may know yourself well and therefore know that you will not do the sensible thing at certain moments. That is, you would not be able to depend on yourself in that respect.

You might not know whether to depend on yourself in some contexts. For example, people sometimes unexpectedly discover themselves to be courageous or cowardly only when faced with a physical threat to themselves or others. We cannot be sure we know our limits when we have never tested them.

A particularly pessimistic vision of trustworthiness is Bob Dylan's (1995, 495) song "Trust Yourself," which ends with these lines:

Trust yourself
And you won't be disappointed when vain people let you down. . . .
Don't trust me to show you love
When my love may be only lust.
If you want somebody you can trust, trust yourself.

Dylan is wrong, of course, about how surely one can trust oneself. Trustworthiness not only requires that one share the interests of the other as directly or indirectly one's own but also requires the competence to serve those interests. Dylan's lyrics are for and about a generation of people who commonly doubted their own competence and who were often as impulsive as Dylan's lyrics suggest.

Bald Dispositions

The cataclysmic events of Wagner's cycle of operas, *The Ring of the Nibelung*, follow from an extraordinary act of commitment in the opening minutes of *The Rhinegold*. Alberich, the Nibelung, is cavorting after the Rhine maidens:

Passionate fevers,
fervid desires,
have set me on fire!
Rage and longing,
    wild and frantic, drive me to madness!
Though you may laugh and lie,
yearning conquers my heart
and I'll not rest till I've caught you! (Wagner 1977, 12)[3]

Only a few minutes later—although this is Wagner, so it may seem much longer—after learning that anyone who can forswear love can gain enormous power from the Rhinegold, Alberich asks,

The world's wealth
can be mine if I utter the curse?
    Though love be denied me,
yet cunning can bring me delight? (Wagner 1977, 16)

Quickly he seizes the gold, swearing, "Love, I curse you forever!" (Wagner 1977, 16).[4] By committing himself Alberich gains extraordinary power. It is no surprise that such a superhuman act should earn great rewards, even magical rewards. Even the great god Wotan, who is unable to make such a commitment to forswear love, is impressed by lowly Alberich's resolve (Wagner 1977, 106–7). The demands made by this commitment might sound commonplace—after all, monks of various religions have chosen celibacy. They do so, however, with substantial social and institutional constraints to keep them celibate, and even then they often fail. Alberich commits himself without any social structure to give him the incentive to stay unloving.

There is, of course, much in Wagner that strains belief. But is anything in the entire *Ring*—or all of opera more generally—less credible than the possibility that any sexually yearning adult male (of whatever Alberich's species was) could turn from lusting to the point of rapacious madness in one minute to credibly forswearing love lust[5] forevermore in the next? (Wagner 1977, 15). Alberich, one of the pettiest figures in all of literature and opera, makes one of the grandest of commitments. Could anyone believe Alberich's conversion, believe that his commitment will carry him through? Unfortunately, Wagner does not tell us enough to know. For all its greatness, the *Ring* turns on this bit of psychological nonsense.

Alberich is preposterous. If we wish to understand real people, we will need a better psychology. What we will have to understand are the capacities for making commitments and the capacities for assessing someone's trustworthiness, capacities that must largely be learned. (The learned capacity to assess trustworthiness is the topic of chapter 5.) One cannot simply start trusting people as of tomorrow unless the people one deals with and one's relationships with them are suddenly different in relevant ways and one is privileged to know this.

The issue for this chapter is what a new person can do to convince me of his or her commitment to fulfilling my trust. For example, it might have been in Alberich's interest to say he would forswear love forever even if he knew he would later cheat. What could have made his curse credible? If he genuinely had forsworn love forever, imagine how forlorn he would have been when, four operas later, he was one of the few survivors in the cast to see the delectable Rhine maidens retrieve their gold. Poor Alberich, now bereft of the gold and its power, would still be bereft of the possibility of love. What was the nature of his commitment? Was it enforced by a supernatural power that would withdraw his power if he violated his pledge? Did the enforcement end when he lost the ring—it was stolen for Wotan through cunning—that was fabricated from the Rhinegold? (He went on to father Hagen with Grimhild, so presumably his lust returned and he acted on it.) Or was it merely an inner disposition? Perhaps it is plausible that some people could actually make as dramatic a commitment as Alberich made and then stick with it merely from strength of character or a remarkable capacity for consistency.

David Gauthier (1986, chapter 6, especially 162), Edward McClennen (1990; but see Skyrms 1996), and others suppose that we can will ourselves to have a particular disposition that, in the future moment when we bring it to bear, is not in our interest. We might, for example, have to do this to secure a present benefit. Perhaps this is what Wagner meant Alberich to do. There are two distinct issues here: First, how can we make a bald commitment in a single interaction? Second, how can we make a bald commitment to behave generally in a certain way in potentially many interactions with different people in the future, as Alberich did? The latter is of central interest here, because the focus is on a disposition for trustworthiness in general. Most of us, however, would probably have to admit that we cannot readily or ever do such a thing. We might think ourselves capable of undying love for and commitment to, say, our child or parent, but we do not come by that love through mere decision, as Alberich supposedly came by his commitment. As Hume (1978 [1739–40], 3.2.5, page 517) says, with his usual confidence, "'Tis certain we can naturally no more change our own sentiments, than the motions of the heavens." With almost as much confidence, we can agree that he is surely right if he means merely by act of will. Yet Alberich committed himself to blocking his own emotions.

Few of our commitments ever have such force as Alberich's curse supposedly had. Our strongest commitments are often merely those that are clearly backed by our interests. For example, Alberich might have been governed by some magical power that would have taken back the Rhinegold if he ever acted on his lust. Then, at least, perhaps he could have ended the *Ring* cycle without the Rhinegold but with the renewed possibility of love and lust. (Romantic love may be characterized as an exquisite combination of lust and devotion—Alberich evidently would have settled for lust.) Our task is to contrive real-world substitutes for such magical powers as Alberich may have faced to keep us in line.

Alberich's curse could be seen as a commitment not to act from lust, a commitment to abjure love. Why is this commitment dubious? Alberich's lust is largely not a matter of deliberate choice. Rather, it is something at least partly in control of him, something that gives him strong motivations, as love would do if he ever stumbled into it. His commitment to defy it means a commitment to ignore those motivations when they come. Typically, we think such a strong motivation cannot be literally ignored, although it can be trumped by a contrary motivation, such as Alberich's desire for wealth and power. His psychological problem, once he has the Rhinegold, is to connect future motivations of love or lust to his contrary desire for power, so that his lust can be trumped in that moment when he already wears the ring made from the Rhinegold and he need no longer abjure lust to obtain the gold and its power.

Our problem in asserting our trustworthiness is similar to Alberich's in asserting his disavowal of ever loving or lusting. When the time comes to live up to our assertions, we may face forcefully contrary motivations. Other things being equal, we might readily fulfill our commitment. Other things are often not at all equal, however. Once we already have whatever led us to our commitment in the first place, we may no longer find it in our interest to keep the commitment, even though, if we had been able to get our benefit and fulfill our commitment in a single moment, we might happily have done so. What we lose when receipt of the benefit and fulfillment of the commitment are separated in time is the coupling of the motivations into, in essence, a single motivation. It would be strange in the future moment to say that we violate our earlier motivation when we no longer wish to fulfill our commitment. This is the central problem of bald commitments into the future: we cannot tie our future and present motivations together to yield a single "net" motivation for action.

Moral Dispositions for Trustworthiness

Much of the literature on trust treats it as an inherently moral matter, although often this is a misconception, because the actual arguments are that trustworthiness is a moral matter. Unfortunately, this is not a simple issue, in part because moral theory is very complex. In what follows, I simplify the issue substantially but without distortion by speaking of two large branches of moral theory whose focuses are radically different. A deontological branch focuses on rules for behavior—that is, on the nature of actions. A consequentialist branch focuses on the results of actions, not the nature of the actions themselves. In either case, if I believe you have strong moral compunctions to be reliable in some context, then I have strong reason to rely on you in that context.[6]

We can imagine a dispositional account of either acting on trust or being trustworthy. In fact, the learning account of coming to be able to trust, in the sense of coming to recognize relevant facts about others, suggests a dispositional, although not moral, account. As argued in chapter 5, if I had an especially benign upbringing, I might have a disposition to take risks on people until they prove to be not worth the risk. If I had a grim upbringing, on the other hand, I might judge few people to be worth the risk of trying to cooperate with them.

One might also say I have a disposition to trust, as though to say I have a disposition to know certain kinds of things and, perhaps, not others. That is a more complex claim that might make psychological sense, but it is not evidently a major claim in the trust literature. What is claimed seems more nearly to be that some people, commonly labeled (misleadingly) high trusters, are more likely to take risks of cooperating than are certain other people, commonly labeled low trusters. These distinctions are drawn in work by many psychologists and social psychologists (Rotter 1980; Yamagishi and Yamagishi 1994).

The more compelling claim, however, is that some people have a perhaps moral disposition to be trustworthy. For example, if I do something cooperative toward you, you reciprocate even though there might be little reason for you to expect to gain anything further in return for your reciprocation. This disposition could be nearly absolute (assuming no external, negative effects of our interaction). You always reciprocate.

Note that this disposition seems genuinely to be a disposition to be trustworthy, not merely to act in a trustworthy manner, although the latter may often be entailed. A comparable disposition to be trusting seems much less likely, because its range is radically larger than that of any disposition to be trustworthy. If I am always trusting, I will be the gullible target of increasingly many people. After losing repeatedly from my excessive trust, I will have overwhelming incentive to alter my disposition. I might still have a risk-taking disposition, but this will be more limited in that it will not lead me to take egregious risks. Hence trust and trustworthiness are not analogous or symmetrical in this respect, because one can be disposed to trustworthiness without significant risk. One will be led to invoke one's disposition only when in fact one has done well, as in a mutually beneficial exchange. A relationship cannot make you worse off if you are merely trustworthy in it. It can, however, make you substantially worse off if you are trusting in it—as his relationship with Trifonov probably made the lieutenant colonel worse off.

Indeed, if one can exhibit a disposition for trustworthiness, as in Gauthier's (1986) moral theory, one can even expect to have beneficial interactions, especially single-shot interactions, that would not have been available otherwise.[7] A disposition to trustworthiness might therefore be in one's interest, so that, if one could arrange to have a disposition, one would choose to have a disposition for trustworthiness. An infant seemingly has something like a disposition to trust because without it the infant would not survive. Much of growing up is learning to override and therefore to shed that disposition when it causes trouble.

In keeping with this distinction between dispositions for trusting and being trustworthy, we might suppose that there are people who are relatively inclined to be trustworthy independently of the immediate payoff from being so. Indeed, if asked, apparently most people in my milieu think that they personally have such a disposition. Most of them have probably never really been tested for just how strong and overriding this disposition is for them, just as most political officeholders who campaign against graft may not have been tested for how strongly they would stand against graft if proffered to them. For many of these people, however, it seems plausible that their disposition to be trustworthy is strong.

Note incidentally that the asymmetry between trust and trustworthiness with respect to dispositions means that trustworthiness might be a two-part relation in a way that trust cannot sensibly be. I might be trustworthy with respect to any and every matter that anyone entrusts to me (again, assuming there are no negative external effects). I am then trustworthy with respect to the class of people who would entrust anything to me. Yet there are few if any people I would trust with respect to everything.

Also note the important potential fact that contrary incentives might not be very effective in altering motivations grounded in moral dispositions. We do not have a good account of the psychological or other force of such dispositions, but they seem to be extremely strong in some cases. We should qualify this claim, however, because psychological research suggests that we tend to overestimate dispositions as a cause of behavior (Jones 1979). On the contrary, we may tend to underestimate the role of interests, as is suggested by the account of supervenience in chapter 3.

Moral Rules   First consider the possibility and coherence of a moral rule for trustworthiness. Suppose I know that you rigidly follow certain moral rules, including your variant of the golden rule, which is always to reciprocate any kind or cooperative action toward you. Hence I am quite confident that in certain contexts you will act in ways that are equivalent to being trustworthy even in the encapsulated-interest sense. Something like this variant of the golden rule seems to have motivated many people I have known on occasion. Indeed, it may have motivated more people than I would have noticed, so that it might be an important source of trustworthiness. It would be of interest to attempt to weigh its frequency against that of the motivation of encapsulated interest in various contexts. It seems likely that the latter is more important for many kinds of relationships that are commonplace in our lives.

It might also be interesting to assess whether there has been a weakening of the force of a moral rule for trustworthiness over time and its possible displacement by considerations of interest, and perhaps therefore by the motivation of encapsulated interest. An enormous literature claims that moral rules are in decline as motivators in our society (see, for example, Schwartz 1986, Bloom 1987)—but a similarly enormous literature has made similar claims in many eras and societies, and one might be forgiven for suspecting that every older generation thinks every younger generation's morals have declined. There may never have been a shortage of moral doomsayers. The issue has not, however, been joined with much empirical research, and there is little one can say beyond the kinds of speculative writings that prevail on the subject.

One thing we can say fairly conclusively is that, in a moral rule system that is articulated enough to cover much of the moral life, the rules must, as in the case of the norms discussed earlier, occasionally be in conflict with one another. For example, in one of the most contested remarks by any major moral theorist, Immanuel Kant holds that one is bound not to lie even when faced with an assassin who asks whether his intended victim is in one's apartment. Kant supposes that effectively turning over the intended victim to the assassin is a less grievous wrong than lying to the assassin. He writes that "although by a certain lie I in fact do no wrong to any person [such as the intending murderer], yet I infringe the principle of justice in regard to all indispensably necessary statements *generally* (I do wrong formally, though not materially); *and this is much worse than to commit an injustice to any individual*" (Kant 1909 [1797], 365, final emphasis added; see further Hardin in press b, chapter 6). A rule to be trustworthy could run aground on Kant's account of his rule against lying. (Beware of such "moral" rules.)

Consequences   The main branch of consequentialist moral theory is utilitarianism. Utilitarianism commends actions that enhance welfare overall and commends against those that detract from welfare overall. To apply the utilitarian principle in the context of a potential trusting relationship we must go beyond the two parties in that relationship. Hence almost all of the analyses of this book and its focus on the encapsulation of the interests of the truster in the interests of the trusted are at best a beginning of a utilitarian account. We can isolate the actions of the lieutenant colonel and Trifonov to speak clearly about the nature of trust and trustworthiness within their relationship; and we can easily enough assess the consequences for the two of them of their actions. To give a fully utilitarian account, however, we would have to assess many other consequences of their exchanges.

The issue for the lieutenant colonel and Trifonov, if we are to suppose they are acting from utilitarian morality, is not whether their actions produced good consequences overall but whether they should have expected them to. It seems unlikely that either of them could have made a good case for the generally good consequences of their dealings with each other, either before or after the fact. After the fact, although Trifonov may have done quite well, the lieutenant colonel's family suffered grievous harm in the loss of status in an excessively status-conscious society. Their financial losses eventually played a role in the conviction of Dmitri Karamazov, who was falsely accused of killing his own father. Before the fact, most of the lieutenant colonel's losses could have been thought to be at least possible risks of his dishonest dealings, although Karamazov's role and fate would not likely have been imagined.

In a utilitarian assessment of our various dealings with another we can commonly suppose that the interactions are more or less decoupled from all else, and we can simply choose according to what's best for the pair of us. In standard mutual trust interactions, I typically cannot justify cheating you on utilitarian grounds because I cannot judge that the pair of us is made better off on the whole unless we complete our exchange. We will know that the move from the status quo ante of no exchange to the condition of a completed exchange benefits both of us, so that it is better overall than not exchanging. If we cannot perform accurate interpersonal comparisons of utility, we cannot conclude that either of the outcomes in which I cheat you or you cheat me is better overall than the status quo ante of no exchange. Hence consummation of a mutual trust relationship is typically utilitarian, so long as it does not have substantial negative effects on others.[8] A strong utilitarian commitment therefore generally implies a strong commitment to trustworthiness.

External Motivations for Trustworthiness

Either a magic force external to Alberich will cancel his wealth and power when he slips and acts on his lust or falls in love, or his commitment is entirely internal. Insofar as we can know what Wagner might have meant about something that he did not write in sufficient detail to tell us directly, we can suppose that Alberich's commitment was strictly internal. He willed himself never again to entertain love. Many thinkers ridicule such willing. As Thomas Hobbes (1968 [1739–40], 2.26: 313) has noted, nothing keeps me from changing my mind if there is only my own will to motivate me.[9] I can be capricious. Superficially at least, this seems so overwhelmingly correct a view that one might think that there is little point in exploring the possibility of direct willing of trustworthiness into a distant future of manifold changes in opportunity.

Nevertheless, one can sometimes "will" oneself into future action indirectly. One can predict well enough how one would act in certain circumstances and can therefore sometimes set matters up to stimulate a particular response. For example, I may know that, once I get out of bed in the morning, I am really up and I will not return to sleep. Therefore I set my alarm clock on the dresser a few feet from my bed, so that I will have to stand to stop its noise. I have then used an external device to get myself on my feet, but it is something internal about me that keeps me from returning to bed and to sleep. If the alarm were too near, I might often turn it off and go back to sleep.[10] (The innovation of the snooze alarm, which sounds like an improvement over the simple once-only alarm, has become a curse to many people.) You might be even better than I am at getting up, and you might find it uncomfortable to stay in bed after first waking, so that the nearby alarm would work for you. Perhaps analogous devices can be called into action for making ourselves trustworthy in certain matters.

When such quasi-internal devices are unavailable or weak, a more forceful move is to invoke external constraints. For example, we can make our commitment in public in full self-understanding that our embarrassment over publicly failing the commitment would most likely trump our costs of keeping to it. Then we do not face motivation from the commitment itself but from social constraints that make it in our interest to fulfill the commitment. That is to say, we no longer depend on contriving commitments to be motivators in their own right. *Indeed, by making the costs of reneging on our commitment high, we can virtually bring our future action of fulfillment into the present so that we tie our present and future motivations into a single net motivation now for action in the future.* In a suggestive term of older contract law, we presentiate that future.

Typically, the external devices that secure our important commitments depend essentially on the actions—often sanctions—of others. We therefore are concerned with social constraints. Society offers three quite distinct general categories of controls to individuals who could benefit from constraining their future actions. First, there are the particular, small-scale controls of ongoing relationships of family, friends, and what we might crudely call geographical associates—those with whom we will almost inescapably be thrown into further dealings. We can include simple reputational effects here as a relatively indirect way of making our relationship ongoing. Second, there are the broad social constraints that commonly support conventions. Third, there are the elaborate, large-scale controls of the law and other institutions in a relatively extensive society.[11] Where these social controls fail we are left with our own personal devices of internal motivations, which all too often means we are left in the lurch.

The first of these social devices—constraint by our ongoing relations with close associates—is spelled out in the encapsulated-interest theory in chapter 1 (also see chapter 5 on the epistemology of trust). As in the case of the relationship between Trifonov and Dmitri Karamazov's lieutenant colonel, trustworthiness involves the reinforcing incentives that come from ongoing relations, such as in the iterated trust game or iterated exchange relations. In such a relationship, my reliability in this moment may be reinforced by my interest in having the relationship continue. Here I focus on the use of the second and third devices—constraint by larger social conventions and constraint by constructed organizational incentives—as they can be made to support trust between persons by making them trustworthy. For example, the legal system of contract enforcement enables me to trust you in some formal exchange. (In chapter 7, the focus is on whether I can trust a particular institution and whether that institution—in particular, government or one of its agencies—has the capacity for trustworthiness.)

Social Constraints

We can use social constraints merely to help us overcome our weakness in keeping to some purpose, such as going to the gym for regular workouts despite our taking little pleasure in the activity and having many other things to do. The self-manipulation to get ourself to the gym is, however, a trivial case. Consider a much less trivial case, that of Maria, who is Catholic but who sees around her a majority population who are not Catholic and a majority of supposed Catholics who are less than faithful. Suppose Maria fears that she herself might slide away in the future—after all, she has seen others do so, including her husband—and she fears that her children may be seduced into the secular world. What can she do to secure or strengthen her future commitment to the faith? She could join a religious order, but that would be too drastic, and anyway she does not wish to abandon her children to the secular world.

Short of such a drastic move, Maria can do something that gets her more involved in the church and that constructs about her a society in which she would lose face if she relaxed her commitments. Suppose her greater involvement in the church leads her into its activities against abortion—not because she is necessarily hostile to abortion but because, by identifying herself with the church's antiabortion movement, she identifies herself more closely with the church and with her friends in the faith. She relocates herself in the world of Catholic political activism not because she shares the activist agenda but rather because she wants stronger connection to the church to keep her safer from the secular world of declining American Catholicism. Fearing for her continued faith, she throws herself in the way of fate, which, as Lady Murasaki Shikibu (1982 [ca. 1010], 234) says, can change our desires. And she ends up as an antiabortion activist and, perhaps, eventually a strongly committed antiabortionist.

In a more securely Catholic society, the fear of falling away from the faith might be less compelling because there are natural reinforcements, and there might be less urgent need to become deeply involved in the activities, including the political activities, of the church. In her society, however, Maria may need to construct her own reinforcements to keep her faith. Suppose that many American Catholics are like Maria—active because they want to be strongly tied to the church rather than because they share all of its politics. Commitment to the antiabortion movement might therefore be much stronger in a less Catholic society, such as the United States, than in a more solidly Catholic society. The difference is, however, not evidence of the greater intrinsic importance of the morality of abortion in the less Catholic society. Rather, abortion is taken on as an issue on the way to something else—namely, maintenance of the personal faith of future selves.

Maria uses fairly specific, almost personalized social constraints to keep herself faithful. We can often turn to the more general social constraints of conventions.[12] Consider the unusually powerful convention that motivated the life of the beautiful young lady Ukifune in Lady Murasaki Shikibu's (1976 [ca. 1010]) *The Tale of Genji*. This convention worked forcefully without need of law to back it.

The fictional Ukifune lives in eleventh-century Japan in the twilight of the world of the shining Prince Genji. She has left her worldly existence at court by having her head shaved, taking vows, and entering a nunnery, as a result of which she can never go back to her previous world. Cutting off hair that has taken her a lifetime to grow to many feet long is, in her society, a step that is visually, symbolically irreversible (Murasaki 1976 [ca. 1000], 1083). Ukifune therefore has little choice but to live up to her sudden commitment to her religious vows into the distant future, although that means a personally and culturally impoverished life compared with life at court. As distressed as everyone about her is that she has become a nun, no one thinks she can renege and return to society. She may grow to hate her life as a nun and wish she had never made such a commitment, but, short of suicide, she is virtually stuck with it. Ukifune wants the commitment that Alberich needs, but she requires neither magic nor bootstrapping to secure it.

Ukifune has chosen to leave her world because she has two potential lovers—the two most desirable men in her world—and she prefers to have neither rather than to have to choose between them. Yet this woefully weak person has made a stalwart commitment. At first, she intends to leave the world by dying, but she fails in her attempt and is rescued by chance to a nearby nunnery. Her decision to become a nun is then purely opportunistic. Her only actual commitment is to leave her world. If she cannot be dead, she can at least be a nun, even though she may have little commitment to any of the ostensible beliefs of Buddhism.

Under the social conventions of her time, Ukifune's was a virtually irrevocable commitment. In our society of radically looser conventions, you and I cannot so readily constrain ourselves as Ukifune did—our shaved heads might be nothing more than a frivolous style of the moment—and we cannot be fully believed if we assert our undying commitment to a particular religious creed or to any other purpose. We can be believed if we say we are committed in this very moment—but we cannot be fully trusted to stay committed into the distant future. The most assertive believers among us are all too often the most fickle. We are like Alberich without magic to control us. We might say, "Love, I curse you forever," but we cannot be sure we will live the sentiment. Ukifune could and did—because she had a whole society to back her commitment.

Why do informal social conventions work to secure our capacity to commit ourselves to trustworthiness? They do so, in part, for the same reasons that organizational devices work. Perhaps the best way to account for such workability is to characterize social conventions that do work. Very often, the rules that can be made to work well are especially economical. They can be simply stated, breaches of them and adherence to them can be easily monitored, and the cost of invoking them bears heavily on the rule breaker and lightly on any sanctioner. In addition, such rules must be relatively stable, so that their effects can be predictably expected into the relevant future.

For example, Ukifune wanted to commit to leaving her world, the world of the court in Heian Japan. She did so by taking vows that would preclude her return to the secular world. First, the rules of her commitment are easily stated: she must live in a convent and not range into the larger world. Second, her actions were extremely easily monitored. If she left, her absence would be instantly noticed by the small group of her fellow nuns, and her presence elsewhere would be instantly seen as wrong even by those who knew nothing of her, because they would be able to see that her hair had been shorn. Third, the sanction against any attempt on her part to return to the court would be essentially of no cost to most of the courtesans, courtiers, and other hangers-on at the court—they would almost all have coordinated on shunning her. The sanction would have been devastating to Ukifune if she had really been intent on returning to the court. Finally, the rules on her behavior after taking vows could firmly be expected to last long beyond her life. They were stable.

Evidently, Ukifune was not confident that she could keep her commitment, and she wanted to put overwhelming obstacles in the way of a future change of heart. She almost perfectly arranged her commitment to leave the court. One might suppose she made a very bad choice, but she would evidently have disagreed at the time of the choice. One might even suppose that she could have left the court in a less degrading and stultifying way. But it is not easy to imagine what more attractive devices she had available in her close-knit society.

For many other forms of commitment through fitting one's desired future actions to social constraints, the use of social pressure may loom large, as in Ukifune's case. Even before the nuns and priests were aware of her aristocratic identity, they attempted to pressure her not to take so drastic a step. Her greatest struggle in the short term was to overcome that pressure and to get the priest to shear her. She, more than most of us who might analyze her problems, knew well the weight and implications of social pressure, and she set herself up to use such pressure against her future self, to guarantee her commitment. Such social pressure may generally work best when the relevant rule works at the small-group level, that is to say, in a context of thick relationships.[13] Indeed, the thick-relationships theory presented in chapter 1 is partly a theory of social pressures to be trustworthy. Ukifune's constraints transcended her small community at court, because everyone in Heian Japan would have recognized that she had left the world.

If Ukifune had merely done something shameful, something that was not instantly visible to one and all, she could still have been excluded by the small world of the court, where her transgression and her identity would have been known to virtually all. Her intent, evidently, was not merely to absent herself from the court but also to block herself, in a weaker moment, from returning later, and she wished to block others from attempting to draw her back. She found a device that made her own commitment reliable into the distant future and that simultaneously de facto committed others not to try to change her mind.

Institutional Constraints

If I trust you to act on my behalf, I set myself up for the possibility of disappointment, even severe loss. To avoid that possibility, I might try to find institutional backing to get you to do what I trust you to do. This might be easy to do. For example, if I wish to get you to pay in several installments for the work I do for you or for your purchase of my car, in many societies I can propose that we sign a legally enforceable contract. Now you are faced with the likelihood of real costs if you renege on doing what I have relied on you to do. If the only reason you comply with our agreement is the threat of contract enforcement, then ours is finally not a trust relationship.

Had his dealings with Trifonov been reputable, the lieutenant colonel could have been protected by a contract that gave both parties the right to be sued. "Who wants to be sued?" Thomas Schelling (1960, 43) asks. Well, he notes in answer to his own question, "the right to be sued is the power to make a promise: to borrow money, to enter a contract, to do business with someone who might be damaged. If suit does arise, the 'right' seems a liability in retrospect; beforehand it was a prerequisite to doing business." The odd right to be sued is the "power to accept a commitment." It enables one to establish that one has a strong commitment to fulfill one's half of a bargain. Trifonov had no right to be sued by the lieutenant colonel, who, indeed, could not even publicly accuse him. Trifonov could therefore be assumed to have only a commitment to gain as much as he could from his dealings with the officer. That is all that the lieutenant colonel should have trusted Trifonov to do.

We can imagine that enhancing trustworthiness in general will increase levels of trust, because people will tend to recognize the level of trustworthiness of others. Hence there will be more productive cooperation. Trust can also be enhanced by introducing devices, such as the law of contracts, to regulate relationships to make parties to them more reliable. More generally, the development of norms with sanctions and of other devices for social control tends to enhance cooperation and reduce the risks inherent in trusting others (Barber 1983, 170; Coleman 1990, 114). The effect of institutional enforcement of trustworthiness may go well beyond making specific instances of trust reasonable.

Let us unpack this claim. How can trust be enhanced by enforceable contract or by audits with the threat of sanction? The contract or audit may protect a relationship against the worst of all risks it might entail, thereby enabling the parties to cooperate on less risky matters. This is a milder and more specific variant of the central argument in Hobbes' theory of political order. The threat of sanctions to protect each makes all better off. Hobbes' sovereign enforces order in the protection of life and property. Once these are secured, we have less reason to be defensive, and we engage in productive investments and beneficial exchanges.

In deciding whether to take a risk on someone, we can often avail ourselves of extant institutions. Hence we can make more credible commitments on some matters than on others, depending on what institutions are available. Given our institutions, who or what can we expect to be trustworthy? Remarkably, economic institutions, such as manufacturers and dealers, are often trustworthy at least in their dealings with their customers. (They might not be trustworthy to the larger society insofar as they might readily pollute or discriminate by neighborhood.)

Of course, when a manufacturer or dealer faces bankruptcy, its usual reputational and legally induced incentives to be trustworthy can deteriorate badly. When future expectations collapse for any such reason—the previously trusted party suffers from radically changed circumstances—there is less reason to expect trustworthiness.[14] Similarly, governments may often be quite trustworthy in carrying out the laws, even though a particular government might be very untrustworthy in designing the laws to be carried out. In both these cases, institutional control devices are often powerful and well directed.

These devices have no match in professional contexts, although control of professional behavior may be changing toward sterner regulation. Similarly, economic relations between individuals are relatively well governed by institutional controls. Other relations are typically much less well governed. Some areas are coming under increasing institutional oversight, as are some gender relations and some intrafamilial relations. Still, contract law, for all its difficulties, seems almost like an ideal type in comparison with many other institutional controls over individual commitments.

Many social critics complain of what seems to them to be the increasingly economic and material focus of modern life. The complaint is that we have let economic concerns and material welfare displace other values. Barry Schwartz (1986, 247–48) argues that, in their misguided scientism, the disciplines of behavior theory, economics, and sociobiology may give an accurate picture of things as they are, of human nature in our circumstances. However, he supposes, this is because these disciplines have contributed to and helped justify the conditions that foster pursuit of self-interest. Schwartz's view sounds suspiciously like a golden-age fallacy—the past was never so good. Some aspects of our relations with others get publicly regulated, as contracts for housing are now standardized in large part to keep us from making special agreements in a context in which one party might have great power to set the terms (Macneil 1980). Hence trust and trustworthiness may be displaced by economic devices. There may, however, be offsetting gains of greater fairness, reduced vulnerability of the economically weak, and so forth; and the displaced trust may not have been substantial in what were primarily economic relations of tenants and landlords even before public regulation.

A deeper problem may be the greatest constraint on what our values can be. Our institutions enhance trustworthiness, and hence the value of trust, far better in economic than in noneconomic relations. One might suppose that this follows because these institutions are deliberately designed to work that way, whereas our social conventions merely arise and grow and are generally not meaningfully said to be intended. Institutions and organizations also grow in unintended ways, however, and they need not be true to any designers' intentions for them. More crucial to the difference in the economic and noneconomic constraints may simply be the fact that the former are easier to assess and easier to build into strong expectations— therefore easier for institutions to enforce. There is great reliability in contracts because performance is easy to assess and enforcement is relatively easy; there is far less reliability in marriage in many societies and times, because performance is too hard to measure to make enforcement work. Not surprisingly, even in marriage economic interests can be monitored well enough to be governed by contractual agreement, and there may be a growing trend toward prenuptial contracts to cover financial matters relating, especially, to prior status and earnings potential.[15]

Incidentally, it is arguable that, if contracts become as shaky as marriage, *then* our society will be in danger of collapse. That is to say, ordinary contractual regulation may be more important to social order in a complex society than is the enforcement of any particular possible convention on sexual and familial relations.

Norms of Trustworthiness

Norms for behavior can be effective because they directly motivate us through our commitment to them or because they indirectly motivate us through the force of social sanctions—rewards and penalties—that back the norms. One might suppose that trustworthiness is backed by social norms. Unfortunately, a simple norm of trustworthiness seems not likely to be a strong reason for widespread trust in society, although such a norm might motivate some people, such as those who adhere to strict codes of honor. The following brief account of why some social norms are quite effective and others much less so suggests why a general norm of trustworthiness would be weak.

We can separate the discussion of the possibility of norms of trustworthiness into internal (more or less moral) and external (more or less interest-based) motivations, but such a separation might lead to a confusing picture of norms and their force. Moreover, a particular norm might actually drive both internal and external motivations. Hence I discuss norms of trustworthiness as a separate category of mixed motivations and have little to say about internal motivations to follow norms. It is commonly supposed that norms become internalized so that they operate directly in the motivations of people. Again, this seems to be a correct view, although theories of how internalization happens are often little more than descriptive accounts of seemingly internalized norms.[16]

Consider a highly articulated differentiation of people into different classes of apparent trust. In Leo Tolstoy's *Anna Karenina*, Count Vronsky's code of social rules is probably well understood by all concerned, who therefore have differential grounds for expecting good or bad behavior from him. As Tolstoy (1949 [1874–76], 1.347) puts it, "The code categorically determined that though the card-sharper must be paid, the tailor need not be; that one may not lie to a man, but might to a woman; that one must not deceive anyone, except a husband; that one must not forgive an insult but may insult others, and so on." Karenin therefore can be confident that Vronsky will be honorable in repaying a gambling debt but he cannot be confident that Vronsky will be honorable with his wife, Anna—and therein lies a long novel.

What was the nature of Vronsky's concern to repay his gambling debt? It was not merely a reciprocal concern with his gambling partner of the moment. It was, rather, a concern to live up to the standards of behavior of the nineteenth-century Russian aristocratic community of which he was a member. If he failed to repay the debt, he would be embarrassed in that community and would lose standing in it, so that his opportunities within that community would be constrained. He faced a norm of exclusion, a norm that required his submission to the group in various ways at the cost, if he did not submit, of being shunned within the group and perhaps even excluded from the group.[17]

Therefore, many of the things that one could have "trusted" Vronsky to do are different from the kinds of sequential exchange that can be modeled by the iterated prisoner's dilemma. Someone's "trust" in him would be a two-part intentional relation, because it would depend on Vronsky's intentional and arguably rational commitments. These would not be with respect to a particular other individual (such as his specific gambling partner of this evening), however, but with respect to the whole aristocratic community as the enforcer of its norms. He would not be motivated by concern with the interests of the person to whom he owes a debt but only with the possibility of enforcement of the communal norms. Hence his stance would not justify anyone in trusting him in the strong sense of supposing his interests directly encapsulated theirs. The second part of the two-part relation would be the range of things covered by the aristocratic norms. Vronsky's commitments were simply rational if Vronsky adhered to the code just in case it fitted his interests to do so. In choosing among debts to pay, he paid his fellow noble gambler, who could harm him socially or otherwise, rather than his tailor, who could only hassle him and refuse him further service.

Many social and moral norms are primarily manifestations of interest, as trust commonly is. For example, my adherence to norms of exclusion is motivated by my group's sanction and even exclusion of me if I violate the norms (Hardin 1995, chapter 4). Because this is so, we can count on others enough even to take an optimistic view of them. It might be difficult to explain the rise of Vronsky's aristocratic class norms; but we might readily explain their maintenance once they have arisen as straightforwardly dependent on the interests of Russian aristocrats to abide by them—in particular, their interests in sanctioning violators of them. That explanation has a simple functional form analogous to the functional explanation of trustworthiness presented in chapter 6 (Hardin 1995, 79–91). Vronsky could only lose by violating his class's norms, because he would find himself shunned or even more severely excluded.

If we wish to break the hold of such norms as those that reinforce the exclusionary status of some group such as the aristocrats, a forceful way to do so would be to offer contrary incentives. That is what the modern industrial economy has inadvertently done to many aristocratic norms, such as the dueling norm (Hardin 1995, 91–100). Some of Vronsky's class norms might, however, seem generally good, so that we might wish to keep them. Unfortunately, if they are merely universalistic norms, so that following them is not motivated by the exclusionary sanctions of the status group, they will most likely have far less force. No one other than the victims of violations will have incentive to sanction violations of them. Universalistic norms that are not enforced dyadically, as the norm of promise keeping or that of truth telling typically is, are generally weak norms (Hardin 1995, chapter 5). They might work in small, close communities that are not status communities, just because, in such close communities, all are relatively well known to all. One can readily escape monitoring only by leaving the community, which can use shunning and even exclusion to induce "good" behavior. For the larger society, reliance on norms to secure or at least encourage trustworthy behavior is not likely to be as thoroughgoing or successful (Cook and Hardin 2000).

Even if there were a widely held norm of trustworthiness, it would commonly run into alternative motivations. For example, suppose Karamazov's lieutenant colonel thought Trifonov should be bound by a norm of trustworthiness, a variant of a norm of honor. Against his hopes, note that the force of a norm of honor derives from the potential public disgrace from dishonor, as in the case of the dueling norm, which is a norm of honor (Hardin 1995, 91–100). Trifonov was not under a norm of honor of such force if for no other reason than that his actions were not on public display and could not be if it were up to the lieutenant colonel, who therefore was helpless to call on enforcement of the norm.

Suppose the lieutenant colonel thought that Trifonov was under a norm of trustworthiness of some internalized kind. Such a belief, while perhaps common, would actually be quite odd in this case. The lieutenant colonel was, after all, engaging in criminal activity with Trifonov, and he was violating the trust of his command and of his nation. Perhaps the lieutenant colonel would himself have felt bound by a norm of trustworthiness in strictly personal relations while blithely violating any such norm with respect to the Russian army and the Russian nation. More generally, any broad system of norms is likely to include within it quite different norms that would commend contradictory behaviors in common contexts. It is perhaps therefore not surprising that universalistic norms tend to be vague and limited, and they might tend to be weakened by their potential conflicts.[18]

Finally, consider how internalization might work. Perhaps internalizing norms is akin to developing habits. In a sense, although it need not be a deliberate move, we economize on thinking and calculating. We adopt habits and norms as devices for deciding in repeat contexts how we should act. Then, following a commonplace but seemingly compelling fallacy, we moralize these shortcuts from being merely devices that we should pragmatically use to being devices that are morally incumbent on us to use. This is the standard fallacy of supposing that what is also ought to be—the is-ought fallacy of reasoning.

Even a norm that is little more than a convention to help coordinate us, such as the convention of driving on the right side of the road, becomes moralized. Such moralization is not entirely wrong in the sense that once the convention is in place and it governs others' actions, it would be morally wrong of me to violate it, because I would cause havoc if I did.[19] It would be odd to say, however, that it is in itself moral to drive on the right when it is equally useful to have a convention to drive on the left, as much of the world demonstrates. If being trustworthy is generally advantageous, because it enables others to enter into cooperative arrangements with us, then we can stop considering the benefit it brings us and merely become habitually trustworthy. For many of us, the difficulty of strategic reasoning might be great enough that the norms of truth telling, trustworthiness, cooperativeness, and promise keeping are useful as substitutes for reasoning that we find burdensome.

Concluding Remarks

It would be useful to have systematic analyses of trust that is grounded in each of the bases of trustworthiness discussed here: internal, external, and mixed motivations. In this book, I focus primarily on encapsulated interest as the ground for trustworthiness, although I also discuss categories that are closely related to encapsulated interest. I think it will be harder to give systematic accounts of trust in all its workings for trustworthiness that is grounded in moral commitments, norms, and bald dispositions. The knowledge problems of assessing such commitments in general seem likely to be harder than those for assessing interests. For example, I would have to have a lot of experience with someone before I could begin to believe he or she has the capacity for the kind of bald commitment that Alberich supposedly had. In addition, the functional arguments for the maintenance of trust presented in chapter 6 work for the encapsulated-interest account and do not generalize to non-interest-based accounts.

Interest is one of the best and most useful of internal motivations. It leads us to and through much of the best that life has to offer. To suppress interest on occasions in which it leads us in directions we might consider wrong is to put ourselves at war with ourselves. In waging that war we are supported by social controls based in our own longer-term interest. A strong network of laws and conventions is needed to make any kind of behavior reliable if it is likely to conflict with powerful considerations of interest. All too often, we have neither law nor convention nor love to make us trustworthy, and it is often only the interest we have in maintaining particular relationships that makes it in our interest to be trustworthy.

Still, trust can be grounded in the belief that another person is guided by norms or moral dispositions. Whether we know that these, and not encapsulated interest, are the grounds for seemingly trustworthy behavior will commonly be important for explaining behavior and understanding social practices and institutions. *We can build institutional devices that mimic the incentives of the encapsulated-interest account, so that we can relatively easily see how to overcome problems of the lack of trust and trustworthiness in many contexts in which, for example, ongoing relationships cannot motivate cooperation.* This is what contract law and legal regulation of such professionals as lawyers and doctors do in their varied, sometimes inadequate ways. It may be difficult to deliberately develop norms and moral dispositions merely for handling relationships that trust as encapsulated interest can handle, but if they are available already, we may benefit from reliance on them.

Typically, strong norms are likely to be embedded in close communities that mobilize commitment to their norms with such sanctions as shunning and exclusion. The deliberate creation of such systems might, however, be more harmful than beneficial (Hardin 1995, chapter 4). Moral dispositions are probably widespread but relatively thin and unreliable for the vast number of quasi exchange relations we have that are not with people we know well enough to rely on their morality. Thin moral dispositions might often be enough, however, to tip our behavior, especially when they are combined with "thin" or weak institutional and other incentives.

Other motivations to be trustworthy might not be so readily mimicked by institutionally devised incentives, especially if those motivations are not matters of simple incentives. When these motivations are at work, trustworthiness might be overdetermined in the sense that one of these motivations might be coupled with encapsulated interest. Hence one might say that one or the other of these is the essential reason for the trustworthiness. In truth, however, parsing the motivations would be quite difficult unless we could compare the same person's behavior over a wide range of interactions. Interests and moral considerations are often aligned. Interests and norms are often identical in what they motivate because norms are commonly enforced through interests, although it is often difficult to see how this complex relationship works (Hardin 1995, chapters 4 and 5).

Trustworthiness may be inherently moral in part for at least some people, or it may be compelled by the force of norms. That many accounts of trust are really accounts of trustworthiness therefore suggests that the moralizing of trust might be more reasonably seen as a moralizing of trustworthiness. Certain standard moral theories, such as that of Kant or various virtue theories, could readily elevate trustworthiness to moral status. Surely there will be fewer theories, if any, that moralize trust itself, although writers whose focus is ostensibly on the phenomenon or idea of trust often do spuriously moralize it.

Chapter 3

Conceptions and Misconceptions

S TRATEGICALLY, trust interactions can take varied forms. Two of the most important are the iterated one-way trust game and the mutual trust interaction of iterated exchange or prisoner's dilemma. In these models of some trust relationships, trust is clearly a reductive term, a three-part relation, and a cognitive—not behavioral—term. Some discussions of trust implicitly or explicitly assume away one of more of these conditions, and in this they are often, though not always, conceptually confused. I canvass these conditions in the first part of this chapter. Readers who are not concerned with alternative accounts can readily skip this chapter without loss of understanding the arguments in later chapters that develop from the conception of trust as encapsulated interest.

In this book, I wish to establish a vision of trust that helps us to explain—and perhaps evaluate—behavior. The same concerns have driven many writers on trust to elucidate quite different visions of it. In the second part of this chapter, I canvass many of these visions to see how they differ in their implications for understanding behavior and, in some cases, to query their conceptual coherence. Many of these visions, especially those of philosophers, are essentially definitional or conceptual. Others, especially those of social scientists, are explanatory. The encapsulated-interest account of trust is both a definitional and an explanatory account. In the vernacular, there are many ways in which the term trust is used, and many of these do not fit the encapsulated-interest account. Many of these are elements in scholarly accounts of trust. I wish to canvass these to see whether they should be seen as partial theories of trust and to judge the force of alternative conceptions of trust.

In discussion, people often assert that trust is some particular thing. As in foundationalist epistemology, we just know it when we see it—or they know it when they see it. This supposition is a constant problem in serious discussions of anything in the social sciences. We often tend to suppose our quick, even sloppy intuitions or insights are foundational and not merely casual, as though they were innate rather than randomly collected from diverse acquaintances and other sources, often misguided sources. Casual accounts might even not distinguish trust in another person, trust in a fact of nature, and trust in an institution, such as money or government. In general, however, we should not indulge a so-called social science that depends on no more than a personal intuition that X must be so and that is not spelled out for others to question, test, and understand it.

In this chapter I address a number of conceptual moves that undercut many discussions of trust. It is a compelling characteristic of the encapsulated-interest theory that it stays the same at all levels without conceptual change. Hence if moving from one level to another makes a difference, that is because doing so changes the possible or likely degrees of trust, not because it changes the conception of trust. For this reason, it is useful to examine various visions of trust, moving from essentially individual-level conceptions to those that are increasingly socialized. Some theoretical accounts of varied aspects of trust are compatible with one another, others are not. For example, the evolutionary account of the rise of trustworthiness—which is explanatory—that is presented in chapter 6 might fit well with the encapsulated-interest account if it is augmented in various ways. Similarly, the functional account of the rise and maintenance of trustworthiness, again in chapter 6, might also fit well with it.

Conceptual Confusions

Consider seven conceptual slippages that are especially pervasive and worthy of brief discussion. Typically, these slippages are not themselves alternative theories of trust or even inherent in any specific theory of trust. Rather, they can often vitiate conclusions in any such theory. Each of these evidently requires vigilance to avoid.

First, there is a commonplace slippage between trust and trustworthiness in what many authors present as accounts of trust. This is especially true of moral accounts, but it is also true of evolutionary accounts. Surprisingly, this slippage is pervasive in academic discussions of trust, which often should rather be posed as discussions of trustworthiness. I have addressed this issue in chapter 2, and I do not discuss it further here except in the context of other visions of trust in which the confusion occurs, such as the views that trust is a good. I treat the accounts of those visions as accounts of trustworthiness, as they must be treated if they are to make sense.

The second and third slippages involve somewhat misleading inferences from the ordinary language of trust. The second is an instance of a common conceptual presumption in the social sciences. It is to assume some notion of trust is an epistemological primitive and not subject to analysis. Third, most accounts of trust are essentially expectations accounts. That is to say, they build on the expectations that a potential truster has. This implies, however, that trust is inherently a matter of knowledge or belief. Many ordinary-language statements about trust seem rather to conceive it as a matter of behavior.

Trust is a three-part relation: A trusts B to do X, and even this is restricted to certain contexts and ranges over degrees of trust. The fourth and fifth slippages involve the reduction of trust to a two-part relation. In our daily invocations of trust we commonly do not include the third part. This might merely be an ellipsis of what we mean, but it might also begin to inform what we think, so that I begin to assert that I trust you, purely and simply, as though with respect to anything and everything. Although this might sometimes be true or very nearly so, it is clearly not so in many cases in which I trust someone. Many writers also suppose we trust more or less anyone with respect to some things, so only the two parts, A and X, are present. Such trust is commonly called generalized or social trust.

Sixth, trust occasionally is seen as analogous to promising, so that the seeming morality of promise keeping attaches to trustworthiness. Seventh, there is a sometime slippage when claims about entrusting something to someone are transposed into claims, which make less sense, about trusting someone.

One might choose to put forward a theory of trust that is actually built on one of the slippages by taking that slippage as a principle. One could then attempt to keep the theory coherently fitted to that principle. I do not think any such theory would be of interest because it would thoroughly misfit actual experiences of trust. One of the moves that is sometimes merely a slippage, however, is basic to some theories of trust, in which it is deliberately asserted that trust is a two-part—not three-part—relation.

Because all of these conceptual slips are standard parts of vernacular discussions and invocations of trust, even careful writers find them hard to avoid. Although I cite some instances of such conceptual confusions in many writers, I suspect that many or even most of them would happily expunge the confusions.

Trust as Reductive Versus Nonreductive

One reason why trust is such a hard term even to define and why it may have so many apparent meanings in the vernacular and even in scholarly work is that it is not a primitive term that is unanalyzable into other terms. Rather, it is essentially a reductive term, in the following sense: Trust is not a primitive, something that we just know by inspection, as the color blue might be a primitive, at least for ordinary people who do not think of it as a problem in optics. Rather, it is reducible to other things that go into determining trust. There are expectations, and these are of a certain kind. In the encapsulated-interest view, the expectations have largely to do with the commitments of the trusted—in particular, a commitment to acting at least partly in the interests of the truster because they are the interests of the truster. Because those commitments might vary in degree, so too trust might vary in degree. Because those commitments can motivate the truster only if the truster knows or believes them, trust is inherently cognitive.

As a reductive term, trust is similar to other major theoretical terms such as power, equality, and justice that must be explained and are not primitive terms but are reducible to other terms.[1] For many trust relationships, we can determine what these other terms are from the structures of those relationships, as in the account of mutual trust in ongoing exchange relations discussed in chapter 1. Academic accounts generally treat trust as reductive, although sometimes it is hard to be sure what trust reduces to.

It is hard even to imagine a conception of trust that is nonreductive and still plausible. One might argue that joy is conceptually not reductive, although it is probably causally explicable in reductive terms. Trust is not merely an unvarnished emotion, however, in the sense that joy is. Emotions might come into particular trust relationships, but trust is not itself simply an emotion.

Finally, note a peculiar implication of an ordinary-language analysis of trust. Anyone who wishes to make trust a simple primitive or who wishes to take it as a deontological moral concept should have trouble with real-world experience, which often lacks any such notion. (A deontological concept is universally applicable and derivable from pure reason.) Even today, many languages have no direct, perspicuous equivalent of the term. In French, one says, "I have confidence in someone"—or, oddly, in something (j'ai confiance en quelqu'un ou quelque chose) or, more strongly perhaps, "I have faith [or almost blind faith] in someone" (je me fie à quelqu'un). According to Unni Wikan (personal correspondence via e-mail, 3 April 2001), there is a noun for trust in Norwegian (tillit) and in colloquial Egyptian Arabic (thiqqa), but in neither language is there a verb for trust. To make a verb form, one must say "to have trust" (ha tillit til) or "there is trust" (fi thiqqa). According to Toshio Yamagishi (personal correspondence via fax, 31 March and 13 May 1998), a common Japanese term was deliberately invented about a century ago, possibly as a neologism from English. A Chinese root form is xin (shin, in Japanese), which means to be honest, true, and sincere (or without cheating). In some combining forms, xin takes the meaning "to believe." Commonly, the meanings include both competence and well-intended. According to Edna Ullmann-Margalit (personal correspondence via e-mail, 2 April 2001), the Hebrew noun for trust is emun. Its root is the same as the root of "belief." There is no verb; instead, one says, "to have trust in." The equivalent verb form from emun means "to believe in." Translations from other languages into English often use the term trust where it is not clearly apt and thereby add to what is being translated (as noted later in, for example, translations from Ludwig Wittgenstein's German). Even in English, as noted later, the word trust has an ambiguous history.

Trust as Behavioral Versus Cognitive

That trusting someone and acting on that trust are different is trivially evident. For example, I may trust you in various ways but never have reason to act on that trust. Against this distinction, Jane Mansbridge (1999) argues for "altruistic trust," which implicitly runs trust into action. To speak of altruistic trust is implicitly to say that it is not trust, that one acts cooperatively beyond what one would do if one acted only from the degree of trust one had in another. One acts altruistically despite lack of sufficient trust to justify the action. Hence to speak of altruistic trust is to make trust a term of action rather than of knowledge. That is peculiar because, again, I could trust you very much without having occasion to act on my trust. It is also true that I can easily act cooperatively toward others even when I do not trust them and I am not even confident that they will reciprocate or will take my interests into account.

We can choose to put ourselves in a position to come to know something, but we cannot look at the evidence and then decide to know. The evidence might compel us or it might not, but we do not choose the degree to which it does compel us. The recognition of this point and its denial are in contest in such claims as that it "is not possible to demand trust of others; trust can only be offered and accepted" (Luhmann 1980, 43). No. My trust of you can be neither offered nor withheld. It just is. I cannot withhold it from you—and it would make no sense to do so even if I could because it would be contrary to my interest as I understand it. Similarly, you can neither accept nor refuse my trust. Both of us, however, can choose to act or not to act on it in various contexts. Moreover, you might be able to act on it to the extent of getting me to do something for you—because I trust you—and then violating my trust, all to your advantage. Again, trust is in the category of knowledge; acting on trust is in the category of action. Niklas Luhmann correctly, if metaphorically, notes that it is "not possible to demand" trust. That is to say, if I do not trust you, your demand that I do trust you cannot be honored merely on the ground of your demand plus the knowledge I already have of you, knowledge that is insufficient for me to trust you. Your mere demand adds little or nothing to my knowledge of you and therefore cannot lead me to trust you if I do not.[2]

Commonplace claims that one chooses to trust entail mistaken implications that trusting is a matter of acting. Kenneth Arrow (1974, 26) speaks of the "agreement to trust each other." John Dunn (1988, 73, see also 80) says that trust is "a more or less consciously chosen policy for handling the freedom of other human agents or agencies." Annette Baier (1986, 244) speaks of "conscious trust the truster has chosen to endorse and cultivate." Luhmann (1980, 24) speaks, as do many others, including Baier (1986) and Virginia Held (1984, 65), of trust as a gamble, a risky investment. Held (1968, 158) also says that one may be obligated to trust.[3] All of this is wrong. I just do or do not trust to some degree, depending on the evidence I have. I do not, in an immediate instance, choose to trust, I do not take any risk in trusting. Only actions are chosen—for example, to act as I would if I did in fact trust or to take a chance on your being trustworthy beyond any evidence I have that you will be trustworthy.

Moreover, when I am not confident of your motivations toward me or of your likely actions, I clearly cannot have an obligation to trust, which would be an obligation to know what my evidence denies; that way leads to the Inquisition, to an obligation that one believe what one does not and cannot believe. Perhaps none of these writers actually would maintain that we choose to trust or distrust rather than that we just do trust or distrust after relevant experience or in the light of relevant knowledge. Luhmann (1980, 88), for example, says elsewhere that trust "is not a means that can be chosen for particular ends." Their apparent claims to the contrary might merely be slips into looser vernacular usage.

Treating trust as a form of behavior is confusing and gets in the way of an explanation of behavior. What we commonly wish to do is to explain various actions and behaviors that derive from trust or degree of trust. If trust is the action, what are we trying to explain in thousands of pages on the topic? I therefore keep trust in the category of knowledge and belief rather than in the category of action and behavior. There is no "act of trusting." Rather, there is trusting or not trusting to whatever degree, and there is taking the risk of engaging with someone. I can take a huge risk with someone I do not trust on a certain matter or hardly any risk at all with someone I trust very much on that matter.[4]

Trust as a Two-Part Relation: Open-Ended Trust

Although it is common to say, simply, "I trust her," this is commonly an elliptical claim in which the condition "to do X" is merely implicit. To say that our trust is genuinely only a two-part interaction in this way is to say that it is utterly open ended with respect to all possible matters. This is extremely unlikely for any but the very closest relationships. We trust only certain others with respect to some things, and maybe an even more inclusive set of people with respect to somewhat less demanding things, and so forth. Unfortunately, however, the vernacular usage sometimes pervades analytical, explanatory, and theoretical discussions of trust. That is an inherent problem with the use of ordinary notions in such discussions. It often requires deliberate effort to avoid falling into vernacular usage and hence drawing implications that are wrong.

There are, however, theories of trust based on the assumption that trust is (or at least can be) a two-part relation of the form A trusts B, without any conditional constraint on the scope of the trust. If trust is unfounded faith, such as Abraham evidently had in his god, it could be as simple as this two-part relation, without any limits. It should be superficially evident that the field of play for a theory of trust that is restricted to such cases is limited. Most of us do not even have it for Abraham's god. Such unfounded faith is not relevant to the trust that most of us sometimes have in others. Nevertheless, the assumption that trust is merely this two-part relation is itself commonly smuggled into discussions of other theories in which it is a conceptual slip that should be avoided.

Trust as a Two-Part Relation: Generalized or Social Trust

The assumption that trust is a rather different two-part relation is also basic to theories or definitions of trust that make it not a sibling of knowledge. Much of the fast-growing literature on the value of trust in society often focuses on the possibilities for social exchange that follow from generally trusting others (Luhmann 1980). Such *generalized* or *social trust* is trust in random others or in social institutions without grounding in specific prior or subsequent relationships with those others and, as is often argued or implied, without taking into account the variable grounds for trusting particular others to different degrees. Such "trust" might seem to be a two-part or even a one-part relation.

There is a substantial literature on such generalized trust, which is loosely seen as unspecific trust in general others, including strangers. This literature is based primarily on standard survey questions of the form, "Can you trust most people most of the time?"[5] People commonly answer that they can, or, on a multilevel scale, they choose a relatively high level. Some researchers read such responses far too loosely. If I say I can trust most people most of the time, I may merely be saying I trust most of those I deal with most of the time. Of course, that is partly why I deal with them and not lots of other people whom I would not trust most of the time. (I might actively distrust some of them and be agnostic about others.)

Moreover, even if I trust most of those I deal with most of the time, that is because most of the time there is little at stake in my dealings with them—I would not trust many of them for very high stakes. My trust is of you to do X, and making X a large matter can drastically affect whether I would trust you. If the survey instrument asked whether respondents would lend a hundred dollars to a random stranger on the street, they would presumably say no. If it asked them if they would lend even a moderately good friend many thousands of dollars without a legally enforceable contract for repayment, again most would presumably say no.

Therefore, it is not credible that the standard survey results really imply merely one-part or two-part relations. It is virtually inconceivable to suppose it is a one-part relation if we pay even slight attention to what it could mean: I trust, period, everyone and with respect to everything. The standard survey question refers to "most" people; but then, it also says "most of the time," which could be taken to mean that the respondents must restrict the range of matters on which they would trust "most people." This is not genuinely generalized trust. The respondents are forced by the vagueness of the questions to give vague answers, and it is a misdescription to label their responses as generalized trust.

At best, in any case, generalized trust must be a matter of relatively positive expectations of the trustworthiness, cooperativeness, or helpfulness of others. It is the stance of, for example, the child who has grown up in a benign environment in which virtually everyone has always been trustworthy. That former child now faces others with relatively positive expectations by inductive generalization (see further, chapter 5). The value of quasi generalized trust is the value of such an upbringing: It gives us the sense of running little risk in cooperating with others, so that we may more readily enter into relationships with them. Of course, such generalized optimism is, again, a value only if others are relatively trustworthy.

Why speak of generalized trust? In any real-world context, I trust some more than others, and I trust any given person more about some things than about others and more in some contexts than in others. I may be more optimistic in my expectations of others' trustworthiness on first encounters than you are, but apart from such a general fact I do not have generalized trust. I might also typecast many people and suppose some of the types are likely to be trustworthy and therefore worth the risk of cooperating with them, other types less so, and still others not at all. However, this is far short of generalized trust. It is merely optimism about certain others. Such optimism from typecasting makes rational sense, just as typecasting of those whom one might employ makes rational sense as a first, crude indicator of competence or commitment.[6]

Many, maybe even most, claims for generalized trust can readily be restated as claims that, in contexts in which trust generally pays off, it makes sense to risk entering into exchanges even with those whom one cannot claim to trust in the encapsulated-interest sense—because one does not yet have an ongoing relationship with them nor does one have reasons of reputation to trust them. This is not a claim that one trusts those others but only that one has relatively optimistic expectations of being able to build successful relationships with certain, perhaps numerous, others (although surely not with just anyone). If the context is even slightly altered, this conclusion may be wrong, as it is in dealings with con artists who propose quick-profit schemes or, often, with sellers in tourist traps. Hence generalized trust seems likely to be nothing more than optimistic assessment of trustworthiness and willingness therefore to take small risks on dealing with others whom one does not yet know. That assessment would be corrected if the optimism proved to be unwarranted because people and agencies in the relevant context proved not to be generally trustworthy.

Promise Keeping and Trust

Note a strangely deceptive parallel between the pair promising and promise keeping, on the one hand, and the pair trusting and being trustworthy, on the other. Trust and trustworthiness are at issue in the kinds of interactions that often involve promise keeping, marital fidelity, or truth telling. Let us briefly consider the analogs. What establishes the good of generalized fidelity or truth telling is that individuals are faithful or truthful. What establishes the good of generalized trust by a *truster* is that the *trusted* is typically trustworthy. The reciprocity is more demanding than in the cases of truth telling and marital fidelity. In promising and promise keeping, *the analog of trusting is believing someone's promise.* Trust can be one-sided in the sense that, in a given relationship, I may always do the trusting while the other always has the burden of being trustworthy.

The moral burden, if there is one, is typically on promise keeping and being trustworthy, not on either promising or trusting. That is because the immediate, short-run incentives in relationships of promising and trusting are on the side of failing to fulfill the promise or the trust. The potential promise keeper, however, is first the promiser. I make a promise to you, and I am expected to keep it. On standard understandings of obligation, I impose my own obligation on myself when I promise. The trust relationship is very different. The one who faces the burden of trustworthiness is not the one who trusts. I trust you, and you are the one who is expected to fulfill the trust. But I cannot impose an obligation on you to fulfill that trust. Moreover, it would be odd generally to moralize promising, as opposed to promise keeping; similarly, it should be seen as odd generally to moralize trusting, as opposed to trustworthiness.

Promise keeping is an issue because there has been a prior act of promising, either explicitly or implicitly, by the party whose promise keeping is at issue. If there is an analog in trustworthiness, it must be a prior *claim* to be trustworthy, a claim to fulfill some charge. It is hard to imagine what such a claim might be—unless, of course, it is by way of making a promise. For example, while it is easy to conceive of someone gratuitously promising to do something, it is harder to imagine serious cases of gratuitously announcing one's trustworthiness in a way that matters apart from promising.

If there were a law to govern personal trust relationships, it would most likely be an analog of the law of promise keeping. If so, it would be a law of trustworthiness, not of trust, because we typically need law not to constrain those to whom promises are made but only to constrain those who make promises. The strategic structure of promise keeping is quite varied, with three distinct kinds (Hardin 1988b, 59–65). First, there are promises made without any reciprocal benefit to the promiser, whose fulfillment is essentially altruistic. Such promises are commonly called gratuitous, and in some societies there is law to govern these while in others there is little or none (Dawson 1980). Second, there are coordination promises, which do little more than coordinate joint actions at future times, as in our mutual promise to meet for lunch tomorrow. Finally, there are exchange promises, which are explicitly a reciprocal part of an exchange relation. In a case of the latter, for example, you may do something for me now in return for my promise to do something for you later.

Laws of promise keeping can have substantial force for exchange promises but little or none for coordination promises. They commonly have little force for gratuitous promises—unless there is subsequent reliance that gives the promisee a loss relative to the status quo ante if the promise is not fulfilled. Even for exchange promises, the law usually enters only if the stakes are relatively high and there has been some reliance that would prove costly if the promise were not fulfilled.

The law, as opposed to the mere practice, of promise keeping is an instance of the substitution of institutions for trust relationships. That law primarily covers some classes of promises, especially exchange promises involving significant values in exchange, while neglecting others, especially small-scale exchange promises for which recourse to the law would be disproportionately expensive and coordination promises, in which there are no values in exchange. In daily life we make coordination promises and exchange promises involving limited values far more often than we make exchange promises involving substantial values. Moreover, we generally make promises at all only to those with whom we have ongoing relations. That is, in daily life we make promises in just the contexts in which trustworthiness is a plausible assumption and in which we therefore fairly confidently act on trust. The law takes over those areas in which there is significant value at stake and in which trustworthiness would be inherently less reliable, because it would face endgame incentives either in a once-only interaction or in an ongoing relationship faced with unusually high stakes in a single interaction.

Apart from teaching children the capacity to trust others (largely by being trustworthy to them), there is little point in cultivating trust. Rather, if the law or political institutions are to be used on behalf of trust, they should be used to cultivate trustworthiness and to block the kinds of action that would most severely abuse trust. If the law blocks severe losses, we are de facto enabled to handle our own lesser problems of reliance on others with greater confidence because we will not be threatened by the potential for large endgame losses. If the law and social conventions can secure trustworthiness even to this extent, we can generally expect trust to follow.

There is a long tradition of claiming that to break a promise is logically to contradict oneself.[7] To make a promise is to proclaim an obligation; to break it is to prove that proclamation false. In more recent writings, the logical entailment of an obligation to keep a promise is tricked up out of the meaning of the ordinary expression "I promise," which is taken to entail fulfillment as though the statement were not merely an instance of presentation but of actually taking the future action now. If we reject such an analysis, we may still suppose that competent people who make promises thereby assume some obligation, which, however, may fall short of actually requiring them to keep all their promises. With trust, however, we cannot even formulate an analog of either the conventional or the logical account of an obligation. It is I who promise and who thereby assume an obligation. But, if it is I who trust, it is the trusted who would have to be burdened with an obligation.

In one philosophical discussion, however, it is supposed that a person who is trusted has an obligation to fulfill the trust. "When someone's trust has been misplaced," the philosopher Lars Hertzberg (1988, 319) writes, "it is always, I want to say, a misunderstanding to regard that as a shortcoming on his part. The responsibility rests with the person who failed the trust." That is more than a bit odd. It is analogous to saying that a *potential* promiser has an obligation to fulfill the potential promise—even though no promise has actually been made—if the potential promisee relies on the fulfillment. One could conclude either that the analogy between promise keeping and trustworthiness is not very close or that this supposition is wrongheaded. Hertzberg goes on to say that "unlike reliance, the grammar of trust involves a perspective of justice: trust can only concern that which one person can rightfully demand of another" (Hertzberg 1988, 319). On this view, I can only "trust" someone to do what that person already has a moral obligation to do. This is a definitional move that, if accepted, makes unnecessary Hertzberg's several pages of argument while it raises many ancillary questions. On whose moral theory do I ground your obligation, one might wonder, yours or my own? Hertzberg's redefinition also makes "trust" a nearly otiose category.

Trusting and Entrusting

Finally, consider a conceptual slip that might be included under the confusion of behavior with knowledge or belief. There is a family of related concepts that includes entrusting, accepting a promise, and contracting. I entrust something to you; I accept your promise that you will do something in the future; I contract with you to do something for me later. I might be forced to entrust something to you even though I do not trust you, just as I might have no better move than to "accept" or rely on your promise or to put myself at risk in a contractual dealing with you even though I do not trust you. I might say to you that I entrust some matter to you as a challenge to get you to live up to my trust, as a parent might do with a child or a therapist with a recovering alcoholic (Horsburgh 1960). Moreover, I can trust you to do something that I have not (could not) entrust to you. Entrusting, accepting a promise, and agreeing to a contract are actions or commitments. Again, trust is not an action or a commitment, nor is it a matter of decision. Hence trusting and entrusting are not equivalent or even parallel, although we might casually use the two terms as though they were interchangeable, especially in contexts in which both might apply.

In actions that come under any of these terms, our purpose is commonly to bring the future into the present in some sense—a move that contract lawyers call presentiation. There may be some joint project or exchange that we cannot complete in this moment, but we might wish to secure our expectations about its future before we expend effort or resources now or make commitments in the future whose value will turn on completion. As Luhmann (1980, 13) says, "Managing complex futures means corresponding performances by people in the continuous present." He then adds, "Trust is one of the ways of bringing this about." The addition is not quite right. We hope to bring it about by entrusting, contracting, or accepting a promise, by turning over some future part of our project to another or others. It is the turning over—that is, an action—that fits that hope. Even then, of course, we may fail to control the relevant future because others may fail to do their part.

Other Visions of Trust

Several other visions of trust that are fairly clearly articulated, sometimes only implicitly in part, differ from trust as encapsulated interest. I discuss each of the main visions not as articulated by a particular advocate but as characterized by central assumptions that differ distinctively from the encapsulated-interest account. These assumptions are that trust is not a matter of knowledge (in other words, it is noncognitive), that it is normative in some moral sense, that it is dependent on the characteristics of the trusted other than the trusted's commitments to the truster, and that it is a good in much the way that various consumption goods are goods or that capital of various kinds is a good. Trust that is dependent on the characteristics of the trusted evokes the issues of dispositions to trust, as mentioned in chapter 2. Martin Buber's (1951) brief account makes trust noncognitive as well as seemingly moral. The extant accounts of trust as a good are misleadingly said to be about trust when in fact they are about trustworthiness. When they are cast as being about trust, they are incoherent; when recast as being about trustworthiness, they can be compelling.

In chapter 2, I survey reasons for trustworthiness other than the truster's interests that are encapsulated in the interests of the trusted. These are both bald and moral dispositions, external motivations from social and institutional constraints, and social norms of trustworthiness. One could have an account of trust in most of the cases discussed there that is cognitive but that is not moral, and in which trust is not a good. In some instances, the account would, however, be dependent on the characteristics of the trusted other than the encapsulation of the truster's interests; or it might be dependent on an account of norms in which the norm following is morally determined rather than determined (as it is for many norms) by interests.

The visions of trust presented in what follows are generally intended as accounts of trust, not of trustworthiness, although, as noted, I think this is an error for the accounts of trust as a good. All cognitive and strategic accounts—necessarily?—ground trust in assessments of trustworthiness. The accounts of trust discussed here do not require a prior account of trustworthiness. Many of these accounts include conceptual moves such as those I have identified as mistakes or slippages, but they commonly do so more or less deliberately, so that in these accounts those moves are definitive rather than erroneous. While the alternative accounts of trustworthiness in chapter 2 are generally credible, none of the alternative accounts of trust considered here (excepting the accounts that are actually about trustworthiness) is credible for more than the occasional odd instance of trusting. Others may be able to show that such doubt is misplaced; if not, the account of any substantial category of trust relations must be based in large part on a prior account of trustworthiness.

Trust as Not Knowledge

Two growing literatures disagree with the view of trust as belonging in a cognitive category with knowledge. They are perhaps closely related, although the hard argument that trust is specifically noncognitive comes mostly from philosophers, and the argument that it is ungrounded faith seems to have a wider following. The former view typically makes noncognitive trust a matter of psychological dispositions. These must partly be grounded in experience, so that cognition may have mattered in the past. The latter view is that trust is in the cognitive category but that it gets there not through learning of relevant facts about others' trustworthiness but rather through the triumph of faith over facts. That people assert these views is reason to suppose that trusting takes these forms in addition to the cognitive form of trust as encapsulated interest. We are left with the question of whether these various accounts model enough of the variance in trusting behavior for us to take them seriously in explaining much of the trusting that we see. Some of them seem far too artful and inventive to be commonplace in the lives of ordinary people. I do not deal in detail with the fit of the not-knowledge accounts with trusting and behavior. The proponents of these accounts have not given us enough plausible examples of them for us to judge whether they are important for a general account of trust.

In some of the claims for these visions of trust as unrelated to knowledge, and for other extrarational visions of trust, the move seems to be definitional. This sounds like an essentialist claim that trust is X, as though we were returning to the worst aspects of Platonic philosophy and seeking ideal forms. We tend instead to think of contemporary notions, such as trust, as having their meanings set by convention, not by some ideal form. In an explanatory theory, we try to explain a range of behaviors that have closely related parts. Rational trust and extrarational trust have similar forms to some extent— they are even family resemblance terms, as Wittgenstein might say. In the case of the accounts of trust as not knowledge, however, even the three-part relational structure of trust and the nearly universal view that it in some way involves expectations are challenged. At their extremes, these views hold that trust is a one-part relation: A trusts (or has a trusting attitude), although they may include a restriction, "with respect to X." Moreover, they generally reject any role for expectations because expectations are very much a matter of knowledge.

Trust as Noncognitive   Perhaps the most forceful and compelling account of why we should view some trust, or some aspects of trusting, as noncognitive is Lawrence Becker's. Becker writes, "Let us call our trust 'cognitive' if it is fundamentally a matter of our beliefs or expectations about others' trustworthiness; it is noncognitive if it is fundamentally a matter of our having trustful attitudes, affects, emotions, or motivational structures that are not focused on specific people, institutions, or groups." Even more forcefully, he continues, "To say that we trust others in a noncognitive way is to say that we are disposed to be trustful of them independently of our beliefs or expectations about their trustworthiness" (Becker 1996, 44, 50; also see Jones 1996). One could say that some people are more optimistic than others about the likely performance of others.[8] Becker intends something stronger. Although Becker supposes that there are two variants of trust, he also says that theorists of cognitive trust "eliminate what they say they describe."[9] Hence the second variant is evidently an empty category.

To understand the claim that there is something noncognitive or irrational about trust, consider how we might deal with a context that makes trust irrational: Thomas Hobbes' state of nature. Hobbes' (1968 [1739–40]) actual view may be relatively modest despite his violent vision of the state of nature. He supposes that, without enforcement, the few who would take adverse advantage of others would finally drive others to be too defensive to enter into beneficial relations that they could readily have sustained without the threat of the few. In essence, his argument is that, in the absence of a political order to secure reliability of certain kinds, the potential costs of misplaced trust overwhelm the potential advantages of taking risks on others' trustworthiness.

Hence trust is virtually irrational in a Hobbesian state of nature. Would Becker and others think trust should be irrational or that we should trust even against reason? No. Against his argument that the category of cognitive trust is empty, Becker thinks that our cognitive distrust should trump our noncognitive trust in such a context (he refers to François "Papa Doc" Duvalier's grim Haiti) but that our noncognitive trust should stay healthy (Becker 1996, 61).[10] One may ask whether this is a credible psychological view. Robert Frank (1988, chapter 3) thinks we are likely to trust even against reason if we develop or inherit moral characters of trustworthiness. He might further think we ought to develop these moral characters (even if we did not inherit them) if doing so is—as he seems to think—the cost of developing a character that will benefit us. Here, however, rationality, or self-interest, stands in the background to justify the character development. For the lifetimes of most of Papa Doc's subjects, rationality worked against any such development with respect to the state and his dreaded personal police force.

If our differentiation of whom to distrust and how much is so fine-grained as to allow us to trust our close associates very much and to distrust our ruler almost entirely, the role of our noncognitive trust in motivating us seems quite limited, and its role in explaining actual behavior seems likely to be limited as well. Unfortunately, if we wish to separate noncognitive from cognitive trusting behavior, we will most likely find them thoroughly run together in any kind of data we could imagine collecting. If my learning of whom to trust fits any standard learning theory (see chapter 5), it will look for all the world like a disposition. Trying to show that such a disposition is noncognitive rather than learned will be extremely difficult if not impossible. Finally, note that so-called generalized trust must be noncognitive in Becker's sense.

Trust as Ungrounded Faith   As a contemporary dictionary puts it, "To *trust* is to have complete faith or assurance that one will not be let down by another [to *trust* in God]" (*Webster's New World Dictionary*, college ed., s.v. "rely"). Abraham evidently had such complete faith in his god as to be willing to sacrifice his beloved son merely on his god's order. Apart from such trust in his god, however, which may amount to a blanket acceptance that whatever that god causes to happen must be right or for the best, it is hard to imagine anyone reasonably asserting "complete" faith in anyone.[11] The theologian Martin Buber (1951, 7) says that in one form of trust, I trust someone "without being able to offer sufficient reasons for my trust in him." This is not so clearly "complete" trust with respect to every possible thing, but it is trust without grounds.

A standard example of such trust without grounds is the infant. The infant, who is not yet able to trust or not to trust, depends on the actions of parents and others and merely lives with those actions. From this early relation, arguably, "there gradually evolve attitudes which may be called trustful" (Hertzberg 1988, 316). If, on the other hand, that early relation is very bad or capricious, the child may develop an utter incapacity to trust. Because the infant has no choice but to depend on its parents, there is no point in saying the infant trusts them. Indeed, it is not sensible to say that Abraham trusts his god, given his beliefs. He might have failed to follow that god's orders because of weakness of will, or he might have revised his view of the goodness of his god and the rightness of following his orders. If Abraham could not revise his beliefs, however, then there would be no question of choice for him of whether to sacrifice Isaac, any more than if his son had been taken from him by disease.

Given the way in which trust seemingly develops from infancy, one might suppose that trust "is not based on grounds" (Hertzberg 1988, 318).[12] On Baier's account, trust is an extension of the infant's relation to its parent, especially its mother. Yet, she notes, a "constraint on an account of trust which postulates infant trust as its essential seed is that it not make essential to trusting the use of concepts or abilities which a child cannot be reasonably believed to possess" (Baier 1986, 244). If this is so, then the encapsulated-interest view of trust is inherently wrong because assessments of trustworthiness could only be based on an infant's instinctive, behavioral learning. They could not require straightforward rational accounting such as we indulge regularly when, for example, we revise a prior supposition and realize that someone is, after all, not trustworthy.

On the infant view, trust is a primitive and somewhat ineffable condition in which we sometimes find ourselves. Such trust cannot very well be applied to people whom we know almost entirely through intellectual apprehension. There surely is some element of the primitive and ineffable in many of our commitments and judgments, perhaps especially in the forms they can take. In particular, our capacity for trust must build in part on evolved instincts. Our trust itself is not, however, necessarily as primitive as the "innate readiness of infants to initially impute goodwill to the powerful persons on whom they depend" (Baier 1986, 242). That readiness may be a necessary or at least important foundation on which the capacity for trust may be built. In any case, although infant experience might be psychologically important in our learning to trust, such experience does not either conceptually or motivationally bind us once we gain the capacity for reason. At that point, we can commonly know better whether someone is trustworthy, and that knowledge constitutes our degree of trust.

Consider an adult instance of Baier's kind of trust. In Richard Wagner's (1887) opera *Lohengrin*, Lohengrin is an utterly incredible, godlike figure who demands of Elsa that she trust him without doubt or query. Elsa is a true Wagnerian heroine, prepared to submit to and adore her hero as her lord. She wants not only to trust him but also to marry him, to fade into him, to give herself up to him entirely, so beautiful a person does he seem to be, and a man at that. By refusing to tell her why she should trust him, Lohengrin puts her in the relation of an infant to her all-powerful parent with no choice but to accept or perish. Elsa's fundamental problem is that she has no good way to explain Lohengrin's existence and powers. He has come from nowhere, no one has ever heard of him. The nearest theory available to Elsa for understanding him is sorcery. That theory would make Lohengrin evil, not good. Given her understanding of the world, it would be stupid of her to trust him merely on his demand. Yet he demands of her to put doubt from her mind, to trust him. That is not a choice available to her as an adult. She cannot choose to doubt or not to doubt. If the evidence is on the side of doubt, she doubts.

What is Elsa's evidence? Lohengrin's initial appearance is supernatural. He is towed in by a swan at precisely the moment he is required to defend Elsa's honor when she is on trial and there is no man willing to defend her in battle against her accuser. Although he has never been here before, he already knows who the people are and what the situation is. How could anyone not wonder? In the end, it is hard for us mortals to avoid thinking of him as inhumane and partly evil in his supreme Wagnerian goodness. The view of trust that Lohengrin imposes is repulsive. Indeed, he proves himself untrustworthy when, as Wagner's punishment for her faithlessness, Elsa is demolished and Lohengrin sails away more in splendor than in sorrow—now towed by a dove. Notwithstanding Wagner's repulsive demand for it in *Lohengrin*, infant trust would be stupid in an adult. Lohengrin is unusual in his magical powers; he is less unusual in the demands he makes on his lover.

Lohengrin's demand is for trust that is analogous to infant "trust." But infant trust is not the trust we have in people once we have left infancy behind. We become too articulate in our understanding to continue to have such an attitude toward anyone. We would not accept Lohengrin on his word, we would want evidence. An account of the life of the infant and its necessary dependency might seem cogent as an account of how we come psychologically to be able to trust or to know (as argued in chapter 5). That is not an account of what trust is or of how it works, however. It is not only preadult, it is prehuman. It is plausibly the way an infant bird works, turning a wide-open mouth to the sky with an instinct behaviorally equivalent to acting on trust that good things will fall into it. In the survival lottery, this works for at least some number of the instinctively openmouthed. Even at poor odds of survival with a dumbly open mouth, however, opening up is more beneficial than keeping the mouth closed, which guarantees starvation.

Such instinctual considerations are arguably a compelling part of an account of knowledge, including knowledge that backs up trust, knowledge of the reliability of any particular other and of others in general. That kind of knowledge is inherently inductive, and one might suppose it wise to be skeptical of inductive knowledge until the run is fairly long. Our normal, biologically inherited proclivities may be to make an optimistic assessment of a short but so-far positive inductive run. If we live in a culture in which that optimism typically is justified by longer-run experience, we develop rich relationships from trusting others. Still, although it befalls us rather than being chosen by us, trusting depends on objective data and is subject to correction if experience recommends.

The most significant sense in which trust may go beyond justified expectations is that many of us—more, no doubt, in some societies than in others—face a new case with optimism, as though with tentative trust. We are not wildly irrational in our optimism, however, and we will revise our optimistic hope if it proves to have been unwarranted. This is a minimally rational constraint on trust: One will not continue to trust another who repeatedly fails the trust. Moreover, we may be more optimistic toward new cases in richly structured than in anomic contexts. An account of the life of the infant child and its inherent dependency suggests the plausibility of evolutionary selection for openness that enables us later to be warily optimistic. That is to say, we start life with an instinctual analog of optimism.

Recall Buber's (1951, 7) supposition that I trust someone "without being able to offer sufficient reasons for my trust in him." Note how peculiar this would be in a real-world relationship. When I first meet you, perhaps I take risks merely optimistically or out of hope. For Buber this could be genuine trust, because it has no grounds, at least no grounds in you. Ten years later, when I have great experience of your trustworthiness, I genuinely do trust you. This would not be trust for Buber, however, because it is based on sufficient reasons. Buber insists that trust is, in the end, ungrounded. Indeed, one could probably say that its beginning is noncognitive, it is not a function of reasons, whether conscious or unconscious. It is something else, something evidently ineffable, which is to say inexpressible in words. Perhaps, therefore, there seems to be nothing more to say about Buber's trust.

Trust As Scant Expectations   A close cousin of the view of trust as unfounded belief is the view of it as grounded in only scant expectations.[13] The impulse for such a view seems to be that trust is a significant issue only when there is doubt in the trusted's likely performance. This is one of the most interesting problems in our relations with others: taking a risk on them when we have little or no ground for trusting them. Prima facie, one might think that this is really what trust is about. Under this view, I have greater trust the less I expect you to fulfill my trust. Superficially this might sound right for the reason that my motivations are especially sharply focused in such a case, which is very different from my normal experience of dealing with close associates about whom I have clear and grounded expectations. The scant-expectations view is implausible, however, even as an ordinary-language notion.

If it is trust only when I have little reason to expect you to fulfill my expectation and not when I have substantial reason to expect you to do so, then I did not ever trust my mother, do not trust my son, close friends, or any of the other people I am most likely to say—in ordinary language—I trust with respect to various things. It seems extremely unlikely that anyone really means by trust what the scant-expectations view entails. On that view, I can trust a complete stranger but not my mother. (This contrasts strongly with the view already discussed that likens all trust to infant trust in one's mother.) Although there can be many contradictory notions of trust in our messy ordinary language, the scant-expectations view cannot stand even the beginnings of ordinary-language analysis.[14]

In the scant-expectations view, what seems to strike us is acting on "trust" despite the lack of adequate expectations of fulfillment to justify taking the relevant risk. The act could follow from many motivations. For example, one might act as if one did expect fulfillment in order to give the "trusted" a moral impulse or to give him or her a chance to establish a cooperative relationship. Alternatively, if one holds that trusting is often a good thing in its own right, one might conclude that trusting in such a case is an especially strong instance of such goodness—a self-abnegating goodness. One who insists that this is one of the ways we use the term trust is surely right. One who insists that this is an important and frequent kind of trust relation is just as surely wrong.

Trust as Moral

Almost everything written on trust recognizes the possibility of accounting for much of what we commonsensically call trust with a rational-choice, expectations theory. Much of the literature, however, including contributions by the economists Oliver Williamson and Robert Frank, the philosophers Baier, Becker, and Hertzberg, and the theologian Buber, suggests or even insists that there is something left over. Some of these people seem to want to say that the rational-choice elements or cases of apparent trust are not trust at all. Williamson (1993, 479) says that what he calls personal trust is "nearly non-calculative." In a gentler claim, Baier at one point says there is still some vapor lurking after she has cleared away everything covered by her theory of trust.

We should try to understand what is the content of these thinkers' claims. Part of the claim in each case seems to be that one just knows there is something else at stake—something moral or psychological or whatever. This putative fact recommends that we try to understand how or why someone comes to think of his or her own actions as other than rational. We want to understand the etiology of the belief in order finally to weigh it. Scholars as diverse as Partha Dasgupta, Jon Elster, Diego Gambetta, and Baier think trust is grounded in more than mere reliance and interests. Many of these scholars have been associated with self-interest theories of individual and social behavior. If even they think there is something beyond rational choice involved in trust, we might expect a compelling case. Oddly, however, there is not "a" case for an extrarational notion of trust. Indeed, there is little analytical agreement at all on any notion of trust, other than perhaps a residual interest notion. What case there is for something beyond this residual is essentially a cluster of descriptive claims about trusting behavior. The case is that it *seems* that more than the self-interest of the trusted is involved in the commitments of the truster.

Luhmann says (1980, 88), for example, that trust is at least partly something other than a reasonable assumption on which to decide correctly whether to risk cooperating with someone, and for this reason models for calculating correct decisions miss the point of the question of trust. Such remarks miss a core element that is captured in the encapsulated-interest account. One part of a reasonable assumption on which to decide correctly is some sense of what the trusted is likely to do as a result of my acting on my trust of him or her. Often the something else is the belief that the trusted will have incentive to fulfill the trust for reasons of his or her relationship with me. That relationship can be direct in the sense that we will potentially be interacting repeatedly over time, to the benefit of both of us; or it can be indirect, through reputational effects.

Clearly, two quite distinct issues are at stake here. First, some moralize the notion of trust itself. Second, some moralize trustworthiness and make trust depend exclusively on such moralized trustworthiness. It is possible that the tendency to moralize the notion of trust follows from a mistaken association with thinking of trustworthiness as a moral matter, so that the first of these issues is less problematic than the second.

Although many writers treat trust itself as a moral matter, this is typically a mistake even on their own accounts because, as argued in chapter 2, trustworthiness is often at least partly a moral matter, but trust typically is not. If we wish generally to moralize the notion of trust, we will have to take out cases of acting on trust to accomplish bad ends. Such a move, however, is perverse in either an explanatory theory or a conceptual account. It is better just to let trust work its way and then to judge the morality of acting on it. Members of a community may trust one another in ways that are commonly all to the good, and yet their trust may enable them to subjugate and brutalize a neighboring community. For example, Ratko Mladic and Radovan Karadzic might well have been able to cooperate to wreak gruesome harm on Bosnian Muslims only because they trusted each other.

To say that something is moral could imply two quite different things: that it is morally required or that it is at least morally a good thing. If trust is a matter of knowledge, then moralizing it seems peculiar in either of these senses. Consider whether it could be required in common contexts. Is it moral or immoral to know or not to know, say, that Afghanistan is ruled by the Taliban? For certain officeholders in the U.S. Department of State it might seem immoral, or at least a failure of professional duty, not to know that it is. Am I immoral, however, if what I know about you is inadequate for me to trust you? Unless you can say, as one might of the State Department official, that I am in the wrong not to know those things about you that attest to your trustworthiness with respect to what is potentially at issue between us, then you cannot say it is morally incumbent on me to trust you. Similarly, to say that it is a virtue to trust is to say that it is a virtue to know that others are trustworthy. This is largely incoherent. It is surely a virtue in many contexts to act as one would if one did trust. It is the behavior or the inclination to such behavior, however, not knowledge, that is a virtue.

Could trust be at least morally a good thing? Acting as though one trusts when in fact one does not might well be a good thing in certain contexts, because it can stimulate good results. Having the knowledge that entails trust can also be a good thing from the perspective of the potential knower, because that knowledge could lead to mutually beneficial cooperation. It does not follow, however, that trust is a good thing in and of itself, because it could be grounded in false knowledge.

Moreover, although one should not conclude too much from etymology, note that a strictly moralized notion of trust runs up against an odd history. The Anglo-Saxon word "trust" is cognate with "tryst." Tryst today has a somewhat salacious ring, as in an appointed meeting with a paramour. In Middle English, it merely meant, especially in hunting, holding one's place in a team effort. I hold my place while you drive the game toward me, and I catch or kill it. In Middle English, I stand tryst. It is my trust to hold my place, so naturally you might come to say you trust me to do so. Note, of course, that it is likely then also to be in my interest to fulfill your trust by holding my place. Also note that you might similarly trust someone's spouse to meet you for a tryst behind the barn.[15]

In defense of the inherent morality of trust, one might argue, for example, that to act as though I do trust someone who is not evidently (or not yet) trustworthy is to acknowledge the person's humanity and possibilities, to give respect to the person, as contemporary Kantians might argue, or to encourage the person's trustworthiness. In addition, one might sometimes suppose that acting as though one did trust someone else, even though one's knowledge goes against actually trusting them, is an altruistic move.[16] Moreover, it might be rational for me to act as though I do trust even when I do not have grounds for trust, because risking cooperation is a good way for me to find out whether someone is trustworthy and to learn whether that person and I might mutually benefit from my developing a cooperative relationship with him or her. All of these possibilities—which are instances not of trust but only of actions that might be justified if one did trust—seem good. These considerations might commend acting as though one trusted others in some matters.[17] However, these possibilities do not entail having the knowledge actually to trust—indeed, they are defined by the lack of such knowledge. To call these actions trust is to slip into making trust a behavioral term, so that the phrase "acting on a trust" would be redundant.

Although it cannot be generally correct, there is some field of play for Hertzberg's (1988) view that one is morally obligated to fulfill a trust in particular instances. Luhmann (1980, 34) notes that in a simple, close society trust may be expected, and distrust or lack of trust may be a moral fault. In quite complex, open societies, "trust" or the requirement of trustworthiness is often defined by a social norm or practice (as discussed in chapter 2), and the requirement may be given legal force. Certain actions legally justify "trust" or, rather, the presumption of trustworthiness, so that one who relies on that presumption can call on the law to enforce the entrusted performance if necessary. Such an obligation can follow from mere reliance, however, and indeed there is sharp controversy over the moral force of entering and fulfilling a contract, with some legal scholars holding it to be merely a rational, self-interested action (Atiyah 1979, 1981) and others holding it to be inherently moral (Fried 1981). If contracts are to be of value, it is necessary that their performance be made independent of the question of whether anybody has in fact trusted.

Hertzberg (1988) wishes to show a difference in the "grammars" of reliance and trust. He draws on discussions of trust by Ludwig Wittgenstein. Unfortunately, he seems to have been misled in some cases by the English translation he uses, because the words Wittgenstein uses in German are as nearly equivalent to "reliance" as to "trust" in Hertzberg's senses. Wittgenstein's (1969, §§159, 509) words translated as "trust" by Denis Paul and G. E. M. Anscombe include "gläubig hinnehmen" and "sich auf etwas verlassen," which mean, respectively, "to take as true" and "to rely on something"—not "someone."[18] Wittgenstein's discussion is about how we come to know things. He says we simply rely on the claims of others. For example, a child begins learning by believing its parents, by relying on them, not by checking out the objective truth of their claims.

Suppose I rely on you more than can be enforced by withdrawing from future interactions with you. I act as though I trust you when in fact I do not. My action is virtually a gift—or, better, it is a gamble and a hope, not a manifestation of trust. You may respond well to my reliance on you, and we may then go on to have a strong and mutually rewarding relationship that is eventually grounded in trust. On the other hand, you may also turn on me when the moment for gain is ripe. One might go further, as Elster (1979, 146) does, to say that "altruism, trust, and solidarity are genuine phenomena that cannot be dissolved into ultra-subtle forms of self-interest."[19] Many writers and many people in ordinary life seem, with Elster, to have some vague sense of a distinctively moral character to trust. In contrast with the case of altruism, however, it does not make sense to cut trust free of mooring in expectations and hence, at least potentially, in interests. We cannot cut it free because our expectations will be grounded in factual assessments of the motivations of anyone we might trust. Among the most important of these must commonly be interests.

Ascriptions of trust may be morally loaded in some ways in specific instances, just as expectations and other interpersonal terms may be. For trust to have moral bite, however, it must entail some degree of obligation. On contemporary theories of obligation, this means that it must depend on something specifically relational as, for example, a contract does. The trusted must do something that morally motivates the claim of obligation. I trust you because we have some kind of relationship or because, at least, you typically have some kind of relationship toward those in a relevant class. For example, I trust you in a relevant context because we have been through a lot together, or because you are a police officer and I am a citizen and think you have professional integrity in fulfilling your duty. Our ongoing relationship or our role relationship may generate mutually reinforcing expectations that each of us sees as obligating to some extent and that each of us may have reason to think the other sees as obligating.

Unless one makes something like Hertzberg's definitional move, ruling out the application of trust to any cases but those of moral obligation, it does not seem likely that trust can generally be moralized. It can be grounded in moral obligations, as public officials may be regarded as morally obligated to behave in certain ways toward their constituents, but it need not be. It also can be grounded in expectations about the moral commitments of others; but, again, it need not be. Even when we think someone is morally obligated to be trustworthy, we might still doubt that he or she will be. For example, we might suppose a police officer is obligated to be fair and helpful in various contexts, but we might have reason to think she will not act from that obligation. Despite her presumed moral obligation, then, we might not trust her. We could conclude that her failure of duty is primarily to be faulted not because it is a failure of our trust but because it is a failure of her duty as supposedly accepted by her.

Trust as Dependent on Characteristics of the Trusted

As discussed in chapter 2, a seemingly natural account of trust much of the time is that certain people are trustworthy and can therefore be trusted. Hence it is characteristics of the trusted, characteristics not dependent on my trusting of her or even my relationship with her, that make me trust her. For Yamagishi and his colleagues in various experiments on trust, "trust" is defined by its dependence on such characteristics as moral dispositions and commitment to norms rather than on the kinds of reasons implicit in the encapsulated-interest view of trust. Indeed, Toshio Yamagishi and Midori Yamagishi (1994) call the latter merely assurance.

Against the view that trust inherently turns on such independent characteristics of the trusted, note that I might trust you though others do not. Somehow, something other than your characteristics must be in play. Most people in their professional lives can probably count some of their colleagues as untrustworthy and others as trustworthy. They might even be able to do this with fine gradations, but let us simplify to the two extreme types. Often, those you trust tend to trust one another, and those you distrust tend also to be distrusted by those you trust. Yet many of those you distrust may trust one another. Such patterns make sense if trusting is a matter of shared interests that make for the reliability of the trusted. They do not fit an account of trust as based on bald characteristics of the trusted.

That some people trust you and others do not means, on this account from characteristics of the trusted, that some are mistaken in their assessment of your dispositions and commitments. Oddly, in their own experimental results, the Yamagishis (1994) find that Japanese subjects tend to trust one another within cliques but not across cliques. How might we explain this as merely the result of mistaken assessments of others' characteristics? It seems trivially easy to explain it as relational, as grounded not merely in characteristics of the trusted but in relationships with them. More generally, it seems far more sensible to suppose that there are many potential reasons for people to be trustworthy (as discussed in chapter 2) and that trust can result from any of these. Moral dispositions or any other dispositions for trustworthiness are not uniquely the reason for trusting someone. Moreover, someone can have a specific, perhaps momentary disposition to be trustworthy in my particular relationship with her even while lacking the general disposition of trustworthiness that the Yamagishis and some others want us to have. It seems sensible to say I can correctly trust her even though others who read her dispositions correctly would not say they trust her.

Instant Trust

An extreme version of supposing that trust is merely a matter of the characteristics of the trusted, characteristics that are not grounded in the relationship between the truster and the trusted, is one-way, one-shot trust, as in the one-way trust game presented in chapter 1, but played only once. Fredrik Barth tells the story of his dealing with a rug merchant in a bazaar in the Middle East. Barth found a rug that he liked, but he had no way to pay for it at the time. The dealer told him to take the rug and send the money later. Many of us have had similar experiences of seemingly being trusted by an utter stranger who would quite likely never see us again and who could not compel our trustworthiness. The experience seems striking and virtually inexplicable in its virtual uniqueness.

What is the role of trust in this interaction? Let us first consider its one-way character. Barth took no risk in walking away with his rug and his likely unenforceable debt; only the rug dealer faced a risk of loss. As a one-way relationship, Barth's interaction with the rug merchant is similar to the dealings of Karamazov's lieutenant colonel and Trifonov. Trifonov was not at risk—at least not from the lieutenant colonel's possibility of cheating him the way Trifonov could and did cheat the lieutenant colonel. (They were both at some legal risk if they were found out.) The distinctive difference in the two cases is that Barth's interaction was once only while that of Trifonov and the lieutenant colonel was iterated over many exchanges.

Now consider the one-shot character of Barth's relationship with his rug dealer. In particular, consider the case from the perspective of the one who seemingly trusts us. For the rug dealer in the bazaar, the difficulty of selling to customers unable to pay on the spot might be commonplace. If experience shows that those customers are reasonably reliable, then the rug dealer might profit substantially from increasing total sales by taking the risk of letting people send the money later. Barth's rug merchant might have had some sense from experience or guessing, rightly or wrongly, that some types of people (those who struggle to speak the local language, women, men, the well-dressed, the friendly, those who seem to be knowledgeable about rugs or who praise the workmanship and artistry) will often enough send the money to make it worth the risk of parting with rugs on expectations—perhaps with less willingness to bargain down to the lowest price to cover for the sometime person who does not send the payment.

In certain richer contexts, trust as encapsulated interest can develop almost instantly. Consider an intense work group put together for a momentary task in which all must perform or all are worse off. For example, the cockpit crew of an aircraft in flight or the members of a military unit in combat might depend on the adequate performance of each person if they are to have best prospects of survival. Just because their interaction is in this forced form, they actually have reason to expect all others to want to live up to the requirements of their own parts in the enterprise. Each therefore at least partially encapsulates the interests of the others. We may call this swift trust (Meyerson, Weick, and Kramer 1996). In contexts of such trust, the relationships are largely depersonalized and are focused on role-related competence (the competence is often well certified for each of the group members, as, for example, by the airline employer in the case of a commercial flight crew). In such contexts, too much personal knowledge and individuating data might even be counterproductive.[20]

For many cases of supposedly instant trust, such as those canvassed by Michael Bacharach and Diego Gambetta (2001), it is hard to see why trust is at issue at all. Some of these cases are purely calculative in a very ordinary way. Williamson (1993, 473) notes, for example, that "cab drivers need to decide whether to pick up a fare or not. Although the probability assessment out of which they work is highly subjective . . . , this is an altogether calculative exercise. There is no obvious conceptual or explanatory value added by describing a decision to accept a risk (pick up a fare) as one of trust." As noted earlier, Williamson is hostile to the use of the term trust for even more complex relationships in which calculation of risks seems to be at stake. For this simple case, however, his hostility seems clearly right.[21] Similarly, my decision whether to give money to a beggar on the street does not turn on whether I trust this person I have never met, will most likely never meet again, and can judge only from appearances this moment. It turns on whether I think my donation is likely to be beneficial and what my stance on such altruistic actions is. Reading the beggar's signs as signals about whether his plea is a scam affects my decision but does not elevate it to a matter of whether I trust him.

The master of scam at the center of the play and movie, *Six Degrees of Separation*, worked his magic on his targets by coming to know enough about them and their family to get them to think of their relationship with him as one involving trust and trustworthiness. They were led to believe that he was a good college friend of their children, and they therefore treated him as such. The trustworthiness they assumed of him was analogous to that in the encapsulated-interest account in that it was, they thought, reputational, because it was grounded in what they thought to be the judgment of their own children and in the scam artist's ongoing relationship with those children. Without the apparent sanction—past and future—of their children, they would not have welcomed him so gullibly into their lives as they did. They fell for the scam, did trust, and were burned—although they evidently enjoyed the ride enough not to feel scarred. My relation with the beggar on my street has none of the qualities of that mistaken trust, although that beggar might also be trying to scam me.

Trust as a Good

In many discussions, trust is treated as a good in itself, not merely as a matter of the assessment of the trustworthiness of others. By this is not meant that it is a morally good thing but, rather, that it is a good much the way goods we buy in the market are. In these discussions, trust seems almost palpable, something that we can create and destroy, use or not use, just as we create and destroy capital and other goods of various kinds. The first way trust is deemed to be a good is that it is a commodity. The second way is that, in a remarkably large and growing literature, trust is treated as a good that is a kind of social capital, capital that enables groups and whole societies to accomplish various purposes.

In both these discussions, the actual concern is trustworthiness, not trust. It is trustworthiness that might be a commodity and widespread trustworthiness that is at least the background of social capital. If there were no trustworthiness, it would, of course, be absurd to suppose trust is a good morally, and it would be a commodity only to others who might exploit it, not to the truster. If there were no trustworthiness, trust would not constitute any bit of social capital because it would enable no larger social purposes but only opportunities for exploitation of the misplaced trust.

More generally, if trust were a commodity, we would invest in it for ourselves. Doing so, however, would be absurd in many contexts. If trust were a form of social capital, it would have the character of a public good, and each of us would have incentive to free ride by not doing our share of trusting. That, too, is absurd. If others are trustworthy, I typically have incentive to trust, not to "free ride" by not trusting. Hence in the two discussions that follow, I am concerned with whether trustworthiness, not trust, is a commodity or an element of social capital.

Trustworthiness as a Commodity   Dasgupta argues that trust is a commodity, something that can be produced if there is adequate demand. In this claim, clearly he is concerned directly with trustworthiness and only indirectly with trust. He treats the general issue as an analog of the business firm's problem of generating a reputation for trustworthiness. In such an analysis, of course, we must look at costs and benefits that give people incentive to be trustworthy. Typically, we might expect that we must have enforcement and punishment that is credible. My trust in you will be a function of my confidence in institutional enforcement. You trust persons (or agencies) to do something only if you expect them to choose to do it (Dasgupta 1988, 50–51, 60). Hence, Dasgupta says, you must think of the trusted's position and likely incentives at the time of the need for fulfillment. Dasgupta's view is in the class of expectations theories of trust; it is an incentive-to-be-trustworthy theory.[22]

If trustworthiness is a commodity comparable to the reputation in which a firm might invest, then we should economize on it, using more formal devices when economically feasible, and we should invest in it or, rather, in the reputation for trustworthiness (not trust). If, on the other hand, trustworthiness (not trust) is a collective good, there may be a tendency to underinvest in it, as there may be a tendency to underinvest in reputation. For example, in the case of Dasgupta's (1988, 51, 64) auto dealer, each dealer's reputation is partly a function of the general reputations of all auto dealers, which no single auto dealer can much affect by its own investments in reputation.[23] Roland McKean (1975) similarly has argued that trust is a collective good, although this should properly be a claim that trustworthiness is such a good.

In general, it seems that, in the end, all that one can invest in is reputation, which is not necessarily correlated with trustworthiness. The only way to actually affect trustworthiness is by changing one's incentives—for example, by entering into long-term ongoing relationships with those whose trust one would like to have. Hence trustworthiness is not a commodity, even though perceived trustworthiness (that is, reputation) is.

Trustworthiness as Social Capital   Kenneth Arrow (1974, 23) implicitly and Dasgupta (1988, 64) explicitly, among others, characterize trust as a public good.[24] Sissela Bok (1978, 28) says that trust is a "social good . . . and when it is destroyed, societies falter and collapse." Luhmann (1980, 64) says trust "accumulates as a kind of capital." These seem to be nascent claims that trust is, or is an element in, what is now widely called social capital. Although he is not its inventor, the term is now especially associated with James Coleman, who gives a compelling overview of the idea of social capital that has had great influence. In his applications of that idea, Coleman (1990, 300–21, 361–63, 590–93, 595–96) considers the lower-level structures of ongoing relationships: family, work groups, and so forth. These structures enable us, as individuals or corporate actors, to do many things, including cooperate successfully with one another in manifold ways. Hence as is true of other forms of capital, social capital is enabling. Other recent users of the term social capital typically do not define it but rather refer to instances of it or give general characterizations of it. By social capital, Robert Putnam (1995b, 665–66) means "social connections and the attendant norms and trust," which are "features of social life . . . that enable participants to act together more effectively to pursue shared objectives." John Brehm and Wendy Rahn (1997, 999) define social capital as "the web of cooperative relationships between citizens that facilitates resolution of collective action problems." Francis Fukuyama (1995, 10) shares this general view and gives the broadest statement of what social capital is: "the ability of people to work together for common purposes in groups and organizations."

What then is the nature of the relationship between social capital and trust? Coleman, Putnam, and others say trust is social capital, or an element of social capital. It appears, however, that the core of the meaning of social capital in the work of these scholars is not trust but rather the social relationships, or the networks of such relationships (as emphasized by Brehm and Rahn), that enable us to undertake cooperative endeavors. These relationships, of course, ground trust among the participants in them. They do so because we have incentive to be trustworthy to those in our networks, therefore making it beneficial to us to trust one another in various undertakings. Hence it seems wrong to think of the trust itself as an element of social capital. As Gambetta (1988, 225) says, trust is "a result rather than a precondition of cooperation" (though Bacharach and Gambetta [2001] hold a contrary view). It is actually both, as is not surprising in an iterated interaction in which there can be feedback from each to the other. Nevertheless, Gambetta's (1988) point seems to be basically correct. I risk cooperating and, if it pays off, I begin to trust you.

There might be some feedback between trust and further development of trust. I cooperate with you, discover your trustworthiness, and therefore cooperate even more or on even more important matters with you. If I trust most of the people with whom I interact, I might also begin to take the risk of cooperating with almost anyone I meet, at least if they are likely to remain in my ambit. Hence my general optimism about others is a benefit to those others when they might wish to cooperate with me (or even to abuse my optimistic expectations). Again, however, it is the high level of trustworthiness of people in my network that generates this benefit. Moreover, their trustworthiness is, on the encapsulated-interest account, the result of their having an interest in being trustworthy toward those with whom they have ongoing interactions that are beneficial and are likely to continue to be. Hence, again, it is the network of exchangers that is the social capital that enables us, not our trust. More generally, what seems to concern most of the writers on social capital is such networks of relationships, so that one might call their social capital "network" or "interpersonal" capital (Hardin 1999e).

Motivations and Trustworthiness

When I act in a way that seems to fit my interests, I might nevertheless assert that I am acting out of moral commitment, character, or something else. Moreover, I may be extremely good at acting in my interests and still be genuinely committed to the claim that my motivation is not that of self-interest.[25] Given that more than one of these motivations—interests, morality, norms, identity—might govern my behavior, trustworthiness, and therefore trust, can be overdetermined. We often begin with a bit of risk taking that leads to simple trust as encapsulated interest, and then we develop such a rich relationship that other motivations come into play. I might also have normative commitments in some context that are quite independent of any grounding in interests, and I may have interests in that context as well, and either might be sufficient to motivate my trustworthiness.

It is a constantly problematic aspect of social scientific explanations of social facts that the social scientist has a vocabulary and a catalog of motivations that those whose behavior is being explained do not share or even understand. Are the subjects whose behavior we wish to explain right and the social scientists wrong? Possibly, of course. Ironically, those who are most hostile to rational-choice and economic explanations, such as many postmodern anthropologists and other critics, use a vocabulary that is radically different from that of their subjects, so that they must assume that, somehow, the social scientist can get explanations right even while defying anything their subjects would claim. Yet the common criticism of rational-choice explanations is that they are contrary to what the subjects themselves think of their own actions.

Perhaps it is not surprising that the differences in explanations seem to be partially culturally determined. In prescientific cultures, there may even be no distinction between acting from supposedly objective facts and acting from supposedly subjective norms; facts and norms are both treated as objective. In our own society, we may commonly make a related move. We act on factual understandings and from our interests, but we suppose these are essentially normative. It is common to suppose that what is is right. The sociologist George Homans has remarked that, as a matter of common practice in the construction of moral norms, "what is, is always becoming what ought to be" (1974, 98). Hume (1978 [1739–40], 3.1.1, 469–70) notes that those who write on morality commonly make the same move without acknowledging that they have let a qualitatively different term into the discussion without justifying it. Most subsequent philosophers would revile the move that Hume criticized, but few people read Hume or take his views seriously.

Indeed, most people may make a move that philosophers often make when they lack an explanation for something, such as, for example, how mind comes out of brain. A common assumption is that there must be a way that this happens, so we can say that mind supervenes on brain. We do not know what this means, but we are sure that something happens there. In part, this is a way of saying "then something happens" when we have no idea what happens. Still, we are virtually certain that something happens because there is no mind without brain. Brain is, from all the evidence that we have, necessary for mind. For anyone trying to explain the phenomenon of consciousness, giving this "something" a label seems to help even though it is only a label on a black box full of what remains yet to be discovered. *Here, the invocation of supervenience is by the theorist who lacks part of the full explanation.*

In a somewhat analogous sense, the ordinary supposition that we act from norms may supervene psychologically on motivation by interests. For example, I develop a collection of friendships, each of which is rewarding to me in its own ways. I value the friendships for what they do for me, and I spend more time on and develop those that do most for me. I also begin to think of them as normatively valuable. I would strongly assert that they are good—and, of course, they are good, in the sense that they are good for me, which is to say that they benefit me in various ways. Once they are in place, however, I think of them as morally grounded. I might have difficulty giving a moral account of why I change and begin to dislike someone who was formerly my friend but whose interests now substantially conflict with my own. But I might readily suppose that the problem is one of moral fault. A similar psychological process might take place for many relationships, such as friendship, love, caring, and so forth, each of which might supervene on a relatively rich background of interactions after a while.

In the case of an ongoing trust relationship, we might now suppose that the whole story of our current trust of the relevant person has the quality of standing on its own without its prior foundation in interests. Just how we might get to this state with a particular person will be hard to explain. Unfortunately, it may also be difficult to establish that this motor is at work. In the case of the brain and consciousness, we are relatively certain that both exist. In the case of the putative supervenience on interests of a trust that is not seemingly based in interests, we can actually give an account of how to get from a relationship grounded in interests to one that is seemingly unmoored. Our problem with the account is that people may often deny that there was ever a background of interests. *The problem of psychological supervenience is more that of the agent than of the theorist who wishes to explain the agent's behavior.* This is a problem that is rife in social explanation. Our task is not simply to accept agents' testimony but, for example, to establish general patterns of development of trust relationships.

For the initial connection between trusting a particular person and the assumption of the morality of that trusting, there are two possibilities. First, finding ourselves in relations that are mutually advantageous, we might develop trust relations, which we then suppose are good and moral. Second, because we are moral, we develop trust relations. The second possibility makes sense only if we have been socialized to think that moral people are trusting, which seems far too contrived actually to be a common practice.

Consider an odd example of a claim that some behavior is normative rather than merely straightforwardly self-interested.[26] In North America virtually everyone drives on the right side of the road, and in any other nation, on the side that is the norm in that nation. I have asked many people how they explain that action. Almost everyone answers that it is immoral or illegal to drive on the wrong side and moral to drive on the correct side. Of course, that answer from morality is analytically true because it would be murderous to drive on the wrong side. It seems motivationally unlikely, though, that we drive on the legally prescribed side because we would feel immoral if we did not or merely because we are law abiding. Indeed, if someone is stopped by a highway patrol officer for going the wrong way on a divided highway, the driver's first reaction must commonly be gratitude for being saved from a potentially devastating accident. The problem is merely coordination of interests, not moral truths.

In this context, the motive of personal safety is so enormous that it seems utterly implausible that it is trumped by the motive of being morally or legally right for almost anyone. Nevertheless, many people insist that the rule is morally binding first and foremost. Models of norms commonly suppose that a norm becomes internalized and that the individual is thereafter driven by an actual preference for adhering to the norm (Scott 1971). This does not allow for an explanation of the rise of the norm in the first place. Psychological supervenience would do so.

Finally, note that there may be a disanalogy between supervenience in the theory of mind and the psychological supervenience of normative commitments on interests. There may be no necessary connection in the latter. For example, we might suppose in many cases that people have learned to have normative reactions to particular matters and that this is their first motivation in many actual instances.

Concluding Remarks

Surprisingly many people have a quasi-Platonic vision of trust. They know what it is. Unfortunately, because they know it to be so many different things the concept is so plastic that we cannot even know what is at issue in many accounts that explain trust or use trust to explain some behavior. If our discussions of trust are to be understood, we must specify more narrowly how we mean to use the term. In this book, I canvass numerous claims about trust, what it is and how it works. I put forward one fairly general model of trust—trust as encapsulated interest—that seems to be what is commonly at stake in many of the interpersonal relationships we have. In particular, it fits the fact that most of our trust relationships are ongoing, not one-shot, relationships and with people we know relatively well, not with strangers. The main scope of the model is in its application to such relationships.

I also consider other models and how they relate to the encapsulated-interest model. In general, any claim of the form "Trust is . . . " is at best a definition. Any statement of the form "X is an instance of trust" must either depend on a definition—perhaps only implicit—or be a Platonic assertion of little interest. For trust under any definition we must want accounts of how it is explained and what it can explain.

Some uses of the term are trivializing in the sense that they reduce trust to some even simpler notion, such as mere expectation or reliance. If trust is only expectation, then, in fairness to our readers, we should probably not use a term that seems far more pregnant with meaning than "expectation" to talk about what interests us in some context. This is not to say that trust is not finally reducible to other notions, as it almost certainly is. On most accounts of trust, it is not a primitive notion but is reducible to some combination of other things. Because it is reducible to other things, there is a great variety of conceptions of trust, depending on which other things are included. The question for us is what is the set of other notions to which it is to be reduced. Among those other things in virtually every analysis of trust are two related matters: some possibility of misplaced trust—and, therefore, risk—and some sense of expectations of another's behavior.

In the encapsulated-interest account, it is the reason for the expectations that defines trust. If I expect you to fulfill my trust because I think you encapsulate my interests to some extent in your own, then I can be said to trust you. If I expect you to fulfill my trust because you would act in the relevant way even if I were not in the picture, then I have expectations but not trust as encapsulated interest. Often, as in mutual trust in an ongoing exchange relationship, the encapsulated interest is simply the interest the trusted has to continue the relationship, because that relationship is valuable to the trusted. Hence the trusted's trustworthiness is not a general characteristic of the trusted but is specifically related to the truster. It is relational, often perhaps even wholly relational.

Chapter 4

Distrust

I F THE evidence sometimes leads to trust, then it can also sometimes lead to distrust. Indeed, on the cognitive account of trust as
a category of knowledge, we can go further to say the following:
If, on your own knowledge, I seem to be trustworthy to some degree
with respect to some matter, then you do trust me with respect to that
matter. Similarly, if I seem to be untrustworthy, then you do distrust
me. There is no act of choosing to trust or distrust—your knowledge
or beliefs about me constitute your degree of trust or distrust of me. If
trust has grounds of particular kinds, we may expect distrust to have
correlative grounds. Moreover, distrust is, like trust, a three-part relation: A distrusts B with respect to X. A might trust B on many matters
but not on others. Like trust, distrust is also a matter of degree. I may
distrust Ruth on some matter more than I distrust George. Finally, far
more than could be true of trust, I might distrust a large number of
people with respect to virtually everything. I typically would not trust
many, if any, people with respect to virtually everything.

It is a peculiar implication of the thesis that trust is inherently
moral, and of much of the current literature on the need for trust in
society, that distrust must evidently therefore be bad. But, distrust is
sometimes the only credible implication of the evidence. Indeed, distrust is sometimes not merely a rational assessment but it is also benign, in that it protects against harms rather that causing them. For
example, parents who do not entrust the safety of their children to
unworthy caretakers, or international institutions that do not entrust
the welfare of the Cambodian people to Pol Pot, are acting morally
according to almost any conception of morality. Although one might
argue that acting as though one trusted some person would be a
moral, praiseworthy act in its own right (see Mansbridge 1999), it
would surely not be in such cases. Because distrust is benign whenever it is justified, it seems implausible that trust is inherently a moral
notion—contra some views canvassed in chapter 3. If there is moral-

ity lurking there, it is, again, in trustworthiness and perhaps some-times in the failure to act on trust when there is adequate evidence of trustworthiness.

One might think of distrust as the complement of trust, so that if I do not trust you with respect to something, I distrust you. As is im-plied in the opening paragraph of this chapter, I treat it here rather as the negative of trust. If I trust you, I have specific grounds for the trust. In parallel, if I distrust you, I have specific grounds for the distrust. I could be in a state of such ignorance about you, however, that I neither trust nor distrust you. I may therefore be wary of you until I have better information on you. Sometimes, I can create the grounds for trust by giving you incentive to be trustworthy. If you then fail, I might sensibly thereafter distrust you and, therefore, avoid putting myself at risk from further attempts at cooperative endeavors with you. The degree of my wariness might be a function of the rela-tive frequency with which I encounter new people who turn out to be untrustworthy rather than trustworthy.

Asymmetries Between Trust and Distrust

Despite parallel definitions, trust and distrust sometimes work in con-trary ways. First, they have asymmetric grounds, both motivational and epistemological. Second, they have substantially asymmetric im-plications for behavior and for society. The chief motivational dif-ference comes from the asymmetric costs and benefits of failed and successful cooperation, which entail asymmetric incentives to risk co-operation. In many contexts, the chief epistemological difference comes from the general fact that we can expect our interests to be in conflict with those of relevant others so that we cannot expect that, even if our interests are encapsulated in theirs, our interests will trump their own.

First, consider asymmetries of motivation. As Coleman (1990, 101) observes, misplaced trust typically entails a large loss, while forgone trust entails only a small loss. For example, the lieutenant colonel lost 4,500 rubles—an enormous sum of money at that time—on one inter-action in a long series, in which the total benefits from many of the previous interactions might even have been less than this one loss. If his benefit from each successful deal was 300 rubles, it would have taken fifteen successful deals to make up for his one unsuccessful deal. Distrust may therefore come more quickly to us than trust. Moreover, the slightest distrust or even a slight degree of trust can recommend against risking cooperation with someone if the potential loss is typically greater than the potential gain.

This assessment is of the immediate choice of whether to risk cooperation this time. Unfortunately, forgone trust can entail enormous losses if it blocks establishing a longer-term relationship (see further Erikson 1963, 247–51). Distrust produces an aggregate of lost opportunities, each one regular and predictable. Trust leads to an aggregate of some real losses plus some real gains. Overall, the gains from acting on trust may far outweigh the losses from doing so, because the gains from any given relationship are repeated over and over again while the loss in any relationship tends to end because we correct our misjudgment that the other was trustworthy and we take no further risks on an untrustworthy person. Hence the gains from trust can far outweigh the savings from distrust, as they typically do in many groups or societies, especially including prosperous societies. In deciding whether to take a risk on another's possible trustworthiness, therefore, we should look to the potential gain from a longer run of repeated interaction and weigh that gain against the loss from a single risk of cooperation. Because of this asymmetry between potential losses and gains, we can further suppose that it is relatively easier to flip from trust to distrust than to create trust where there has been distrust for very good reasons of the risks at stake.

Although, potentially, trust is far more productive than distrust, it leads to greater variance in piecemeal outcomes because it offers both greater potential gains and greater potential losses. A cartoon by Ted Rall captures the problem well. Two men are walking along; one suggests they have a beer and shoot pool, and the other says sure. A label says: "Warning: Relationship (friendship) imminent. Relationships are known to lead to trust. Trust erodes certain protective personality traits, particularly suspicion, wariness, and caution. [This can lead] to heart disease, stroke, bulimia, obesity, insomnia, and premature death" (*New York Times*, 28 November 1999, 4.6). That is a downside risk of going after the pleasures of friendship.

Turn now to epistemological asymmetries. Distrust comes easily because it can be built on a limited bit of behavior by the distrusted. Trust, however, requires too rich an understanding of the other's incentives for it to come easily to many people.[1] In a world in which there are many potential partners in cooperation for various purposes, the standard, relatively friendly tit-for-tat strategy might be too generous. In that strategy, I cooperate with you if you cooperated on our last round, and I defect if you defected on our last round. If we both start out by cooperating and we both follow the tit-for-tat strategy, we may readily establish a long-term cooperative relationship. Just because we have many potential partners available, however, we might often use the more draconian trigger strategy of dropping efforts with anyone who fails an initial attempt at cooperation. One failure at the outset of our potential relationship and you are out of my ambit. (Incidentally, the equivalent of a trigger strategy would be even more compelling for acting under theories of trust that ground it in the moral or other normative commitments of the trusted.)

This asymmetry might not fully deter us from trying to work out cooperative arrangements if we are in a trapped relationship, as we might be with colleagues at work, neighbors, or relatives. In such a relationship I might work a bit on leading you to realize the foolishness of being uncooperative, and others in our group might also work on you. In such relationships we might wait until after a few persistent failures finally to pull the trigger and stop attempting cooperation. It may often be easier merely to live with surliness than to work with it. Outside such a trapped relationship, we need not even bother to live with it. Of course, the trigger strategy can be misguided in some cases in which there is merely a mistake and not an exploitative intention on the part of the other. On the other hand, when there are many alternative potential partners, there can be too little benefit in trying to distinguish mistakes from anticooperative intentions to justify the effort, and so we simply move to an alternative partner.

Two important ways in which there are likely to be asymmetries between trust and distrust are discussed in later chapters. First, trust and distrust of government and its agents may be asymmetric because we have knowledge and theory to distrust them when it would be hard to have knowledge or theory to trust them (see chapter 7). Second, fairly generalized distrust might make sense in a way that generalized trust does not (see chapter 8).

Finally, consider some asymmetric effects of trust and distrust. As is argued more fully in chapter 5, one consequence of distrust is that, if I generally doubt the trustworthiness of new people, I am likely to take few risks of cooperating with others, and I will therefore acquire little information about their trustworthiness. Hence those whose early years are spent in relatively hostile and unsupportive environments may be generally distrustful ever afterward, even if their environments later change. This is true in part because those who are initially distrusting will take few risks of cooperative endeavors with others and will therefore have few opportunities to learn that their environments are now relatively cooperative. (Those who begin from a cooperative background will take risks sooner and will, if their environments have changed, discover the change quickly.)[2]

Similar problems can afflict ongoing relationships in later life even without any differential experience in early, formative years. For example, one study reports that "low trust couples avoided focusing on contentious current issues. . . . This lack of commitment to confronting ongoing issues in the relationship removes the opportunity to restore trust by showing concern and caring. As people pull back, di-

minished evidence of concern by one person is likely to be reciprocated by the other, creating a reality that mirrors their fears" (Holmes
1991, 95; also see Rempel 1987). Instead of taking chances on the relationship, distrustful parties put more effort into securing themselves
against its breakdown by use of devices outside the relationship—
and this reduces dependency on the partner. Hence distrust is circu-
larly reinforced by the actions it provokes.

The asymmetry between trust and distrust can also be heightened
by a related but distinct effect. Albert Breton and Ronald Wintrobe
(1982, 70) note that the role of the effects of reputational and other
indicators of trustworthiness will be transitory if they foster the development of trust between you and me. After a few interactions, it is
your responses in these cooperative efforts that will govern my expectations and behavior thereafter. If, on the other hand, those indicators
suggest your untrustworthiness, their role can become essentially permanent because I never risk cooperating with you. Again, if there are
many alternative people with whom to deal, initial reputational effects will be especially damning to future prospects of our attempting
to deal with someone for whom the indicators are not promising. This
fact can compound the problems of learning, because one who has
learned not to trust, perhaps for very good reason, is likely to give
signals of cynically low expectations from cooperative endeavors.
Those signals would then suggest the inutility of trying to cooperate
with them. Hence those whose backgrounds worked against developing trust in their early years not only fail later to grasp opportunities
when they are available, they may also be offered fewer opportunities
than others are offered.

Uncertainty and Distrust

It would be impossible for individuals in their daily interactions to
escape the suspicion of distrust, because that suspicion is inherently
well grounded. The slogan, "Every betrayal begins with trust," suggests not only that it is principally when we trust or rely on someone
that they can betray us but also the sense that we cannot be sure of
another. There are at least four reasons for this. First, the other might
change between the time we place our trust and when the other must
act on it. Second, people can and often do strategically misrepresent
themselves in order to gain advantage. When you and I discuss some
matter of significance to both of us, there is always the possibility that
we do not put our views fully and honestly but, rather, put them
strategically in terms that would appeal in some way to the other.
Often, we do this relatively innocently because we are, in fact, unsure

of our actual desires. I think I more or less share your interests now, but after reflection I may realize I do not.

Third, if my trust is grounded in iterated exchange interactions (which take the form of the prisoner's dilemma), our conditions can change so that you now face a much larger than usual incentive to defect. That is to say, in game theoretic jargon, we eventually face endgame effects that give you reason then to violate my trust (Hardin 1982a, 200–5). This can happen for varied reasons, of which two are perhaps most important: the stakes of our interaction can change, or that interaction may seem soon to be at an end. If the stakes change dramatically, then the formula, A trusts B with respect to X, may still be true, but with a big change in X it is no longer relevant for our relationship. If our interaction is coming to an end, the usual incentive for cooperation in an iterated exchange fails, as it did for Trifonov.

Fourth, and even more fundamentally, as Georg Simmel (1950, 311–12) observes, "All we communicate to another individual by means of words or perhaps in another fashion—even the most subjective, impulsive, intimate matters—is a selection from that psychological-real whole whose absolutely exact report (absolutely exact in terms of content and sequence) would drive everybody into the insane asylum." The niceties with which we cover our true feelings are, as Thomas Nagel (1998, 6) says, "not dishonest, because the conventions that govern them are generally known." They often do cover the facts, however, which commonly will not be known in particular cases.[3] Moreover, the niceties that are expected and understood well enough in one milieu need not have the same implications in another.

All of these reasons for uncertainty and even doubt at the individual level have institutional analogs. Many institutional deliberations change the views of the participants and, therefore, the collective intention. Institutional groups also strategically misrepresent and face endgame effects. On the latter, indeed, there is a widely held suspicion that corporations begin to pay their bills later and perform their contracted duties later to any business that faces potential bankruptcy. The mere hint of potential bankruptcy can therefore make it actual.

Finally, in many contexts, it seems only reasonable that the underlying messiness of an institution's deliberations should be concealed lest it lead to conflict and complications. For example, a jury should arguably deliberate outside the public eye. The National Academy of Sciences in the United States was recently burdened by the general requirement of public openness under the 1972 Federal Advisory Committee Act.[4] Such openness would make it, in the view of many, virtually impossible to reach reasonable judgments about scientific matters of public importance that affect specific interests. In particular, advisory committees whose purpose is to give unbiased scientific judgments would be subject to heavy influence from government officials (Lawler 1997). A standard argument in defense of the secrecy of the deliberations of the U.S. Constitutional Convention in Philadelphia in 1787 is that openness would have been inflammatory and would have inhibited the serious, open debate necessary for working out a constitutional arrangement. The results of those secret debates compare favorably with those of the virtually public debates of the revolutionary French parliament soon thereafter (Elster 2000).

The inherent problems of inconsistency over time, strategic misrepresentation, changing conditions that end or threaten to end an interaction or that radically change its stakes, and reasonable concealment make distrust potentially the correct prima facie judgment in many relationships. These problems may reduce confidence in the expectations of what parties to the relationships will do when their moments for trustworthiness come. Indeed, they must often cloud even good, trusting relationships.

The shambling, slightly dishonest nature of the niceties of private discourse and the concealment of official debates behind closed doors may actually contribute on balance to the possibilities of trusting relevant individuals and groups. In fact, your willingness to say polite things to me, whom you may dislike or otherwise harshly judge, may be a clue to how committed you are likely to be to fulfilling some agreement we make. By covering your feelings, you focus on the benefits from dealing with me, and you give yourself reason for trustworthiness in our dealings. Indeed, as Nagel (1998, 6) argues, there is a sense in which we actually know that others are concealing much of what they think of us, because, after all, we do likewise.[5] We also know from our own concealments that they are civilizing, that they invite others to take us to be civil and quite likely cooperative.

Pervasive Distrust

Luhmann (1980, 71) says that trust and distrust are functional equivalents. The function to which Luhmann refers is that of reducing uncertainty. If I either trust or distrust you, I have fairly clear grounds on which to act toward you, either by cooperating with you or by not doing so. Hence trust and distrust are functionally equivalent in a rather odd and even perverse sense, roughly the sense of saying that "off" is functionally equivalent to "on" for an electric light. Trust and distrust are functionally very different in their implications for your actions or for social organization more generally. In a group or society in which people are trustworthy, trust enables mutually beneficial cooperative endeavors and complementary competitive endeavors. Distrust blocks both of these.

Distrust in a world in which others are untrustworthy does, of course, protect one against losses that would follow from taking the risk of cooperating with others. But it can wreck one's own opportunities in a society or context in which others are generally trustworthy. The meaningful result of trust, when it is justified, is to enable cooperation; the result of distrust is to block even the attempt at cooperation. Trust is functional in a world in which trust pays off; distrust is functional in a world in which trust does not pay off.

Contemporary writing on trust is sometimes afflicted with reasoning from the fallacy of composition. We commit this fallacy whenever we suppose that what is true of a group or set is similarly true of the members of the group or set or vice versa. A commonplace argument in the trust literature is that we would all be better off if we were all more trusting, and therefore we should all trust more. If we found a society in which distrust was endemic, we might readily conclude that its members would all or almost all be better off if we could somehow lead them to be more trusting, perhaps by creating institutions that would substitute for trust while educating them to be trusting. Yet we should still recognize that it would not be in the interest of an individual in that society simply to start acting as though he or she trusts.

Consider several social orders in which distrust has been pervasive and, therefore for each distruster, functional. Fredrik Barth argues that two of the societies he has studied as an anthropologist were organized by pervasive distrust.[6] The Swat Pathan of northern Pakistan were an acephalous society of pastoralists loosely organized without anything vaguely like a state or higher authority. They were politically egalitarian, with a headman in each locality. The headman could be replaced at will by the other men. All were therefore constantly watchful of one another, and they could not be sure that the others would not betray them at any moment in struggles over leadership. The men spent most of their time together in the men's house. In a sense, therefore, they had the natural possibility of having trust in one another grounded in rich, ongoing, and unending relationships. Instead, they lived without trust.

In Omani society, the social implication of pervasive distrust was very nearly opposite that in Swat. Men had limited dealings with one another, and these were managed with a formality that required circumspection, civility, and grace without any insults or critical remarks. Families lived in compounds behind high walls and had little contact with people outside their own compounds. Yet this society was for centuries a prosperous international trading society. The society had an all-powerful ruler who had the willful power of life and death over his subjects. He was about as near to a Hobbesian absolute sovereign as one can imagine in an actual society.[7]

The so-called culture of honor of the American South is similar in some ways to that of Oman. The culture supposedly comes from Scotland in its days of relatively anarchic shepherding—anarchic in the sense of having limited legal devices so that individuals had to defend their own interests against others. Because sheep are relatively easily stolen, shepherds armed themselves to defend their flocks. The culture that developed was one of quickness to anger and violence coupled with remarkable gentility and politesse in ordinary relations. Richard Nisbett and Dov Cohen (1996) find that, still today, male southerners are typically polite and even respectful to strangers but quick to anger and hurtful to others when their anger is aroused.

Those who worry about supposedly declining trust in the United States and some other industrial societies might suppose that social organization based on such pervasive distrust is fragile, that no society could survive such lack of trust. Indeed, it seems unlikely that Barth's accounts tell the whole stories of trust in these two societies. For example, because there was presumably no good legal system covering the vast regions in which they traded, the Omani must have been able to trust one another in their commercial dealings; otherwise they could not have been such successful traders. Their society might have been organized to secure trust in some areas while lacking it in many other areas. In this, their pattern was not so different from much of commercial relations in many other societies or of various other relations. We trust one another with respect to some matters but not with respect to all. Still, the extensiveness of Omani distrust seems extraordinary.

Data from the General Social Survey in the United States for the years 1972 to 1994 show that blacks have much lower levels of so-called generalized trust than do others in the society (Patterson 1999, 175, 190–91). This could follow for various reasons. Life in poor ghettos and in broken families most likely tends to offer less trustworthy relationships than does life in more prosperous conditions. If these conditions produce little experience of trustworthiness in early life, they might lead to a pervasive distrust that is hard to overcome through later experience (see further chapter 5). In addition, blacks individually have proportionately far more interactions with whites than whites have with blacks. This follows from the simple mathematics of the differences in the sizes of the two groups. (Suppose there are eight whites for every black and that on average each black has eighty interactions with whites every month. Then on average each white has only ten interactions with blacks every month.) Hence if relationships between whites and blacks are less trustworthy than those within the two races, blacks are likely to have far more experience of untrustworthy interracial relationships.

Perhaps the greatest deliberate experiment in pervasive distrust was that of Joseph Stalin's Soviet Union during the purge years of the 1930s. Although the apparatus of those years was not fully dismantled soon thereafter, the war with Germany required enough cohesion to make such deep distrust harmful even to Stalin's personal rule. Pol Pot's rule of Cambodia similarly depended on radical use of distrust. In general, pervasive distrust is more quietly used than it was in these two dreadful cases.

Robert Merton (personal letter of 4 May 1995) notes that "anomic distrust presumably makes for a widespread, reinforced sense of the functions served by inter-personal and institutional trust." Therefore, many Americans in 1943 were reachable through an appeal that featured Kate Smith, an often inspirational singer who was popular with a wide slice of the American population and who seemed to personify believability and trustworthiness to many of her fans. She was "a symbol of sincerity, of truth amid duplicity, of forthrightness amid deceit, honesty amid guile" (Merton 1946, 84). Americans may have craved just such a person—a "flag-wrapped symbol, inseparably associated with . . . abiding patriotism" (Merton 1946, 101)—to mediate their connection to the nation.

Subsistence Communities

There may also be systematic distrust that sustains a destructive equilibrium.[8] For example, familial trust can turn exclusionary, so that outsiders may become actively distrusted. Various studies of impoverished peasant subsistence communities in southern Italy, Mexico, and Peru suggest that people in such communities sometimes develop what the political scientist Edward Banfield (1958) calls amoral familism (also see Aguilar 1984; Westacott and Williams 1976; and, for a brief survey, Govier 1997). Family members stick together and both lie to and distrust others. Many peasant societies are very different from such subsistence societies, which are often at a level of poverty and hunger that is daunting. People in these impoverished societies seem to see life as a zero-sum competition with others. There are at least four reasons for this.

First, they are overwhelmingly dependent on land because theirs is an economy of agricultural subsistence. Land is essentially a zero-sum commodity: If my family has more land, some other family has less. Second, if we are all producing the same things (basic food for our families), there are few opportunities for division of labor outside

the family. Some of the opportunities for exchange or cooperative behavior in more complex societies are therefore not available in some
subsistence societies, so that there are limited opportunities for learning the advantages of cooperation. Third, the form of agricultural production in these societies does not depend on joint efforts, so that
there is no natural reason to have a system of broadly cooperative
agricultural effort that might spill over into other realms.

Finally, in a subsistence system it is natural, because sensible, to be
highly risk averse and to develop practices that are sure to have the
least likelihood of crop failure in especially bad years, when many
would starve, rather than the greatest likelihood of producing a sur-
plus in the average year. In the longer run, though, this risk aversion
undercuts the possibility of escaping from the poverty of subsistence.
If there is variation in the productivity of particular pieces of land,
yours being very good this year and mine next, we can introduce a
system of mutual insurance to cover for the variation and to allow us
to plant more productive strains. If, on the other hand, the variation is
from year to year across all our lands, such insurance would have
little value, and we would have no incentive to develop the cooperative institution of mutual insurance.

People in these societies therefore fail to cooperate, in part because
it would do no good in many contexts and in part because they naturally focus on the competitive, zero-sum aspects of their lives. If there
is no point in cooperation, there may even be advantage in deceit,
secrecy, and cheating, as there typically is in a zero-sum conflict. Of
course, if everyone outside my family is likely to cheat me, I have
good reason not to trust them.

We may sum up the distinctive quality of these societies by noting
that they lack networks that go beyond the family. They have neither
a multiplicity of networks nor a multiplex, all-inclusive network.
They have only a collection of unrelated, mutually exclusive familial
networks. Hence they can achieve trustworthiness beyond the family
neither through the imposition of group sanctions nor with the imposition of network or extended dyadic sanctions. Locke (1955 [1689],
52) supposes that no one can be trustworthy without the threat of
punishment in the afterlife. In these societies it appears that one cannot be considered trustworthy without the threat of extrafamilial
sanctions. Their worlds are predictably dangerous and grim places.

Such perverse equilibrium states might be extremely stable, unless
there is finally intervention from outside. They are stable because
anyone who tries to be cooperative is at risk of being exploited by
others. To move away from pervasive untrustworthiness, and hence
distrust, requires moves by several or many at once and cannot easily
be started by a single member of the community. An endogenous

change that might break the equilibrium would be a change in the relative wealth and prosperity of one family that made it willing to take the risk of relying on others for their services. Thus initial inequality would often be mutually beneficial just because it would lead to new kinds of useful networks and relationships.

Power and Distrust

The worlds of courtiers to various kings, dukes, and other leaders have often been pictured as rife with distrust and intrigue. Giuseppe Verdi's opera *Rigoletto* and Shakespeare's play *Othello* present conflicts between subordinates and their powerful superiors, conflicts that turn lethal. In these conflicts, between the jester Rigoletto and the Duke of Mantua and between Iago and his general, Othello, the weaker men turn on the more powerful. That we might not trust those who have power over us, especially when they have little reason to care for us individually, is no surprise. I depend heavily on your favor, while you depend not at all on mine. You can therefore do me substantial harm, while I can do you little or none. The mutual trust that depends on reciprocal relations cannot easily develop in such unequal, nonreciprocal contexts.

There is a further problem in power relations. The subordinates may come actively to distrust one another. For example, courtiers are commonly in contest with other courtiers over who has the greatest favor of the powerful king. The French court in Versailles elevated vacuity to its high status in self-defense against the harms that could befall anyone who ventured to say anything with real content that might be reported to the king. The result is presented, perhaps with rococo exaggeration, in the 1996 French film *Ridicule*, directed by Patrice Laconte. Courtiers gain status at the expense of others whom they best in vicious repartee.

The intrigues of the court of Henry VIII in England are captured in the fascinating *Lisle Letters*, written in the "grim unlovely years" from 1533 to 1540. They were written to and by the family of Arthur Plantagenet, Lord Lisle, in the years of his service in Calais. Many of those letters tell a story of deep distrust. Lisle's London agent, John Husee, responded to Lisle's urgent requests for news at court with the following report: "There is divers here that hath been punished for reading and copying with publishing abroad of news; yea, some of them are at this hour in the Tower and like to suffer therefor. . . . It is much better that I stay from writing than to put your lordship to displeasure and myself to undoing" (Byrne 1983, 154). In Calais, Lisle was too far from Henry to be able to look after his own affairs, which

were continually at risk at court.[9] Therefore his actions and desires
were put into writing in those potentially damning letters, which
were assembled for his trial for treason, after which he was sent to his
death in the Tower of London.

There are inherent problems in trusting another who has great
power over one's prospects. In an iterated exchange between two relatively equal partners, both stand to lose more or less equally from
the default of the other. If a much more powerful partner defaults,
however, she might be able to exact benefits without reciprocating.
Moreover, she might be able to dump partners willy-nilly and replace
them with others, while they cannot dump her with such blissful un-
concern because there may be few or no others who can play her role.
Hence as in the discussion of endgame effects, the weaker party to an
unequal trusting relationship is at threat of seeing the interaction ter-
minated at any time but is most likely not in a position actually to
terminate it. In general, therefore, the weaker party cannot trust the
more powerful much at all. Inequalities of power therefore commonly
block the possibility of trust. One might mistakenly suppose that a
powerful Henry VIII is trustworthy, but this supposition cannot be
grounded in a belief that a mere courtier's interests are encapsulated
in Henry's interests, at least not over the long run.

Moreover, in the context of great differences in personal power,
distrust is malignant. I cannot trust the egoistic Henry VIII, and therefore I cannot trust anyone else at court much either, because they
might use anything I say or do to undercut me with Henry, to my
great peril. Indeed, I may merely not trust Henry while actively distrusting my fellow courtiers. Henry need have no competitive interest
with me, but my fellow courtiers do. In the actual case of Henry
Tudor and Arthur Plantagenet, however, Henry might reasonably
have been suspicious of the loyalty of the Plantagenets, who might
have been thought to harbor ambitions for regaining the throne for
their family. Hence Henry would have needed little evidence to suppose Lisle was actively working against him. In contexts in which the
powerful partner of various weaker parties need have no such fear,
however, the weaker parties themselves might still have reason actively to distrust one another and little reason to trust their powerful
partner.

One of the most important achievements of many societies, and
especially of modern democratic societies, is the regulation of various
kinds of organizational relations to make them less subject to the ca-
prices of power. That regulation is partly spontaneous rather than
politically determined. For example, there are too many interests at
stake in corporate contexts to allow bosses to use their power exten-

sively for their own ends if these go against corporate ends. More generally, people in ostensibly powerful positions have need of cooperation from those under them if they are to succeed in their organization's purposes and in their own personal interests. When this is true, the less powerful might well be able to trust the more powerful. Even in the most sanguine cases, however, the one-sidedness of power relations must often cast doubt over the trustworthiness of the more powerful partner.

Annette Baier (1986, 247) argues that "voluntary agreement, and trust in others to keep their agreements, must be moved from the center to the moral periphery, once servants, ex-slaves, and women are taken seriously as moral subjects and agents." Great power differences undercut the very possibility of agreement that is voluntary and uncoerced. For example, Immanuel Kant's kingdom of ends—that is, rational beings—makes little sense where there are gross inequalities. "Modern moral philosophy," Baier writes, "has concentrated on the morality of fairly cool relationships between those who are deemed to be roughly equal in power to determine the rules and to instigate sanctions against rule breakers" (Baier 1986, 249).

The implicit claim that all of modern moral philosophy has this quality is false, but much of it does. As Carole Pateman notes in *The Sexual Contract*, the most influential "story" in political theory is the story of the contract by which we supposedly create or have created political society. The vision of agreement on social order is carried to perhaps its most exaggerated level in the arguments of Hugo Grotius and Samuel Pufendorf that even slavery is contractual: The slave benefits from steady employment, and the master benefits from the slave's services (Pateman 1988, 68–69). The idea of the social contract has often been subjected to harsh criticism, as, for example, by Hume (1985 [1739–40], 465–87) in his derisive essay on the "original contract" (also see Hardin 1999d, chapter 3). Despite the brilliance of various rejections of the idea of the social contract, however, that idea still today drives some of the most influential works in political thought. For example, on his own account it drives John Rawls (1971, 10–11, 14–15) in his *A Theory of Justice*, easily the most important work in political theory in the twentieth century. Pateman (1988, 1–4, 221) makes arguments that are prima facie incontrovertible and that cut persuasively against the idea that the supposed agreement in our reputed social contract merits our moral respect. Her most important criticism of the idea is the conspicuous lack of participation by women in the social contract of any past time and, arguably, even of today, but her criticisms are more general than this in that, with Baier, she thinks much of moral life is grounded in the assumption of agreement. Agreement between those of unequal power is inherently suspect.

Social Uses of Distrust

Distrust and even merely the lack of trust can be very useful and can be strategically manipulated. As Anthony Pagden (1988, 127) notes, "Although it may be the case that no central agency is capable of intentionally creating trust where none previously or independently existed, it clearly does lie within the power of most effectively constituted agencies to destroy it." For example, the structure of prisons and the behavior of prison guards often provoke distrust between prisoners. Among the most obvious devices, setting up the cells so that any one prisoner cannot see any other but every one of them can hear the noise of every other creates tensions and hostility between individual prisoners. They can become virtual enemies rather than allies who might pose a common front against the guards of the system. Some of what critics think of as unnecessarily punitive and insulting treatment is functional in provoking interprisoner distrust and hence in blocking group mobilization. Jeremy Bentham's panopticon was a relatively benevolent device for monitoring prisoners while encouraging their self-correction, in part by protecting them against the backsliding influences of their fellow prisoners. Modern prisons seem to be designed far more for quotidian control than for rehabilitation. The two seem clearly to be contradictory purposes and, given the choice between the two, American prison designers and administrators have opted for control first, for prisoner incapacitation over rehabilitation (Lin 2000, 115–32).

In his novel, *A Bad Man*, Stanley Elkin (1996) portrays a prison in which the inmates are mobilized by the warden to control one another, especially to control the relatively ordinary protagonist, Feldman, who seems to be entirely out of place in prison and who cannot quite understand why he is there. The prison goes well beyond the usual in putting the convicts into conflict with one another to maintain rule by the warden. After publishing that novel, Elkin was invited by a prison warden to visit a genuine prison to see what it was really like. Elkin related the story of his visit and then, with a tiny laugh and a big grin, he said, "Mine was better."[10] Indeed, it was. In Elkin's prison the warden directed the prisoners in their harassment and beating of Feldman.

In 1710, the Neapolitan social critic Paolo Mattia Doria gave us an account of the Spanish destruction of Neapolitan society in the previous century. This is a remarkably subtle account of how to dissolve trust relations within a society while still preserving order in the society, at least order enough not to require substantial Spanish investments in maintaining the order. The Spanish created a new aristocracy dependent on Spanish support and thereby replaced a society based on trust by one based on honor (Pagden 1988, 133). This is reminiscent of Hobbes' concern with glory seekers in seventeenth-century England. Hobbes supposed there are two groups who cannot be included within a stable society because their values are essentially against order. These are religious fundamentalists, who prefer disorder to an order that does not center on their religious views, and glory seekers, for whom strife provides opportunity to gain glory or honor (Hardin 1991b).[11]

Doria shares with Hobbes the sense that the system of competitive honor undercuts the possibility of decent order. Such honor is an inherently positional, not universal value—I gain a higher level of it by besting you in some way. There can be noncompetitive honor systems in which honor is accorded to anyone who meets relevant standards of behavior. For example, honor might be a criterion for inclusion in some group, such as the Bedouin (Stewart 1994, 54), the Swat Pathan (Barth 1981, 115–17), or the French aristocracy (Hardin 1995, 90–100, 115–17). Under the Spanish hegemony over southern Italy, however, as in the England of Hobbes' day, competitive honor was the value of a small and potentially destructive aristocracy. Doria supposes that a society based on honor cannot respect the impartial justice that is a necessary condition of trust—or, rather, that the system of honor undercuts the possibility of trust between the hierarchically ordered groups of the society. To undercut such cross-group relationships even more, the Spanish also destroyed the normal rule of law by setting up separate, privileged courts for both the barony and the priesthood (Pagden 1988, 136–37).

The Spanish were evidently less concerned to mobilize the people of southern Italy for greater contribution to Spain's wealth than to block their mobilization in any way at all to maintain easier control over them. Sicilians were able to rely on neither the fairness nor the protection of the law. Not having confidence in the state leads to not trusting other individuals in many contexts, because the state cannot be relied upon to prevent the worst possible outcomes from various joint endeavors and contractual relations. Rather than risk such outcomes, individuals may refrain from cooperating at all. Hence by wrecking the conditions for trust between pairs of individuals or families, the Spanish could substantially reduce the prospects of cooperative endeavors to oppose or hinder their rule (Pagden 1988). In this, Spanish Italy and contemporary American prisons have much in common.

As Hobbes supposes, social relations in the absence of government are likely to be grim and conflicted. This might particularly be true after the attainment of any great measure of economic advance and consequent social and economic inequality, as in Sicily after the Habsburg intrusion or during the breakdown of order during Hobbes' lifetime, when conditions in England were, in some ways, dreadful beyond anything known for centuries, perhaps since the devastating plague years of the fourteenth century.

Reduced prospects for cooperative mobilization impair efforts that would produce general economic advance in an ordinary market economy in which every person's prosperity depends more on the efforts of others in other productive activities than on his or her own efforts. The general economic backwardness produces little opportunity for personal advancement. Indeed, the only way to advance significantly may be to prevail over others in one's own society (see further Hardin 1995, especially chapter 6). Hence advancement and even prosperity are positional goods and not the generalized social goods of a functioning market (Gambetta 1988, 162–63). In such contexts, absence of conditions for trust may breed distrust through paranoid cognition (Kramer 1994). Economic backwardness in these polities exacerbated conflict because it gave little opportunity for advancement through productive endeavor. Economic stasis is sufficient to produce such positional conflicts, which can become lethal, as has occurred in Rwanda and elsewhere in recent times.

Under these conditions, one might expect two general responses. First, people turn inward to concentrate on relations with those with whom they have rich enough ongoing relations to establish trust and trustworthiness. Hence social and economic organization tends toward familism or even Banfield's (1958) amoral familism. Second, alternative organizations for social control might arise in the relatively anarchic vacuum left by the Spanish neglect of normal governmental functions. Thus we might expect to see the rise of such organizations as the Mafia (Blok 1974, 89–102).

Unfortunately for Sicilians, members of the Italian Mafia themselves engaged in the promotion and selective exploitation of distrust. In this, they mirrored the devices of the Spanish overlords of southern Italy in the seventeenth century (Gambetta 1988, 159). Whereas the Spanish merely suppressed Sicily, the Mafia were parasites who exploited Sicilians. The Mafia system survived changing governments into the twentieth century for at least two reasons. First, out-migration of those hostile to the Mafia left less opposition to it. Second, in the early, weak days of democracy, participants in the political system dragged the Mafia into politics as an ally. This move strengthened the Mafia by helping to block legal suppression and, to bring the history full circle, by reinforcing Sicilian hostility to corrupt and unjust central government (Gambetta 1988, 166–67).

Breton and Wintrobe (1982, 140–46) present an analysis of the organization of the Japanese large firm that suggests the sophisticated use of barriers to the "wrong" kinds of trust, wrong in the sense that they are dysfunctional for the firm. In a variant of the Spanish legal system in southern Italy, even workers on the line in Japan are in a hierarchy of ranks. These ranks are not functionally determined by tasks but determined only by some combination of merit and seniority. In such a system, individual opportunity does not depend on group success so much as on individual differentiation from the group. Hence ties within the group of workers on the line are overlaid by ties with those above that must often be more compelling to many workers than are ties with other workers in general. Indeed, many workers must develop relationships of trust with their superiors, with whom they have reciprocal relationships, while their relationships with nominal peers are competitive and perhaps even distrusting. Weakening ties among peers works against their succeeding in group action against their employers.

The prison, Mafia, and Habsburg overlords and to a lesser degree perhaps the managers and owners of Japanese firms all benefit from the same structural failure of their subjects. Their subjects do not cooperate when it would be mutually beneficial to do so because they lack the seeds of trust and the institutional backing that would allow them to risk reliance on one another. As Hobbes (1968 [1651], 1.13: 184–85) argues of his state of nature, they may even become preemptively hostile and untrustworthy—indeed, they rationally ought to do so for the sake of their own survival. Furthermore, they compete in harmful ways, taking advantage of one another because, unable to cooperate for mutual benefit and unable to protect what they have, they struggle over shares of what exists rather than producing more to use in trade. In the Habsburg and Mafia worlds, they also refrain from competing in contexts in which they could, as in a Smithian economy, all gain from competition (Gambetta 1988, 158–59).[12] At the extreme in all these and similar cases, they even individually engage in the promotion of distrust so that they can exploit one another.

Gambetta (1988) calls these behaviors the conditions for the Mafia's existence.[13] They are conditions that Mafiosi, prison designers and guards, political overlords, factory owners, and others can manipulate and contrive to gain or maintain control. The Habsburg rulers and prison overlords have power that they can use to create these conditions so that their power will not be challenged by their wards. Because Habsburg rule produced these conditions, the Mafia was able to rise to power.

Incidentally, an unfortunate implication of the policy of prison overlords to help secure control by instilling distrust is to educate prisoners for the longer term in untrustworthiness and distrust, which must make them less fit for return to society than they would otherwise be. Hence, once outside of prison, they are more likely to exhibit the self-destructive and socially destructive behaviors described in the previous paragraphs. This is especially likely to be true if the argument of learned trust and distrust (see chapter 5) is correct, so that distrust is harder to unlearn when conditions change to justify trust than is trust when conditions change to justify distrust. This follows, again, because distrusters enter fewer joint endeavors than do trusters and they therefore get less feedback on how trustworthy others are. It is peculiar but possibly true that encouraging prisoners to mobilize rather than blocking their mobilization would be more effective in gearing them for return to society. The apparent need for control could be exercised by keeping opportunities for mobilization available only to relatively small groups. Appropriately learned distrust may be the greatest obstacle to success in life in the larger society for the person who eventually goes to prison, and then prison reinforces that incapacitating distrust.

Distrust and Liberal Government

With the possible exception of the organization of the Japanese large firm whose productivity arguably has broad social benefits, the examples discussed here have been instances of the use of distrust for the benefit of some against others. Distrust may often have positive social effects, however, in specific contexts or even in general. On the self-interest view of government as forever at risk of having its power used by its officeholders for their own advantage and against the interests of the broader citizenry, it is commonly supposed that we should openly distrust government. This is, of course, a view that has arisen primarily in the context of democratic thought, especially in the era of modern representative government, rather than in earlier political philosophy that typically justified obedience to rulers whose claim to rule was other than the acquiescence of the ruled.

Hence in a perhaps strange and counterintuitive way, representative democracy and distrust go together in political theory.[14] That is, a certain amount of distrust may be useful to a society or government. Certainly, large, modern democracies work better if we can be sure that there are professional distrusters or cynics or skeptics, people who act as watchdogs, raise alarms, or provide contrary information. Such skepticism is fundamental to liberalism, as in the visions of Montesquieu and James Madison. The American colonial leaders invented popular constitutional government and the institutionalization of distrust of government and its agents as though the two inherently go together. They therefore adopted a constitution that created a weak government (Hardin 1999d, chapter 3).

On some accounts, John Locke, an early democrat of the modern era, put trust and democracy together.[15] He supposes that governors are to act on trust. He was already, however, an implicit advocate of wariness toward political leaders. He suggests that if leaders violate the tacit trust in them, then they should be overthrown. In the later era of relatively stable democracy, the supposition is not that we should be ever prepared to overthrow our leaders but rather that we should be ever vigilant to see that individuals within that government are acting in our interest. Hume (1985 [1739–40], 42–43) supposes that government institutions should be designed so that they work well even if staffed by knaves—or, rather, that the power of governmental position is corrupting enough to makes knaves of many government agents. Madison (1961 [1788], 322–23; see further chapter 7) more directly supposes that government will be staffed by knaves. Hence he proposes that institutions give their agents little power by instituting "opposite and rival interests" to limit the role of each officer.

Cooperation Without Trustworthiness

Our problem in many contexts is that relevant people do not trust or even distrust certain others, often for good reason. Clearly, outright distrust is well founded in many important contexts, contexts in which we would like nevertheless to be able to organize cooperation. In those contexts we therefore would benefit from having institutional or other arrangements to enable us to cooperate in the absence of trust. In many such contexts in an actual society there may therefore be good reason to escape from the need for relying on others' trustworthiness to handle various issues. A central value of contract and even criminal law is to reduce the likelihood of severe losses from cheating, such as the lieutenant colonel's loss of 4,500 rubles. Had he been in a contractual relation with Trifonov, he would not have been completely protected, but the asymmetry between his potential gains and losses would have been much less acute.

The most important institutional alternatives to trust in our lives are government and the market, but there are many others, including various institutions and customary devices. Indeed, one could arguably go far toward explaining various institutional structures by showing how they obviate the need for acting as though we trust, at least when doing so involves risk of great loss. Organizations have, of course, many capacities to recommend them. In particular, they can organize collective actions that could not be organized readily or at all by spontaneous individual action. They are also important in mediating between potential partners who do not trust each other.

It is not only Hume's government but also institutions in general that are at least partially designed to make them work even if they are staffed by knaves. Trusting in the strong encapsulated-interest sense cannot be sensible with respect to the large numbers of people with whom we typically deal in modern societies. I might be able to develop relationships that ground trust with a substantial number of people but not with the vast number with whom I deal directly and indirectly over my lifetime. Someone living in medieval Iceland might have been able to do that. Among the most striking differences between life in medieval Iceland and life in a large, modern industrial society are the change in scale and, corollary to that, the massive role of institutions in our lives. The law commonly fills in where trust would not be likely.

Much of our ability to trust others on ordinary matters of modest scope depends on having institutions in place that block especially destructive implications of untrustworthiness. Indeed, this is, in different vocabulary, Hobbes' argument for government and submission to it (Hobbes 1968 [1651], 2.30: 376–94). If the potential losses of interacting with others are always high, our interactions are like prisoner's dilemmas in which the loss payoff for one who cooperates while the other defects is very large, so that the prospective loss trumps the gains even of several successful cooperations in repeated play. In such games, we may not ever be able to initiate joint cooperation and may therefore never enter into repeated play.

In addition, institutions can be the source of the knowledge requisite for trusting someone (Coleman 1990, chapter 5). In a sense, institutions certify many of those with whom we interact. Of course, individuals can do the same for us. Hence institutions often play for us the role of intermediaries in trust for our relationships with others. Individuals can also play that role, as is the case when you trust someone who vouches for me more than you could trust me. James Coleman supposes that such third-party guarantors of trustworthiness are especially important in commercial relations but rare in non-economic systems (Coleman 1990, 186–88). (I discuss this issue more extensively in chapter 6.)

Government generally protects us against the worst that might happen so that we may take risks on modest cooperative ventures. Even while we are often wary of government and its agents, we rely on them to reduce the need for trustworthiness in many realms that government regulates or otherwise oversees. We rely on contract law and court enforcement to achieve successful cooperation in contexts in which, without such protective institutions, we would not risk cooperating with others. Similarly, instead of relying on purely individual trust in individuals to handle monetary relations, for example, we use banks.

We commonly also rely on relatively informal institutions, such as the market that, to varying degrees, protects us against our ignorance of producers and sellers. That ignorance would make it hard for us to provide for our own welfare without great risk and without paying too much for what we receive. The market produces reputations for producers and sellers, and it produces prices for goods that overcome these two problems to substantial degrees. We rely implicitly on the market to select for us out of the array of goods we might buy. Of course, none of these devices is perfect—indeed, there is a huge literature on the imperfections of the market. Still, we would generally be worse off without such devices.

The claim that we need institutions to obviate the need for trust and reliance on the dubious trustworthiness of others in many contexts is not analogous to the argument of Kenneth Arrow (1972) against organizing the supply of blood for medical uses with a system that depends on altruism. He argues that this would be a misuse of altruism because we can secure a good blood supply readily enough in other ways. That argument turns on the supposition that we may have a limited supply of altruism and the bit of it that we have can be used better for other purposes, especially purposes that cannot be so readily handled by institutional structures. We save our limited altruism for such issues. On this view, altruism is a kind of expendable resource or capital.

It is argued by some that trust is similarly a resource—indeed, that it is a matter of "social capital." However, as I argue in chapter 3, trust is not a kind of resource and is therefore not a candidate for social capital. Rather, if there is social capital involved in trust, it is the capital of rich relationships that ground trustworthiness and enable trust and therefore cooperation. Trust is not, as altruism may be, a motivation that we must use sparingly because we have limited amounts of it.[16] It is a cognitive judgment that depends on perceived facts. It may or may not be in short supply, but using it—that is to say, acting on it—does not reduce the supply. In some contexts people can trust one another across broad ranges of issues. Indeed, establishing trust in one area might lead to expanding it to other areas by generating diversified or higher levels of trustworthiness. Hence trust can build on trust.

Concluding Remarks

In many discussions of trust the authors assume a benign situation or society. Under this assumption, they can argue that trust is a good thing in the sense that it makes society work better. Clearly, this background assumption may be violated, and it often is. When it is, trusting may be generally harmful to the truster and many others. One might, in such a context, be able to develop a small number of intensive relationships in which trust is justified, but even then, as in Stalin's cruelest years, the people one trusts may finally see it as in their interest to abuse the trust or perhaps to violate it, for example, in order to protect loved ones. The only sensible way to read the sanguine arguments is to suppose their point is to support a stable social order in which trustworthiness prevails and therefore trust works for good rather than for ill. This raises the question of how to create a stable order in which trustworthiness prevails and those who are trusting therefore prosper.

Part of the answer in large-scale societies is to create stable governments that are relatively open, which generally, although not necessarily, means democratic governments, and to balance these with other institutions that have relatively autonomous power to stand against the government. At other levels and in societies of lesser scale, part of the answer lies in social structures that create incentives for trustworthiness. Much of the literature on the social benefits of trust neglects the question of how to stimulate trustworthiness; and in any case, there is relatively little on this question in general other than for the problem of creating orderly, liberal government.[17] In chapters 6 and 8, I address the nature of some lower-level structures that enhance the prospects for trustworthiness.

From such discussion, one could go on to issues of institutional design, which I address in chapter 8. We could presumably create institutions that enhance trustworthiness that is grounded in any of the considerations canvassed in chapter 2, ranging from moral commitments to encapsulated interest. A signal advantage of trust as encapsulated interest is that it can be supported by institutions whose motivations are similarly grounded in incentives, which can be fairly straightforwardly understood, designed, and implemented. Modern industrial societies have proved to be adept at designing institutions on such bases.

Even social order is, of course, a tenuous guarantee. Generally, everyone coordinates on order in stable, working societies as, for example, in Los Angeles most of the time. But if something can signal a breakdown of order sufficient to ensure the failure of law enforcement, there can be a sudden dramatic tipping to disorder, as in the Los Angeles riots of 1992. If everyone seems to be relying on the police or the banks or the government, it is relatively safe for me to rely on them too. Still, this may be an unstable relationship that can suddenly tip.

In a less benign world, such as that of impoverished subsistence communities, distrust can become self-reinforcing. Because I distrust virtually everyone, perhaps rightly, I have difficulty establishing trust relationships with anyone who might be trustworthy with me. As Dunn (1988, 85) remarks, the determination to avoid being a sucker, "if generalized to the human race, would subvert human sociality more or less in its entirety." That is the dreadful consequence of pervasive distrust.

Chapter 5

The Epistemology of Trust

I F WE wish to understand trust for real people, we will have to understand the capacity for trust, which is the capacity to read the commitments of others, a capacity that must largely be learned. Hence we must understand trust from the commonsense epistemology of the individual in a position to trust or distrust. One cannot simply start trusting people as of tomorrow. When I meet someone new with whom I wish or have to deal, I may start with considerable skepticism. Of course, my skepticism will not primarily be directed at the new person in particular. I may not yet know enough about the person to judge his or her trustworthiness or rationality in being trustworthy. I make my skeptical judgment largely by generalization from past encounters with other people. In that sense, my expected degree of confidence in the new person has been learned before we ever meet.[1]

My prior experiences with trust may have been so charmed that I optimistically take the risk of cooperating with this new person. On the other hand, they may have been so disastrous that I pessimistically avoid that risk. The new person is no different in the two cases; my prior experiences, unrelated to him or her, are the source of difference. Hence my experience molds my expectations of trustworthiness. If my past experience too heavily represented good or poor grounds for trust, it may now take a long run of contrary experience to correct my initial expectations. Indeed, even my capacities for assessing trustworthiness will reflect a commonsense learning process.

My capacity is constrained by the weight of past experience with all of the reassessment and revision of my views that this experience has stimulated. In a Bayesian account of knowledge, for example, I make a rough estimate of the truth of some claim—such as that you will be trustworthy under certain conditions—and then I correct my estimate, or "update," as I obtain new evidence on you. If I take the risk of cooperating with you, I soon have some evidence on whether you are trustworthy in that single context. I might test further and further, updating until I have a good sense of your degree of trustworthiness in various contexts. I might do this—indeed, typically would do it—not necessarily to test you but rather to benefit from cooperating in new ways. Hence trust—the belief in another's trustworthiness—has to be learned, just as any other kind of knowledge must be learned.

Raymond Chandler's cynical, distrusting Hollywood agent ruefully says to private detective, Philip Marlowe, "I'm going to find myself doing business with a man I can trust and I'm going to be just too goddamn smart to trust him" (Chandler 1955, 118; quoted in Coleman 1990, 100). In his milieu, unfortunately, he was probably as smart as he ought to be, and part of the cost of being so smart was the occasional error on the side of failing to cooperate. The dumber person who would cooperate with the rare trustworthy man in Hollywood would, alas, also cooperate with some others who were not trustworthy. Perhaps the agent took risks at the optimal level. Epistemologically one can do no better.

Because general optimism about the trustworthiness of others enables us to enter mutually beneficial relations, we might readily conclude that a utilitarian should encourage such optimism. It does not follow that the utilitarian should be more trusting, however, because a person's degree of trust is determined by the knowledge that the person has. I speak in this chapter of the street-level epistemology of trust, which is the knowledge—good or bad—that a person develops through ordinary life experiences. That knowledge includes the capacity to assess the trustworthiness of others in light of relevant evidence. This epistemology is subjective in the sense that it is a theory of the knowledge of a particular person rather than of the correctness of claims of knowledge in the abstract, which is the usual focus of philosophical epistemology. All that the utilitarian should do is encourage pessimistic distrusters to take risks on cooperating with others up to the level that the utilitarian thinks is justified in the relevant population. In the model discussed in this chapter, one might go somewhat further and say that the utilitarian should encourage people to take somewhat greater risks than what the utilitarian, on present expectations, thinks correct, because the more open person will have greater opportunity to learn from experience than the less open person. Hence erring on the side of optimism is more readily corrected than erring on the side of pessimism.

Note the nature of the beliefs one must have about another to trust that other. In the encapsulated-interest account, one must know something about the incentives the other has to fulfill the trust (and something about their understanding of those interests, as well). Although valuations of various things are idiosyncratic, we are apt to be fairly adept at assessing someone's interests in many things; thus we might learn to assess trustworthiness that is grounded in the potential trusted's encapsulation of our interests. Trust that is grounded in moral commitments, norms, or bald commitments may be much less generalizable and therefore less easily assessed.

Consider an oddly important but simple case of a seemingly bald commitment. During the recently ended Cold War, rabid anti-Communists in the United States proclaimed, "You can trust the Communists." What did this mean? It did not mean you could rely on them to follow their clear incentives. It meant you could rely on them to act from their more or less malevolent ideology. Why would anyone follow such an ideology? Those who thought you could "trust" the Communists could only answer this question with "I don't know, it's crazy that anyone would follow that ideology, which is contrary to human interests, and which certainly violates the interest structure of Adam Smith's economic and social theory." These trusters had to be true believers about the true-believership of the Communists, that is, they had to be true believers in what they took to be the continuing stupidity of the Communists. That is an odd stance. One might well wonder how their beliefs were established.

Many market economists have long asserted that eventually the people of the Eastern nations would give up on communist command economics. Interests must eventually trump an ideology that runs counter to interests. Market economists and rabid anti-Communists agreed that the ideology was counter to interests. But the economists had better (more generally applicable) grounds for understanding citizens of communist states than did the American far right because their conclusions were grounded in expectations of rationality, not expectations of irrationality.

Street-Level Epistemology

The philosophy of knowledge and belief is a highly developed inquiry. Much of it focuses on particular beliefs or types of belief and the criteria for truth or what philosophers call "justified true belief." For the understanding of trust and knowledge more generally, we require not a philosophically general epistemology of knowledge but an economic or street-level epistemology. The economic theory of belief and knowledge focuses on the individual believer, on the costs and benefits to the individual in coming to have various beliefs, not on the matter of belief (for example, the height of Mont Blanc). In such a theory we cannot speak of the justification of belief X *tout court*; rather, we must speak of the justification of belief X by person A. For this we require a theory that focuses on the individual and on the ways the individual comes to know or believe relevant things, such as how trustworthy another person is.

In addition, we require a theory of how to act on relevant street-level knowledge. I presume here that this theory of decision is a simple commonsense learning theory. You may start with such limited information about me that you can only estimate the likelihood that the typical person in my position would be trustworthy with respect to what you might entrust to me. You might even have such limited information about me that you can only assess from your past experience whether cooperation has paid off in similar circumstances. Suppose it did, and now you risk cooperating with me. (This is not to say you choose to trust me. Rather, gambling on me seems to you the rational thing to do.) You either gain or lose from your cooperation, and this experience is added to your evidence on trustworthiness for future occasions. If I am somehow a new kind of person in your experience, your initial estimate may be unstable, and my behavior might tilt your assessment heavily for or against my kind in future encounters.

The Learned Capacity to Trust

Some writers speak of a greater ability to trust. Typically, they run the likely state of the world—whether those who are trusted will prove trustworthy—into this "ability." There is a genuine problem in whether I can trust, however, that is independent of the outside world I now face, that depends only on my capacities as developed up to this moment. Suppose there is a reasonable degree of trustworthiness in my present community. Now I can benefit—if I have an adequate capacity to trust, which is the capacity to assess trustworthiness. Someone who lacks such capacity will be a relative loser. More generally, we can give a literal meaning to Roland McKean's (1975, 29) claim that "greater ability to trust each other to stick with agreed-upon rules would save many costs and make life much pleasanter."[2]

The best condition for humans is an environment in which they are fortunate enough to have well-founded confidence (Dunn 1988, 84). This is not an individual-level problem but is, rather, a collective problem. For me to rely on not locking up my home or shop would require that I have confidence or trust in almost everyone. The individual-level problem here is to judge rightly what the collective behavior on trustworthiness is.

Being an optimistic risk taker or cooperator opens up the opportunity for great loss and for great gain, neither of which might be possible without risking cooperation. If optimism does lead to good returns on average, then optimism in social relations contributes value. Indeed, one might gain more from increased optimism about others' trustworthiness than from increasing one's trustworthiness, and the external effects of greater trusting might outweigh the external effects of greater trustworthiness. There is no a priori reason to suppose that either trust or trustworthiness is the dominant consideration in general. Teaching our children to be trustworthy is likely to be good for them. But teaching them the capacity to trust and to be optimistic about the cooperativeness of others—for example, by being trustworthy and supportive of their trust in our dealings with them and giving them many opportunities to test our trustworthiness—is surely also fundamentally important for them if they are going to live among a reasonably cooperative populace.

If we must develop such a capacity at an early age,[3] two potentially large groups are at a cruel disadvantage: those whose early years are spent in fractured conditions of caprice and neglect, as in the case of many children of American inner-city communities wrecked by poverty, drugs, and broken families, and those who have suffered substantial abuse in their early years from the very persons who might have provided the first experience of trustworthiness.

The sense that, on average, the middle class have tremendous social advantages over the poor may have some of its grounding in the greater propensity of their children to expect trustworthiness and, therefore, to risk relations that could be beneficial to them. This propensity may have been learned from the apparently justified trusting of family, friends, and others while infants and children. The terrible vision of a permanent underclass in American city ghettos may have its grounding in the lesson that the children of the ghetto are taught all too successfully: that they cannot trust others, especially not outsiders or strangers but often also not even closer associates. Providing opportunities of educational and economic mobility does not equalize prospects for the ingrained distruster, who cannot be optimistic enough to take advantage of opportunities that entail risks of betrayal.

Similarly, an adult who was abused as a young child, perhaps by parents or other close relations, may have been deprived of the normal evidence that trust is justified. For such a person, it too often was not. The woman who was sexually abused as a child may find it hard to be sexually at ease or even close to anyone as an adult. Her incapacity to enter relations with others is merely a well-learned distrust. That ingrained distrust may exact a severe additional cost of the earlier abuse if the distrust is no longer justified by the conditions of the world she has grown into.[4] Substantial additional experience would be required to update her assessments of others' likely trustworthiness.

On this account, in some societies trust must be beneficial. It would be in the interests of one's children to teach them to be optimistic about others. Trust cannot be produced at will, although it can be willfully instilled, as in children. Moreover, acting as if one trusts can be willed repeatedly so that one may slowly develop optimistic expectations of trustworthiness. In many potentially iterated prisoner's dilemma interactions, one should open with a cooperative move in the hope of engaging the other also to be cooperative. This is not merely a moral injunction. It is a rational claim of self-interest (see discussion of the iterated prisoner's dilemma in chapter 1). One should open with cooperation when the expected long-run benefits of iterated cooperation outweigh the short-term risk of loss.

Optimistic assessments can be beneficial only if the general social conditions the optimistic assessor faces are relatively favorable, so that statistically acting on this optimism will be rewarded by trustworthiness. The huge genre of post-apocalypse films and novels of our time portray conditions in which trust is generally not justified. Life is impoverished beyond measure, with the demands of survival and struggle preempting almost all else. To have optimistic assessments in these conditions might be to risk suicide. Even under ordinary circumstances, a central issue for optimistic assessment is how well past experience corresponds to future opportunities.

The psychological development of a propensity to trust involves extensive "investment," especially by others, such as parents. If there has been little investment during early years, far greater investment may be required in later years to compensate. If my early experience led to pessimistic expectations, I may now find it hard to act as if I trust when I do not, and I may find it hard to distinguish those likely to be trustworthy from those likely not to be. If relevant investments were not made, I may always have been pessimistically so wary that I have little or no learning of the value of trust. I may seldom have put it to test. Early trust may be rewarded enough to stimulate its further development and reinforcement. If relevant investments were made in my development, I may have optimistically assessed enough people to begin to learn fairly well when trust is warranted and when not.

The failure of early investment by my parents and others need not correlate with the untrustworthiness of my associates in later life, but it might. The very fact that I have a hard time trusting even those who would turn out to be trustworthy may mean I fail to establish ongoing cooperative relations with such people and therefore disproportionately face short-term relations with people who, on average, are less trustworthy, thus reinforcing my attitude of distrust or wariness. Trusters and the trustworthy may interact chiefly with each other, leaving distrusters and the untrustworthy with reduced opportunities for successful interactions.

If trust is learned from experience, there is little sense in the claim of some that trust is "a more or less consciously chosen policy for handling the freedom of other human agents or agencies" (Dunn 1988, 73, 80), as discussed in chapter 3.[5] I just do or do not trust. I might choose to take a risk on someone that goes beyond what I would trust of that person. But my level of trust is defined, either fairly accurately from experience with that person or vaguely by generalization from my experience of others, limited though it may be.

On a reasonable view of the epistemology of trust, it also follows that common claims that trust is a gamble or a risky investment are at least elliptical and perhaps confused, as discussed earlier but as might be made clearer now. Baier (1985, 61) says that trusting someone is always a risk, "given the partial opaqueness to us of the reasoning and motivation of those we trust and with whom we cooperate" (also see Gambetta 1988, 235). Trust is not itself a risk or a gamble. It is, of course, risky to put myself in a position to be harmed or benefited by another. However, I do not calculate the risk and then additionally decide to trust you; my estimation of the risk is merely my degree of trust in you. Again, I do not typically choose to trust and therefore act; rather, I do trust and therefore choose to act. In some circumstances I might even go so far as to risk cooperation with someone I genuinely distrust if that is the best option open to me. The degree of trust I have in you just is my expected probability of the dependency working out well. On Luhmann's general account, trust is a way of dealing with the risks inherent in complexity. To say on top of this, as he and many others do, that trust is itself a risk is to compound the single risk at stake (Luhmann 1980, 24).

Low and High Capacity for Trust

On a commonsense learning account, those who start life badly are disadvantaged by the continuing loss of welfare in forgone opportunities from low capacity for trust. The disadvantage must continue until they have enough experience to update their estimates of the general trustworthiness. Consider how devastating the early abuse and development of low trust is in the learning account. Suppose that, in our society, trust at reasonable levels usually pays off. If I was so heavily abused as a young child that I now expect almost no interaction to pay off, I will enter into few of the potential interactions I face. I will suffer from what former president Jimmy Carter calls "hopelessness based on sound judgment."[6] I am objectively wrong in my assessments, but my assessments make eminently rational sense given the perverse experience I have had.

As I gain new experience, I may eventually correct my earlier assessment of how poor the prospects are. To do so, I would have to have many interactions that typically paid off well, so that my aggregate experience, from early to recent, begins to approach the average experience. Because I have such low expectations, however, I am willing to test very few interactions. If you had a generally good experience of the benefits from trusting, you would readily enter into far more of these interactions. It therefore would take me longer to gain enough information to recommend changing my pessimistic assessments. All the while, I also enter fewer interactions and therefore benefit less than you do as you enter many, which, on average, pay off well. If we start with similar levels of welfare, you soon outdistance me.

Suppose, on the other hand, that I started life with such a charmed existence that I now am too optimistic about trusting others, so that I often overdo it and get burned. Because I am optimistic, I enter into many interactions, and I coincidentally, therefore, collect information for revising my estimates of the trustworthiness of others very quickly. My aggregate experience soon approaches the aggregate average, and I reach an optimal level of trust that pays off well in most of my interactions, more than enough to make up for the occasions when I mistakenly overrate the trustworthiness of another. Oddly, therefore, if parents are to err on one side or the other in instilling a belief that others are trustworthy, a simple learning account suggests that they should err on the side of instilling greater optimism in their children than they think is objectively warranted, at least with respect to modest issues of cooperation for which the losses at risk are not major.

Modeling Learned Capacity to Trust

The alternative conditions of high and low capacity for recognizing trustworthiness may be modeled as in figure 5.1. To simplify the problem, make the following assumptions: (1) The objective world that we now face is one in which the distribution of trustworthiness is linear, from 0 percent to 100 percent trustworthy. (2) We are all competent to assess the *relative* trustworthiness of people, but we may have different mean estimates of how trustworthy they are *absolutely*. That is, you and I would both rank the same kinds of people as most trustworthy and the same kinds as most untrustworthy. But you might optimistically expect all people to be more likely trustworthy than not, while I pessimistically expect all to be more likely untrust-

Figure 5.1   Low, Optimal, and High Trust

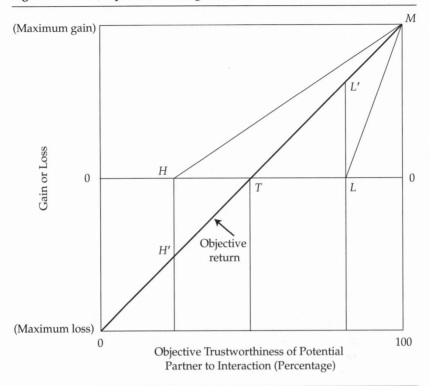

Source: Author's configuration.

worthy than trustworthy. (3) There is a net, positive payoff from cooperating with someone who fulfills the trust and a net loss from cooperating with someone who defaults on the trust. (4) The objective value of the potential loss and gain is the same for all potential partners to interaction, but the probability of getting the gain ranges from 0 percent to 100 percent. Hence the payoff on average will be lower for trusting the less trustworthy than for trusting the more trustworthy. The objective return from cooperating with potential partners is represented by the diagonal line from the lower left to the upper right corner at *M*.

There is an objective breakeven point (any point on the zero payoff axis 0–0) at which the average return from trusting a person of a particular degree of trustworthiness is neither gain nor loss. This is represented by the line 00. The difference between a very optimistic truster and a very pessimistic distruster is that the latter supposes that this breakeven point is reached only for interactions with (objectively) very trustworthy people, while the former supposes it is reached already at significantly lower levels of (objective) trustworthiness. One who trusts at the optimal level for this population supposes that the breakeven point is where it is objectively.

For the person of low trust in figure 5.1, the breakeven point occurs (in the subjective estimate of the low truster) at point L, or about 80 percent objective trustworthiness. For the optimal truster it occurs at point T, or about 50 percent, and for the high truster at point H, or about 25 percent trustworthiness. All three will trust only above their respective breakeven point and will not trust below it; therefore each will risk cooperating only above the breakeven point. The low truster will therefore trust and risk cooperating relatively seldom, only in the range L to 0. The excessively optimistic truster will trust and risk cooperating very often but will lose, on average, in cooperations in the range from H to T. These losses will be offset by gains from trusting and risking cooperation in the range T to 0. The optimal truster will trust and risk cooperating in the range T to 0 and will have an expected net gain throughout that range.

The optimal truster will have the largest actual payoff from risking cooperation, as represented by the large triangle $T0M$. The distruster pessimistically expects the much smaller expected payoff represented by the small triangle $L0M$ but receives the larger actual payoff represented by the trapezoidal area $L0ML'$. The high truster overoptimistically expects the payoff of the very large area $H0M$ but receives the smaller actual payoff that is the optimal trust payoff $(T0M)$ less the loss represented by the small triangle HTH'. The latter triangular area represents the losses from too optimistically trusting those who are unlikely to be trustworthy. The difference in payoffs for the three conditions of trust could be enormous, with the optimal truster several times better off than the distruster. For the values given in figure 5.1, the optimal truster's payoff is somewhat larger than that of the high truster, and slightly larger still than that of the low truster. Note that the optimal truster expects the benefit that he or she receives. These results are presented in table 5.1.

Finally, note that the excessive truster will enter far more interactions than the distruster and will therefore have many more direct opportunities to correct his or her judgment of the breakeven point and the actual distribution of trustworthiness. The distruster will have far fewer direct opportunities to correct his or her judgment.

Great distrust essentially implies that one expects a loss from most interactions. Total distrust would seemingly lead to no interactions, resulting in zero payoff with neither gains nor losses. It would utterly subvert individual existence as well. With a complete absence of trust, one must be catatonic, one could not even get up in the morning. You can learn in this context only if you assume some positive probability

Table 5.1   Returns to High, Optimal, and Low Levels of Trust

Level of Trust	Expected Gain	Actual Gain
High	$H0M$	$T0M - THH'$
Optimal	$T0M$	$T0M$
Low	$L0M$	$T0M - TLL'$

Source: Author's compilation.

of a cooperative response from a first-time interaction with me. If you assume zero probability of cooperation, you do not risk interaction, and you gain no information about me for the future. Moreover, by being extremely wary toward me, you give me information that suggests that I should look elsewhere for cooperation. One reason for stereotyping people is to set a baseline estimate of their trustworthiness in order to get the analysis and its revision of information under way.

Luhmann (1980, 72) says that neither trust nor distrust is feasible as a universal attitude. This follows as an analytical claim for distrust. For trust, however, the claim is empirical and wrong. Trust as a universal attitude could pay off for someone in a benign world in which the level of trustworthiness is quite high. There have surely been such worlds, although Luhmann's claim is likely to be true for most people in modern industrial states. Even in only modestly supportive worlds, however, adopting a policy of taking modest risks beyond one's level of trust can be beneficial. That policy opens up the possibility of discovering the trustworthy. It is risky, but the gains can far outweigh the losses.

Great trust implies expected gain from most interactions. If the optimal-trust line crosses the breakeven line at 50 percent, then never trusting and always trusting have the same net payoff of no gain or loss. The 100 percent truster, however, has many interactions from which to learn better about the world, whereas the 0 percent truster has none. The high truster does the equivalent of as-if testing; the distruster does not. Suppose we wish to correct the deficiencies with which low trusters face the world. *Simply providing equal opportunity for trust will not accomplish this end.* In figure 5.1 and throughout this discussion, the various trusters are assumed to face identical opportunities as of the time of their current interactions. The low truster nevertheless loses ground and suffers severe relative welfare losses. An equal opportunity program cannot stop that morose trend.[7] The losses are not merely of opportunities but *of the capacity to capitalize on opportunities.*

There may be other correlates of high and low capacities for trust from early learning. For example, one may develop a capacity for spontaneity from being able to trust people not to react badly, even to react positively, to one's bold experiments or odd ways. Narcissists are also characteristically spontaneous—yet they do not get that way from a supportive experience. Indeed, the source of narcissistic personality disorder is thought to be severe neglect. If parents and other caretakers are neglectful, perhaps because of alcoholism or severe illness, during the first year or two of a child's life, the child may learn not to take others into account, neither to trust nor to distrust.[8]

Shortcomings of the Model

There are many complications that are not captured in the model of figure 5.1. These include the stated simplifying assumptions, such as, for example, the linearity of distribution of objective and expected trustworthiness. In addition, a number of other limits of the model are noteworthy.

First, the model ignores the relative size of loss and gain at risk. If the downside of risking an interaction is extremely bad compared with the benefit of a successful interaction, as was true for the lieutenant colonel's dealings with Trifonov, one will require much higher probability of gain to offset the occasional losses. The breakeven point in figure 5.1 would move to the right. In experiments on the iterated prisoner's dilemma, as the sucker's payoff (the loss from cooperating with another player who defects) increases, rates of cooperative play decrease, and eventually there is no cooperation. This shortcoming can easily enough be accommodated in the model by making the area below 00 much larger, by moving the bottom edge of the area of returns far lower.

Second, in a point that is related to the first limit, the model ignores the possibility of varied weights of potential interactions. Such variety is implicit in the claim that trust is a three-part relation: A trusts B to do X. In one interaction I might merely trust you to put a quarter in my parking meter, while in another I might trust you to take care of my small child. I might loan you a dollar or a thousand dollars. If there were no correlation between the scale of what is to be entrusted and the likelihood of any person's trustworthiness in fulfilling the trust, this issue would not matter. In general, however, there must be a correlation. We are likely to be lower trusters for high stakes than for low stakes.

Third, the model ignores strategic effects such as as-if trust behavior to test the trustworthiness of people of a particular kind and, more generally, the incentive effects of iterated interaction with the same person. It seems likely that one will tend initially to trust a new person only in limited ways and will trust on more important matters only after building up to them.[9]

Fourth, the model has the shortcoming of Cournot models of economic processes in that it assumes strategic calculation by the potential truster as to whether to enter into interactions but does not attribute any sophistication to the potentially trusted person. The model is only half strategic. This is related to the third deficiency.

Fifth, the model ignores the complexity of possible ways of learning. One might learn indirectly from others' experiences as well as directly from one's own experiences (as discussed in chapter 6). In the light of the second problem of the model, we may note that learning might be quite cheap with minor risks and grievously expensive with major risks. In addition, there is greater value from learning in contexts of likely iteration of interactions.

Sixth, the model may not accommodate complex skews in trusting people, such as the trust many automatically put in managerial or professional persons even in matters outside their professional competence.[10] This shortcoming may, however, be easily addressed within the simplified learning model.

Seventh, the model ignores a particular kind of strategic behavior: deceit. Many people, such as successful con artists and lotharios, may be very good at signaling apparent trustworthiness, because being thought trustworthy opens up potentially valuable opportunities for them (see Bacharach and Gambetta 2001).

The worst of these shortcomings for an account of trust as encapsulated interest are the failures to accommodate strategic considerations, especially incentive effects in iteration (either directly or through reputational effects). Some of the other problems may be easily addressed in the more general encapsulated-interest account of trust, and some may be easily fitted into the model of figure 5.1. Even with its shortcomings, the simple model implies most of Julian Rotter's standard conclusions about interpersonal trust. Rotter (1980) finds that high trusters are more likely to give others a second chance (this sounds almost definitional), and they are less likely to be unhappy and more likely to be liked by others.[11] If they are in an environment in which trust leads more often, on balance, to gains than to losses, they should be less unhappy. As well, their openness to trusting others should lead others to select them as partners in various activities.

Further Implications of the Learned Capacity to Trust

Note some other important implications of the account of learned trust. First, a newcomer to a community may be disadvantaged in ways that are perversely reinforcing. Second, enforcement and sanctions may have a strong positive effect on capacity for trust in contexts well outside the coverage of the sanctions. Finally, the learning account undercuts conceptual claims that trust is a form of human capital.

The Outsider

Consider the condition of an outsider or new immigrant to a community. The outsider may initially seem untrustworthy to others in the community. This could follow merely from a guess, a judgment of that person as less likely to be trustworthy than those who are long well known. Until more knowledge of the newcomer's trustworthiness is generated, he or she is given fewer opportunities to demonstrate trustworthiness. Hence it may take depressingly long for the outsider to become trusted. Since, again, the combination of trusting and being trusted conveys benefits in various kinds of exchange and mutual aid, the outsider faces greater difficulties getting ahead and may begin to seem less able and worthy. Superficially, we might suppose a group that held off from trusting an outsider for a long time was prejudiced in a racist or related sense, although the rational expectations of the wary assessor of trustworthiness might be sufficient to explain the community's attitude.

Alejandro Portes and Julia Sensenbrenner (1993) describe an informal financial system in the Cuban immigrant community in Miami in the 1960s following Fidel Castro's rise to power. Newly arrived immigrants with no collateral could obtain so-called character loans based on the entrepreneurial reputations they had in Cuba. Reputedly, these loans, ranging from $10,000 to $30,000, were invariably repaid, and their recipients often went on to great prosperity.

These loans involved seeming trust by the Latin bankers who made them. Portes and Sensenbrenner call that trust enforceable. Why? Because the Cuban exiles were virtually trapped. They could prosper in this transplanted Cuban community only if they proved reliable in repaying their loans. They could not prosper as well anywhere else. They could not return to Cuba, and there was no welcoming community elsewhere. No other community of people had natural access to their reputations and could have trusted them, in the sense of having good reason to believe that their incentive to be trustworthy was compelling, even overpowering. They were an unusual case: outsiders with almost insider status in one exclusive community on which they were fully dependent. The availability of that status was brief. By 1973, character loans ended, because the newly arriving Cubans were no longer known to the local banking community, and they might also have had little or no recent entrepreneurial success in Cuba on which to ground a reputation.

The Bangladeshi economist Muhammad Yunus created a similar but much more elaborate system of loans to the poor. The loans are made to one or two members of a group of several indigent applicants who need money to become relatively independent in their entrepreneurial activities. No one else in the group can get a similar loan until the first recipients have begun to repay their loans. Hence all the members of the group have strong incentive to be trustworthy because they face sanctions from their neighbors and friends and because they want to keep open the possibility of further loans in the future (Yunus 1998, 1999; Holloway and Wallich 1992).

Many of us, of course, might start by being optimistic toward newly encountered people or people in newly undertaken areas. Even then we would not trust in important matters without a substantial prior history of trustworthiness. If we are outsiders, we might be open to as-if trust to get started. If we are fully outsiders or if we have other communities to turn to, however, we might readily prove to be untrustworthy in the face of large burdens. Hence we could not be trusted as readily as the Miami Cubans in the 1960s.

Sanctions and Trust

Sociologists writing on trust are generally concerned with social mechanisms that generate trust (for example, see Luhmann 1980, 95). Luhmann supposes that the structure of trust relations requires that calculation of risk remain latent. Yet contractual relations may require that such calculation be overt and present and may therefore introduce an atmosphere unfavorable to trust. When such interdependence already exists, so that the risks are openly known to all without need of specific present discussion, mutual understanding and trust may be enhanced (Luhmann 1980, 36). This merely means that the transition from informal to formal regulation of relations may be uneasy, as the street-level epistemologist should expect. New conditions that have ill-defined prior expected probabilities generally introduce initial instability, but the result of successfully completing the transition to formal regulation can be to enhance trust.

Coleman (1990, 114) says development of norms with sanctions enhances cooperation. This is also Hobbes' theory: Creation of strong sanctions to protect each from the others makes all better off. In Hobbes' account of the need for a powerful state, what is mainly needed for most people is merely enough security to be able to enter into exchange relations with others without fear of being killed for what one has or merely preemptively to prevent one from stealing from or killing another (Hobbes 1968 [1651], 1.13: 184; Hardin 1991b). Trustworthiness is underwritten by a government that enforces contracts and punishes theft. Without such a government, cooperation would be nearly impossible, and trust would be unfounded. Without the background of police protection I may be wary of you altogether. With police protection I may readily engage with you in varied activities for mutual benefit. If I no longer need distrust you for possibly having violent motives against me, I can begin to trust your minor motivations to gain from mutual interaction.

At the more mundane level of daily life, we may note, with Bernard Barber (1983, 170), that trust can be enhanced by making distrust and devices for social control more effective. How can trust be enhanced by enforceable contract (or by audits with the threat of sanction)? As noted in chapter 4, the enforceable contract or audit may protect a relationship against the worst of all risks it might entail, thereby enabling the parties to cooperate on less risky matters. Without the threat of sanctions, they might have been able to do none of these. Recall the problem of prisoner's dilemma games with large losses to those who cooperate with a defector (called "sucker's payoff" in the trite vocabulary of much of the prisoner's dilemma literature). If you and I can arrange to have the worst possible payoffs blocked—by legal sanction, if necessary—we can go on to cooperate to our mutual advantage.[12] As McKean (1975, 31) says, we value enforcement mechanisms partly because we recognize how grim life would be without cooperation, "even if the basis has to be created in part by such enforcement mechanisms."

Recall the discussion in chapter 4 of Mafia influence in Sicily. Sicily was not a fully Hobbesian state of nature, but it had Hobbesian tendencies because ordinary Sicilian citizens were not able to rely on the state as a fair enforcer. Lack of legal enforcement on major matters leads to not being able to trust other individuals (Gambetta 1988, 163). A stronger regime capable of coercively overriding the influence of the Mafia could enhance the grounds for trust for most citizens. Most Sicilians would not be coerced by the law that coerced the Mafia. Rather, they would be freed of Mafia coercion if such law worked.

Of course, sanctions need not come from legal authorities. They commonly are built in from iteration and expectation of continued gain that outweighs momentary gain from defection. The incentive to cooperate (or to fulfill a trust) and the sanction not to do so are one and the same. They are the benefits of future interaction that ride on present trustworthiness.

For an apparently extreme case of taking a risk without legal backing, Coleman discusses a 200,000 pound spot loan from the Hambros merchant bank in London to a foreign shipper to allow his ship to leave port in Amsterdam. The loan was negotiated almost instantly over the telephone and delivered immediately, with no security. Coleman (1990, 92) says the loan was made with nothing more substantial than the shipowner's intention to repay and the Hambros man's belief in both the shipowner's honesty and his ability to repay. It seems unlikely that this was really true. There was some threat (surely left unstated) of suit and court enforcement. Even if enforcement was not guaranteed, suit could be initiated and, once undertaken, was likely to have reputational consequences that would have been costly to the shipowner in the future. Even this sanction, though, is largely informal. Hence there were risks in making such a loan, because even with legal action the loan might not have been repaid in full. Still, legal action can keep the scale of losses from misplaced trust substantially lower than the stakes involved in the initial trusting agreement. The possibility of occasionally having to go to court can therefore be counted as a relatively slight cost of doing profitable business.

Most parties to Hambros loans probably prove to be fully trustworthy to repay. The background possibility of sanction greatly enhances this trustworthiness, however, and justifies Hambros's general risk taking. We might say that the use of courts is the centrally important consideration to Hambros in making any particular loan, but such a statement is likely to be misleading. What is centrally important is that the existence of the court sanction changes relations drastically across the board, making Hambros's relations with virtually all potential borrowers more cooperative than they would otherwise be.

To judge fully the Hambros loan, we must back off from the instant case and consider the question of whether it is in the interest of such bankers to do what Hambros did. The answer seems likely to be yes if a sufficiently high degree of trustworthiness can be assured through legal, reputational, or other incentives. Acting as though one trusts relevant others opens up opportunities for doing business.

Concluding Remarks

In many accounts of trust, including Coleman's (1990, chapter 5) strictly rational account, one might suppose those who are to trust are all interchangeable in the following sense: given the same incentives (potential objective payoffs), we would all trust to the same degree. There is an important prior element, however, that some might think of as psychological: we may have different capacities for trust. This issue should not be treated as psychological in the sense of irrational or not rationally justifiable but, rather, as essentially epistemological and hence as pragmatically rational. The sometime claim that there is a psychological dimension to trust that is different from the cognitive or calculative or rational may be little more than nascent recognition of this epistemological problem (see Aguilar 1984).

The encapsulated-interest account of trust is inherently subjective in that what it is sensible for a given individual to expect depends heavily on what that individual knows about both the past and the future of the person or other party to be trusted. Obviously, assessments of the future matter for an expectations analysis. But why the past? Partly for reputational reasons, but also because the past reveals the other's capacity to trust and be trustworthy. To a great extent, this is merely the capacity to judge the likely risks and benefits of entering trust relationships.

These retrospective and prospective views imply that there are two, perhaps causally related, kinds of knowledge about another that play a role in assessments of trustworthiness. First, there is simple inductive knowledge of the kind that goes into reputation. The American anti-Communists, discussed earlier, presumably had some limited inductive knowledge on which to base their conclusions about the supposed "trustworthiness" of the Communists. The second kind of knowledge is theoretical. Economists had theoretical knowledge about people in general and about the working of centrally determined and market-determined economic outcomes. Many economists thought their theoretical knowledge must eventually trump inductive knowledge about loyalty to communist ideology.

A general problem with inductive knowledge, if it is completely atheoretical, is that it cannot justify a claim that what has always happened before must happen again. Most of us are willing to live with inferences that various things will continue to happen in the ways they have always happened so far. Often we are apt to suppose that there are reasons for this, though we may not know the reasons. The economists' theoretical knowledge about economic productivity gave an explanation (perhaps wrong) of why the trend of loyalty to communism must eventually end. A relevant answer to the economists would have to be grounded in an alternative theoretical claim. The anti-Communists generally proposed no alternative theory, they merely asserted the certainty of the Communists' continuing irrationality.

A full account of rational trust must be grounded in reasons for expecting another to fulfill a trust and in reasons for holding general beliefs about trustworthiness. These are addressed, respectively, by the incentive account of trustworthiness that justifies and explains trust and by the commonsense account of the learned capacity to trust. The commonsense learner is little more than an inductivist who generalizes from the past to the future, as in the model of figure 5.1. To break the hold of a bad and misleading past, the inductivist requires a lot of new experience or a bit of theory that runs counter to prior experience. The model of figure 5.1 suggests that the process of correcting pessimistic estimates of trustworthiness merely by amassing better experience may be very slow, so that these misestimates produce a long string of lost opportunities. Understanding that others will be trustworthy when their incentives are right, as in the encapsulated-interest account of trust, may hold greater, quicker promise for grasping those opportunities. This requires seeing the choices of others from their perspective to comprehend their incentives. Then trust becomes fully strategic. It is no longer merely induction on senseless facts.

There is a further implication of the fact that, if I generally distrust people, I will discover little about their actual trustworthiness because I will choose not to interact with them. It follows that I will have to make choices with less information to go on than other, more optimistic people have. Although there might be specific instances in which information is deleterious to my well-being, it is generally beneficial to have more information about one's circumstances. It is not an intention, but merely an effect, of distrust that it can put one at a relative disadvantage on this score. Hence in a society with pockets of distrust, such as in hostile ghettos or in the cases of individuals with particularly bad experience of misplaced or undeveloped trust, some people will have to act from crippled knowledge.

In a relatively benign society, we can afford to take chances with people in general until we discover any of them not to be worthy of cooperation. If, in contrast, we had come to be distrusting in general, the result in a benign society would surely be far worse than what would follow from taking risks on people. Presumably, it would seem much more akin to much of international relations, as in the Cold War between East and West, in which distrust often seemed to be the baseline and trust to be an unreachable goal. Still, to be generally distrusting—or at least to fail to trust—would not be irrational or immoral in some contexts.

Would it make sense for an individual to go through life without taking initial risks with new acquaintances? One might be always distrusting until reputational or other evidence led to trust in a particular case, and no doubt some people are initially distrustful to such a degree. For many people, such a stance would be too tedious and would cost far more in lost opportunities than it would save in avoided harms. To act according to the backward induction argument against cooperation in the iterated prisoner's dilemma would not generally be in their interest (see discussion of the iterated prisoner's dilemma in chapter 1). Once you have a cluster of associates on whom you can rely, however, it might not seem worth the risk of developing new relationships. At its extreme, this might mean a society of close-knit families closed off to most of the rest of the world, as in the impoverished subsistence economies discussed in chapter 4.

For many people in contemporary urban societies, however, openness to new relationships must be a relatively common, even the modal, stance. Those who argue for the good of trusting assume such a benign society. Otherwise, their injunctions are malign.

Finally, note that the simple learning account of figure 5.1 might seem superficially to be poorly fitted with the encapsulated-interest model of trust. To fit that model it must include the incentive effects of iterated interaction with the same person, as in the iterated one-way trust game or the mutual trust interaction of an iterated prisoner's dilemma. If the account is to fit the encapsulated-interest model, then part of the learning that goes into revising one's assessment of another's trustworthiness is learning of the other's interest in continuing the interaction. It is easy to misread the learning account as grounded in a purely dispositional view of trustworthiness, as discussed in chapter 2. If it is taken as an account of my assessing your capacity to judge your interests in cooperating with me, however, then it is fully consistent with the encapsulated-interest view. Hence with relevant simplifying assumptions the commonsense learning model fits with either the dispositional view of trustworthiness or the encapsulated-interest view of trust. The differences between the two are chiefly in the nature of the information another uses in updating his or her assessment of your trustworthiness or the way another reads your actions as grounded either in interests or in some moral or other disposition other than a concern to look after your interests.

Chapter 6

Managing Trust

T HERE ARE many questions we might wish to ask about how trust relationships come to be and why they last or fail. I wish to discuss three general stages of this range of problems: How do individuals come to be optimistic enough to risk the cooperation that often leads to trust? How do they initiate trust relationships with others? How do they maintain the relationships they have once started? The first of these questions is complementary to the discussion of learning in chapter 5, but here I focus on the psychology of cooperativeness as it might be determined by psychological development or by evolutionary selection. In discussing all of these issues, my purpose in part is to test the encapsulated-interest vision of trust against common trust phenomena.

The second question, how we initiate trust relationships, has numerous answers that are diverse in form. The devices available to us may display no logic or natural order. They include taking risks with new people, reliance on reputation, the use of intermediaries in trust, quasi thick relationships that give us information and support, learning by example, escalation from minor to increasingly important matters on which we might trust someone, and, perhaps most appealingly, falling in love or into friendship. These are not all entirely distinct. For example, learning by example from others and the informational sides of quasi thick relationships and intermediaries may be cousins of reliance on reputation.

The third question has two classes of answers. First, we discover fairly directly that a trust relationship is rewarding, and we therefore continue it. Second, we are rewarded indirectly for being in such a relationship in the sense that we are rewarded for actions related to the relationship. These indirect rewards induce us to continue those actions, and the result is maintenance of our trust relationship.

Developmental Accounts of Trust

Several discussions in earlier chapters (especially chapter 5) suggest that there is a developmental path to trust and trustworthiness. Capacity to trust and comprehension of the value of being trustworthy might develop through experience or learning, as they surely do to some extent. On an ethological account, I can trust at all only because I have had relevant experiences at formative moments, without which I could not even imagine myself into the frame of mind of another to guess that other's intentions toward me. Without those developmental experiences, I would, for example, suffer such a severe narcissistic personality disorder that I would be oblivious to the interests and concerns of others and would see all others as merely objects to be used for my purposes. Alternatively, as some writers argue, evolutionary mechanisms might lead us to trust or to be trustworthy. These could be genetic or social evolutionary mechanisms. Models of learning or of evolutionary mechanisms are clearly explanatory rather than conceptual. What is explained can be dispositions, or behavior, or both. In yet a third view, a developmental account is simply about the acquisition of understanding or information about the trustworthiness of others.

Psychological Development

The bulk of the psychological literature on trust is concerned with psychological correlates of trusting or, rather, of being a high truster as opposed to a low truster (for example, see Rotter 1980). Some of it, however, is about the development of a capacity to judge trustworthiness. The simplest psychological path for such development would merely be a learning model, as discussed in chapter 5. The more I encounter people who reciprocate my cooperative gestures, the more I come to understand the nature of our potentially beneficial interaction, so that I become trustworthy in the sense that I begin to take others' interests into account in deciding what I do in joint undertakings. When furthering their interests furthers mine and I recognize this fact, they will have potential reason to judge me to be trustworthy.

The simple learning model of chapter 5 would explain why some people grow up with optimistic expectations of the trustworthiness of others, while other people grow up with pessimistic expectations. If I have optimistic expectations I will more readily take risks on the trustworthiness of others, and if others in the context are relatively trustworthy, I will benefit greatly from the cooperation that we can achieve. If, however, others are not trustworthy in the context, I may quickly learn that and will protect myself against betrayal by them. If on the contrary I have pessimistic expectations, I will not readily take risks with others. Hence I may not even gain the experience to revise my expectations when I come into a context in which others would commonly be trustworthy.

A behavioral learning account, such as that of Erik Erikson, supplies an essential part of an economic or rational account of trust. It is about how particular expectations develop from experience. Such expectations are, of course, central to the rational account. "The firm establishment of enduring patterns for the solution of the nuclear conflict of basic trust versus basic mistrust in mere existence," notes Erikson (1963, 249), "is the first task of the ego, and thus first of all a task of maternal care." What is needed is not simply quantities of food and so forth but the quality of the maternal relationship. "Mothers create a sense of trust in their children by that kind of administration which in its quality combines sensitive care of the baby's individual needs and a firm sense of personal trustworthiness" (Erikson 1963, 249). Annette Baier (1986) and Lars Hertzberg (1988) use discussions of infant trust to try to establish the conceptual nature of trust. One should think, rather, that the infant instinct for waiting happily for good things to happen must be an important learning or developmental experience. John Bowlby and his colleagues have assumed that the child faces ethological constraints during development. For example, if language is not learned before a certain young age, it cannot be learned thereafter. So too, they argue, there are developmental stages in attachment (Bretherton 1992, 762)—and, one might suppose, in trusting, in learning to distinguish those who are trustworthy and those who are not in various interactions, and in grasping the value of trustworthiness over time.

Genetic Evolutionary Development

Trust and trustworthiness often involve a severe commitment problem that may be hard to resolve. A particularly absurd resolution of it is that of Wagner's (1977, 16) *The Rhinegold*, in which Alberich adopts celibacy and forswears love forever to gain the power of the Rhinegold (see chapter 2). The sniveling Alberich has impossibly great willpower (as perhaps befits the ego of Wagner). A somewhat less absurd resolution is offered by David Gauthier (1986) as a matter simply of adopting a relevant disposition to be cooperative with others who are cooperative. This is a less extravagant demand on willpower, but it is still an impossible demand. One nonabsurd way to resolve the commitment problem is genetically. One who blushes when lying may be able to establish credibility easily without any willful commitment or manufactured disposition. One who does not blush when lying may have to create a reputation for honesty that is worth more than any gain he or she might make from cheating on that reputation.

Sentiments of vengeance, guilt, and so forth often incur substantial avoidable costs—hence, Robert Frank (1988, 54, 57) supposes, they must also confer some sort of compensating gain to have persisted socially or genetically. These sentiments will be most effective if they can be properly communicated to deter or encourage relevant actions from others. If devices for communicating, such as blushing, are genetic, we may then explain the genetic selection as the result of interests—it may even develop through intensive cultural conditioning.

Frank has a tendency to conflate the language of self-interest with shortsightedness. He says defectors are pure opportunists who "always make whatever choice will maximize their personal payoff." The choice that maximizes personal payoff in the longer run, however, is the one the self-interested person will want to make, and that is not defection in Frank's iterated prisoner's dilemmas (see discussion in chapter 1). Frank (1988, 57, 11) poses his "commitment model" as counter to the "self-interest model." It seems, on the contrary, to be a simple matter of self-interest as intelligently weighed. In any case, *his account is a resolution of the problem of my capacity to be trustworthy; it is not an account of trust.* If there is an evolutionary account of trust, it is presumably roughly that of the infant "trust" argument of Baier and others. The infant must accept offered sustenance or die. Hence infants of species that survive tend to accept it. They at least act as if they trusted, although it would be perverse to say that a cognitively undeveloped infant bird or human actually does trust.

Frank's model of trustworthiness is merely his model of cooperativeness more generally. (Indeed, experimental work that not long ago was characterized as being about cooperation is increasingly described as being about trust. Unfortunately, this move sometimes conflates data on what is to be explained—cooperation—with data on what is to explain it—trust.) Frank's model yields four conclusions. First, if cooperators and defectors look alike, then cooperators will be extinguished. Second, if cooperators and defectors are easily identified, defectors will be extinguished. Third, if mimicry has no cost or delay, cooperators will be extinguished. Fourth, if mimicry entails fixed costs of detection, there will be a stable mix of cooperators and defectors.[1]

Albert Breton and Ronald Wintrobe (1982, 69–70) suppose that individuals, if they are to prosper, must develop reasonably good instincts for assessing indicators of others' trustworthiness even absent institutions and reputations to certify them. Hence we might suppose Frank's fourth state is that of human societies. Most of us are reasonably trustworthy, and the costs of mimicry are not negligible for most of us. We thus have reason to be confident at least to some extent—but we may occasionally be done in by a master deceiver.

If sentiments for vengeance, generosity, trustworthiness, and so forth have developed genetically, one may act from them even when it is not in one's interest to do so. Hence there may be something left over from or conflicting with the rational-choice account. Generally, however, a person with observable character traits for trustworthiness "will benefit by being able to solve important commitment problems. He will be trustworthy in situations where the purely self-interested person would not, and will therefore be much sought-after as a partner in situations [in which trustworthiness matters]." (Frank 1988, 14–16)[2]

Social Evolutionary Development

The evolutionary account that Frank and many others present is an account of developing dispositions for trustworthiness or of essentially biological signals that belie untrustworthiness or falsity (see also Bateson 1988). Such evolutionary selection of dispositions may be important in enabling us to be trustworthy and therefore in enabling others to trust us; but this must be a small part of the story of why it is the case that we trust those whom we do trust and distrust many others, even though many of those we distrust are themselves well trusted by still others. We almost certainly require social and experimental, not genetic, accounts to explain such variation. The learning account of chapter 5 and many of the arguments that follow go beyond the merely enabling developments of genetic evolution.

Robert Axelrod (1984) proposes not a genetic but a social evolutionary model of cooperation. He supposes that people in a large society use various strategies when they face an opportunity for beneficial cooperation with another. They can do relatively well only if they can take advantage of the cooperativeness of others or if they can selectively cooperate only with others who are contingently cooperative. In particular, he proposes following a strategy of tit for tat, in which one tries initial cooperation and then continues cooperation if the other also cooperates but stops cooperating if the other does not initially cooperate and cooperates thereafter only if the other starts cooperating. Players who follow this strategy prosper, and those who defect instead of cooperating get excluded from relations with the cooperators.

One might call this a model of the rise of cooperativeness. One might also call it a model of trustworthiness, because those who reliably cooperate fit the encapsulated-interest account of trust in being trustworthy with respect to other cooperators. Because they do, they are enabled to cooperate beneficially with others who are trustworthy. Axelrod's social evolutionary model is a model of trustworthiness and not directly a model of trust, although trustworthiness begets trust by giving others the incentive to trust. The Axelrod model, because it is specifically about mutual cooperation in the prisoner's dilemma, does not apply to the one-way trust game. In a social evolutionary account the strategy of choosing to risk cooperation in a one-way trust game might, however, readily survive well against the refusal of such cooperation.

Similarly, according to one of Partha Dasgupta's (1988, 58) evolutionarily stable models of reputation, if everyone assumes everyone is trustworthy, then it is in the interest of everyone to be trustworthy. What evolves socially, then, is trustworthiness, which begets trust and, increasingly, actual instances of cooperation. (It is perhaps this close causal connection between trustworthiness and the possibilities of cooperation that makes it seemingly easy to label many experiments as about either cooperation or trustworthiness.) In particular, of course, this social evolutionary model fits the mutual trust model of the iterated prisoner's dilemma, which is merely one variant of trust as encapsulated interest.

Social evolutionary models would fit better with our experience if two additional elements were included in them. First, in repeat interactions the stakes should rise in later interactions. A good reason for risking cooperation early is, of course, that the loss will be small in absolute terms while later gains promise to be large in comparison with the initially risked loss. Hence repeat interaction with the same person is doubly valuable. Second, partly because of the first point, encounters will not be random; rather, we will tend to develop ongoing relationships. *The natural evolution of cooperation will therefore be toward social structure*, with groups and closely related dyads developing as the milieus for cooperation.

Initiation of Trust Relations

Every initial effort to establish a trust relationship or even to cooperate a single time entails some degree of risk. The account in chapter 5 suggests, however, that in some contexts, it makes sense to take risks in order to discover with whom one can expect beneficially to interact further. One reading of the apparently varied levels of so-called generalized trust is that some people have a greater disposition to trust than others. Studies of trust therefore often divide subjects into those who are high trusters and those who are low trusters, as one might suppose is done in chapter 5.[3] Again, however, note that variant levels of seeming trust might simply be variant degrees of risk taking or of learning about others. Some people may be much more ready to take risks, even given similar assessments of the likely reliability of their potential partners, than others. They will therefore tend to discover more quickly who is and who is not trustworthy in various contexts, and they may even provide a collective benefit in the form of information on others. A modest risk taker who has enough successes may even feel free to take more substantial risks and might benefit enormously if the world turns out to be relatively benign.

Reputational Incentives

Several things follow for the rest of us if you take risks of cooperation. First, of course, you begin to seem a likely candidate for cooperative ventures. Furthermore, my response to your risking cooperation with me may substantially affect my reputation and therefore affect whether I can get anyone thereafter to cooperate with me when I need them to do so. Hence we both develop reputations as a result of your risk taking.

Reputational effects can be restated in an illuminating way. Reference to reputation is commonly about the past, as though to say that someone has demonstrated reliability. In such a claim, the reputation is made to seem like a disposition for certain kinds of benign or cooperative behavior. It is more illuminating, however, to view reputational effects as *future oriented*, because a reputation for cooperativeness or trustworthiness gives the person or group or institution with the positive reputation compelling reasons for a future orientation. If I have established a relevant reputation, it enables me to start new relationships with seemingly less risk to my new partner than he or she would face in a new relationship with someone with no or a bad reputation. I therefore have strong incentive to live up to my reputation. That is to say, you have reason to suppose my interest encapsulates yours. This is just to say that you trust me to some extent, that your relationship with me is future oriented.

Of course, some people might tend to rely on others' reputations inductively as though reputations were merely evidence about their dispositions for trustworthiness, as they might be. Even if that is false, however, their reliance on positive reputations as evidence of trustworthy dispositions may lead them to take risks with those whose reputations are positive. That will be sufficient for a forward-looking person with an established reputation to gain new partners for beneficial exchanges and other interactions. In this case, following a wrong theory can take us in the right direction.

Once we have reputations for some level of cooperativeness, we may begin to push that level to escalate expectations and the value of our future interactions. We are not likely to escalate very high for the simple reason that we will not frequently stand to benefit from extremely large cooperative efforts, although sometimes we will. But we might begin almost all relationships at a low level of risk and then eventually escalate, perhaps slowly step by incremental step, to a more substantial level that makes our relationship much more richly valuable.

Intermediaries in Trust

Intermediaries in trust can help two parties connect even though they do not otherwise know enough to trust each other (Coleman 1990, 180–85). For example, certain institutions can give us the knowledge for trust and therefore they can, in this limited but important sense, play the role of intermediaries in trust. In the commercial world they may actually act as guarantors of someone's trustworthiness. Outside that world, they may still be important for their knowledge of the reputations of people and organizations with whom we might wish to deal. Moreover, it is a common occurrence in daily life—both non-commercial and commercial—that we are assured by a mutual friend or, in some communities, a matchmaker that someone we do not yet have grounds for trusting is in fact likely to prove trustworthy. Indeed, the fact that you, my friend, assure me that Mary, your friend, will be trustworthy may give Mary special incentive to be trustworthy to me just because her reputation with you will be damaged if she is not.

Consider an odd use of an intermediary in trust. When I spent a year in Italy more than three decades ago, I arranged with my bank in Texas to hold funds in an interest-bearing account and to transfer from that account to a checking account whenever I drew a check on the latter. The first time I needed money, the bank failed to keep its agreement and sent me a letter telling me that my checking account was nearly empty (presumably the failure was one of incompetence rather than of bad motivations). By the time that letter arrived through the Italian mails, I was almost entirely broke. I took the letter to one of the banks in Perugia to attempt to get a small loan. The teller who handled my request repeated over and over that this was a matter for a consulate. A colleague, apparently an officer of the bank, came out of the office behind him and asked what was at issue. The teller explained, adding yet again that it was a matter for a consulate.

The officer asked me to explain it all again. He then took my letter into the office for a couple of minutes and returned to ask how much money I would like to have. Thinking now about the slowness of the mails, I asked for the entire amount mentioned in the letter, not the small loan I had originally hoped to receive. His English was not as good as the teller's, but evidently he had more power. He returned to the office and came back almost immediately with the sum I had requested, the equivalent of several hundred dollars. He asked me to sign a receipt for the money and then said that the bank would deal with my bank to get the funds. Naturally, I was floored by the whole transaction, but I asked no questions and acted as though this was, of course, the normal way to do business, asking for no collateral from a foreigner who just walked in off the street and who could as well leave the country tomorrow.

As I left the bank, I noticed a brass plaque beside the entrance, which said that the bank was the correspondent bank of the Irving Trust Company, a major, world-renowned New York bank. My bank was the very small Irving Bank and Trust Company of Irving, Texas. My letter had been signed by the president of that bank. It seemed likely that the officer of the bank had read the signature as that of the president of his correspondent bank. Of course, the president of the Irving Trust Company surely had more important things to do than to write personal letters to insignificant customers. With his enormous prestige and his apparently high regard for me, he was my intermediary in trust, no matter that I had never met him and presumably never would. He handled his role splendidly, however, and his correspondent bank in Italy took care of all my further dealings with the Irving Bank and Trust Company in Texas. My Italian bank was roughly in the position of Karamazov's lieutenant colonel. It would make very small profits from the exchanges of my money, but it risked a substantial loss. Moreover, like the lieutenant colonel, the Italian bank was essentially the first mover in the first round of our play, taking its risk alone.

Of course, intermediaries in trust may be more available to some kinds of people than to others, giving the former great advantages over the latter, as was evidently true for me by error, so that, unlike many people stranded without money abroad, I did not have to go to a consulate. Among the many groups that have long had difficulty owing to a lack of relevant intermediaries to help establish their trustworthiness have been wives seeking credit, the self-employed, and new arrivals to a community.

Most people we meet and come to trust may be people we meet through others, who are de facto intermediaries in trust. This fact might make optimism about others plausible in many cases. Experience must still trump if the new person fails our optimistic cooperative gestures. Personal intermediaries are a central aspect of the Confucian vision of social interaction (see further Cook and Hardin 2000).

When dealing with someone new, a Chinese might ask a guanxi contact for assurance that the new person will be trustworthy. This is often equated with influence peddling in Western understandings—or misunderstandings—that presumably generalize from the use of a guanxi to break the ice with a new person or business associate; but the Chinese in question might merely be seeking an intermediary's recommendations that another is competent, honest, knowledgeable, or trustworthy (discussions with James Hsiung at New York University, 29 October 1997; also see Boyer 1997 and Holan 1997). One might imagine that such devices grew up in a very small-scale society in which family networks controlled many opportunities.

Falling in Love

Suppose that, when meeting new people without much knowledge of them, my initial stance is to be wary, neither trustful nor distrustful. I might be optimistic from past experience, either in general or with respect to certain apparent attributes of a given new person. Of course, wariness means that I will be less forthcoming than I would be with an already trusted person. Hence I may give a new person little evidence on which to judge me. If this were always true, I would develop close relationships only over a relatively long period. Two psychological phenomena might overcome this initial wariness and let me move on to closer relationships much faster. These are falling in love and its near equivalent, falling into friendship. Consider falling in love, which has the richer literature and the sweeter ring.

When I fall in love with you, I partially take your interests as mine. I actually want you to be happy—and not only because I will benefit from your happiness. This is, de facto, a strong instance of my encapsulating your interests in my own, which is to say that you can trust me to some perhaps substantial extent. My love of you grounds your trust because it makes me a trustworthy agent for your welfare and happiness. One might suppose, on the contrary, that trust is absent early in a relationship because the parties have little basis from past experience for trusting (Scanzoni 1979). It is the fact of falling in love or, less forcefully, into friendship that can give people grounds for being trusted virtually at the initiation of the intense relationship. John Holmes (1991, 66; also see 99) writes that "in the early romantic stages love [appears] to be the basis for trust, however inarticulate or unfounded the latter might [be]." He seems to mean "unfounded" in the sense of not based in actions. It is founded, however, in the shared interests, and this can be a strong and deep foundation for trust.

Note, of course, that my loving you does not make you trustworthy toward me. It only makes me trustworthy toward you; and therefore it gives you ground to trust me. Mutual love is far better than one-way love because it gives us reciprocal trust.

Perhaps this account of love as leading to risks that, in the presence of trust, would not be risks suggests the wisdom of Jane Austen's eventual marriages between cousins and other longtime but not too close associates, as in the case of Emma Woodhouse and her neighbor, Mr. Knightley. In her wisdom, Austen (1985 [1816], 419) notes that Knightley "had been in love with Emma, and jealous of Frank Churchill [of whom Emma briefly thought herself enamored], from about the same period, one sentiment having probably enlightened him as to the other."[4] In many societies today, it would be much less common for two people to have such a long-term basis for trust before they happen to fall in love, so that it is often love that leads to initial trust. Alas, that trust can turn out to be misplaced, and the love can prove costly.

Falling in love and into friendship work in two ways at once. First, they stand in for initial knowledge of the other that would be definitive of grounded trust. Second, they imply a commitment that justifies reciprocation from the other in the expectation that one will continue the relationship and that one has much to gain from doing so. Of course, falling in love, if it goes very far, is commonly mutual. If I begin to love you, I become far less wary, thus opening up and giving you knowledge that enables you to trust me (or, if it fails, actively to distrust me). Therefore, the psychology of falling in love (or into friendship) enables us to develop crucial relationships much more quickly than we could otherwise.

Note that in this view, trust and hence trustworthiness are motivated by the fact that I take on my beloved's interests as my own. If my love fades, this ground for trust between us fades and, more pointedly and painfully, this ground for my trustworthiness fades. My initial love might be romantic love. If this fades and is not transmuted into a more stable kind of love, our relationship might therefore seem to be quite foul.

Annette Baier (1985, 58) says that "it is fairly obvious that love . . . involves trust," but this is not obvious at all. Many people have had the doleful experience of deeply loving someone they did not trust. The pattern of "misplaced" love in some cases recalls a spoof of the standard theme of country and western songs: "I can't love you, baby, if you won't leave me." Even reciprocal love need not require extensive trust. It seems likely that falling in love leads to experience that justifies trust, so that love commonly begets trust rather than the other way around. Loving typically gives one a strong motive for trustworthiness, which should beget trust from the beloved, although, sadly, this need not always happen.[5]

Shared Interests

When I trust you in the sense of believing that your interests encapsulate mine in at least the matter with respect to which I trust you, we can, naturally, be said to share interests to some extent. We might share interests in two quite different ways. First, we may merely share them causally, because what serves your interest serves mine as well. Second, one of us may genuinely adopt the other's interests as our own (see further Hardin 1999c). If I love you, I may literally encapsulate your interests in mine to some extent in the sense that I value your happiness so much that I act as though for your benefit without full regard for my own benefit.

In this case, again, I do not cooperate with you merely because it benefits me to do so; I do it because I want you to benefit. If I go much further and virtually assume your interests as mine, you can trust me almost completely. Ours is then virtually a pure coordination interaction. There might be problems of information and understanding, but there are none of motivation. If I only share your interests to some extent, we may have conflicts despite our love, and those conflicts might finally trump. For example, suppose you cannot imagine living anywhere other than the East Coast and I cannot imagine living anywhere other than the West Coast. It will be hard for us to coordinate. The Midwest is not a compromise.

Love can be a one-way relationship, of course, so that, say, a mother might love her child and include her child's welfare very much in her own. The child might count the mother's welfare for little in comparison. The mother may go so far as to share the child's intentions, but the child might not share hers. It is this kind of relationship that allows the child to develop at all in the account in chapter 5. In the end the child's independence or autonomy as a person may depend on the parents' capacity to love and give without commensurate reciprocation. In the one-way trust game that the lieutenant colonel and Trifonov played out, there was some mutual trust so long as they expected the game to continue indefinitely. As did their relationship, a parent's relationship with a child might have unequal shares of trust, so that it is nominally a mutual trust game that they play, but it is the child who can count on being able to trust almost totally, whereas the parent is almost totally trustworthy but might not be able to trust very extensively.

The striking thing about a love relationship, whether it is mutual as between two lovers or more nearly one-way between a parent and child, is that the trusted genuinely encapsulates the interests of the truster in the trusted's own interests. Moreover, this is commonly true ab initio for the mother of a newborn child, and it is very nearly true ab initio for lovers who fall suddenly in love. The lovers need not have known each other for very long, and they need not have a rich array of associates in common to protect them in their risk taking with each other. Their love allows them to escalate the risks they take very fast and relieves them of the need for support from a larger community. Falling in love moves everything ahead much faster, and the thrill of such momentum may even enhance the love just because it is associated with the beloved.

For the ordinary trust relationship, such as in an iterated prisoner's dilemma or exchange or in a trust game interaction over a relatively narrowly defined range of issues, you and I might share limited interests and might not genuinely care much about each other's general welfare, but we can still trust each other because we need each other's contributions to some common effort or production. In this case our interests are weakly shared through the causal effects of our efforts on our joint good. For the lover and the parent, the interests of the other are much more strongly shared: they are directly included in the parent's or lover's own interests to some substantial extent because the lover and the parent care directly about the general welfare of the other. Therefore, the other has strong reason for trusting. The range of matters of concern to the lover or parent is typically very broad; for the ordinary trust relation, it is typically narrowly defined.

Maintenance of Trust Through Feedback

Once they have been initiated, trust relationships are maintained in at least two large classes of ways: through direct recognition of the value of the relationship and through indirect feedback, which stimulates continuation or iteration of the reciprocal dealings that constitute the relationship. The mode of direct recognition may be the whole story for many dyadic trust relationships. You and I each know that continued interaction with each other will benefit us. One reason mutual trust seems, on a subjective assessment, to be so commonplace in the range of all trust relationships is that it is so easily maintained and understood. Additionally, as noted in chapter 1, mutual trust gives each party an extra reason for thinking the other trustworthy: that the other benefits from being in the relationship.

Our chief problem is not maintenance in this sense but only the prevention of the collapse of our ongoing interaction in the face of anything that might disrupt it, such as sudden escalation of the stakes that lets one or the other of us treat the next round of our interaction as though it were part of a new, perhaps only one-shot, interaction. In such an interaction, the modest level of trustworthiness that we might have maintained through many iterations might no longer be enough to prevent opportunistic actions—such as that of Trifonov at the end of his interaction with the lieutenant colonel—that will wreck the relationship and maybe even harm one of us.

Carol Heimer (2001) sees trust as a way in which actors in social relationships can cope with the uncertainty and vulnerability that pervade relationships. Niklas Luhmann (1980, 8) more elaborately wishes to explain the existence of trust by its value to us in causing good things. "Where there is trust," he says, "there are increased possibilities for experience and action." In this view, the function of trust is that it gives us the present sense of understanding and reducing complexity. Complexity is the central problem, because the individual cannot know enough to handle everything and must therefore rely on others as agents for some matters (Luhmann 1980, 15, 5). At least casually, these claims sound like a functional explanation for the existence, rise, or maintenance of trust. Such explanations are often shallow metaphors without genuine explanatory content. Let us unpack this one to see what it contains.

An institution or behavioral pattern X is explained by its function F for group G if and only if it fits the following paradigm:

1. F is an effect of X;

2. F is beneficial for G; and

3. F maintains X by a causal feedback loop passing through G (Elster 1979, 28).[6]

The pattern X is trust; its function F is that it leads to cooperative interaction; G is the society. Let us fill in this paradigm, adding a strong condition (in italics).

1. *If enough others are trustworthy,* cooperative interaction (F) is an effect of trust (X); that is, interaction is enhanced by trust.

2. Cooperative interaction (F) is good for the members of the society (G).

3. Cooperative interaction (F) maintains trust (X) by a feedback loop passing through the members of the society (G). Why? Because cooperative interaction leads to ongoing relationships and institutions that induce and support trust (as in the encapsulated-interest account).

Hence, given the condition that enough people are trustworthy, Luhmann's theory is a functional explanation in the demanding sense of this paradigm.

What does this tell us? It does not say that because trust is functional it will happen. Rather, it says that if the causal chain producing trust ever gets under way, it will tend to be sustained by the feedback mechanism of the explanation. That fact raises an additional question. How does the causal chain get under way? If others are generally untrustworthy, we can generally expect everyone to learn not to be readily open to cooperative gestures. We could imagine that trusting would be a result of social evolution from a prior, less complex world in which ongoing interactions are dense enough to ground trust, as in the thick-relationships variant of trust. This would work because each or many of us might see that trustworthiness is in our interest, and our trustworthiness would then beget trust from others even outside our close, norm-governed community. Alternatively, perhaps the devices for initiation of trust would get trust under way.

It would be sloppy reasoning to suppose that this functional account necessitates or automatically leads to trust in a complex world. It is only an account of the maintenance of trust in such a world.

Note, incidentally, that trustworthiness would fit this account without a strong caveat parallel to the one required for the functional account of trust. I do not automatically have incentive to trust when I enter a relationship, but I often will have incentive to be trustworthy in order to make that relationship beneficial over the longer run. Hence the condition required for Luhmann's functional explanation of trust to work may be fulfilled through a functional explanation of the maintenance of trustworthiness. It is not a morally grounded trustworthiness that is required or explained here. Rather, it is merely the trustworthiness of anyone who understands the implications of being reliable in various potentially beneficial interactions if those interactions are likely to be repeated or continued, if they work out beneficially to both (or all) parties, or if there are beneficial reputational effects of being trustworthy.

Here is the quick functional account of trustworthiness (X is now trustworthiness rather than trust, but F and G remain the same).

1. Cooperative interaction (F) is an effect of trustworthiness (X); that is, interaction is enhanced by trustworthiness.

2. Cooperative interaction (F) is good for the members of the society (G).

3. Cooperative interaction (F) maintains trustworthiness (X) by a feedback loop passing through the members of the society (G). Why? Because cooperative interaction leads to ongoing relationships and institutions that give incentive for trustworthiness (as in the encapsulated-interest account).

Acting on the incentive for trustworthiness is to be trustworthy on the encapsulated-interest account of trust. In his functional explanation of the maintenance of trust in a complex society, Luhmann does not make the direct mistake of confusing trust and trustworthiness. Nevertheless, it is much easier to account directly for trustworthiness, which then begets trust. It begets trust because trust is essentially in the category of knowledge, and evidence of trustworthiness ultimately defines trust.

Luhmann does not confuse trust and trustworthiness conceptually, because it is genuinely his interest to explain trust, which he supposes is the individual's device for dealing with complexity—although, of course, the device can work only if others are trustworthy. My own trustworthiness does not directly help me deal with complexity, although it might do so indirectly by begetting trust. On this account, trustworthiness is, in a sense, prior. Hence there is reason to suppose that *it is the rise of trustworthiness that allows for the development of complexity, which actually results from successful trust.* Trustworthiness not only enables us to handle complexity when we have it, but it also therefore enables us to develop complexity. This would make sense, in a way that his own general argument does not, of Luhmann's (1980, 7) claim that the "increase and reduction of complexity belong together as complementary aspects of the structure of human response to the world."

Also note that, although trust fits the paradigm of functional explanation on the encapsulated-interest theory of trust, it might not under some other theories or definitions of trust. Indeed, it cannot fit a functional explanation under some of the noncognitive or ungrounded definitions because trust under these definitions cannot be affected by its effects, so that feedback plays no role in it. Trust that is inherently normative is also not likely to fit an analogous functional explanation. Luhmann's functional account works under the condition that enough people are trustworthy. Evolutionary accounts typically are functional, and the account of trustworthiness as social capital (presented in chapter 3) can be constructed as functional, although these accounts need not suppose, with Luhmann, that the problem to be resolved is complexity.

In Barber's (1983) account of professionalism, trustworthiness is achieved by indoctrinating the professionals. As a patient with limited medical understanding, I trust a doctor to take my interests to heart and to serve me well. In this account, there is a functional relationship between my trust and the trustworthiness of doctors. Because the relationship is fully understood and is deliberately secured through indoctrination and monitoring of doctors, however, Jon Elster (1979, 28) would reject it as not fitting a functional explanation. For him, a functional explanation is valid only if the feedback is not understood by the relevant actors. This condition means that, once we begin to understand our feedback relationship, that relationship ceases to fit the functional explanation. The explanation of the maintenance of trustworthiness in many societies has surely fitted Elster's condition, although it no longer does in a society with rich enough social science to analyze the relationship.

Still, the nature of the doctor-patient relation, if Barber's account is descriptively correct, might be functional in a more limited, yet still meaningful sense, if the institutions for indoctrination and monitoring are supported by the actions of patients and doctors, who are the beneficiaries of those institutions. Alternatively, one might suppose that the reliability of doctors is secured by a strong institution, much like the institutions that secure compliance with the law, that stands on its own and does not depend on feedback from patients and doctors in the form of actions that support it, anymore than the institutions of justice are dependent on feedback from citizens and criminals.

In general, functional explanation fits especially well with rational-choice understandings because the feedback can work through the creation of incentives for acting according to the pattern of behavior that is to be explained (see further Hardin 1980).[7] The relevant functional pattern of behavior commonly just is a response to incentives. No one need know the general implications of everyone's acting from those incentives. Robert Merton (1968, 103) notes that the requirements of functional explanation in the biological sciences "come to be met almost as a matter of course." Elster (1979, 29) supposes that it is nearly impossible to find cases of functional analysis in sociology that meet the conditions of his paradigm. The correct claim is that few extant accounts that are called functional meet these conditions. But sociology and the social world are rife with cases that do fit it, such as the functional maintenance of trustworthiness and many other cases.[8]

Recall the pervasive distrust of the harsh subsistence societies studied by Banfield and several anthropologists that are discussed in chapter 4. As already noted, such distrust is self-reinforcing. Indeed, one can give a functional account of distrust in these societies. X is now distrust rather than trust, F is self-protection of the individual from gullible harms, and G remains the members of the society. Thus,

1. Self-protection (F) is an effect of distrust (X); that is, self-protection is enhanced by distrust.

2. Self-protection (F) is good for the members of the society (G).

3. Self-protection (F) maintains distrust (X) by a feedback loop passing through the members of the society (G). Why? Because self-protection blocks relationships and institutions that would generate trustworthiness and trust.

In this account, distrust is functional for individual protection, even though successful development of trusting relationships would be far more beneficial. Unfortunately, no individual might be able to break the functional reinforcement of distrust. Distrust therefore might have a stranglehold on the community. To break the pervasive distrust would require a major act of risk taking by some member of the community, outside intervention, or successful collective action. Collective action would be very nearly impossible in the face of such distrust. Note, generally, that the likely prevalence of contexts in which we can give a straightforward functional account of essentially negative, collectively self-destructive behavior patterns suggests the silliness of functionalist theories that suppose functionalism is good. It also suggests the silliness of cultural claims that the present culture is right or good because it serves the interests of members whose identities were formed by that culture.

Concluding Remarks

Other issues in the management of trust could be addressed. For example, we might suppose that trust relationships develop in one arena in response to distrust in another or others. If the larger society is a place of distrust or the government is a source of threat, we might develop stronger local relationships to protect ourselves against intrusions from the larger, malevolent society or government. The threatening world of the Omani (briefly discussed in chapter 4) leads to strongly maintained familial homes that are virtual fortresses, with high walls offering protection against the outside. The awful world created by Stalin led later to the rich underground culture of the samizdat. Pernicious race or ethnic relations might lead a minority group to define its own ghetto.

We might also analyze the range of things that can disrupt trust relationships, as the endgame effect in the disreputable dealings of the lieutenant colonel and Trifonov disrupted their relationship. Some relationships seemingly have to escalate to some relatively high level or else founder, and that gives opportunity for breakdowns that mimic endgame effects. For example, after a period of successful arms control by spontaneous proclamations, American and Soviet leaders began to push for so-called hard treaties (there has never been a hard treaty, except in the sense of its being hard to negotiate and ratify), and the effort stalled (Hardin in press b, chapter 2). Soon thereafter, the United States planned the missile defense system popularly known as Star Wars, the greatest single escalation in the history of the nuclear deterrence system.

Chapter 7

Trust and Government

A LARGE and growing literature focuses on the theses that, if it is to function at all well, government needs the trust of its citizens and that such trust is now declining in the United States and in certain other nations. Hence there is a crisis of trust. At most, this claim is misstated. It should, rather, be made merely about confidence in government's actions and policies. I argue that, in any strong sense of trust, trust in government is not a major consideration in the working of a modern society. A claim to trust government is typically implausible if it is supposed to be analogous to a claim to trust another person. The implausibility of trust in government is true for all the standard conceptions of trust, including the encapsulated-interest view articulated in this book, views that ground trust in the moral commitments of the trusted, and views that make trustworthiness a matter of character. In all of these views, trust is inherently cognitive in that it turns on assessments of commitments of the trusted. The difficulty with "trusting government" is that the knowledge demanded by any of these conceptions of trust is simply unavailable to ordinary citizens. I do not constantly include these other views in the discussion that follows, but they are easily accommodated.

One might still wish to say, as in the vernacular, that a citizen can trust government, but the "trust" in this case is almost certain to be different from the trust that I might have in you. Hence the seeming goodness and importance of ordinary interpersonal trust does not clearly transfer to any meaningful notion of trust in government, because the possibilities for trust in government are not analogous to those for trust in a person.

The contemporary claim that democratic government needs the trust of citizens raises another critical question. While my trusting you may enable you in certain ways, will citizens' trusting government enable government at all? Citizens must often be compliant if government is to work, and they may more readily be compliant if

they are confident that government actions will serve their own interests or some broader public good that they support. For example,
H. L. A. Hart (1961, 201) argues that the Hobbesian vision of using
coercion to motivate obedience to law or to the state depends on the
background fact that most people comply willingly, perhaps for normative reasons. It is their compliance that makes it possible for the
state to focus its limited resources for coercion on the potentially dis-
obedient.[1] This sounds like a fundamentally important claim. In fact,
of course, for most of us most of the time in a benign society, the
police generally work in our interest, and compliance is easily motivated. This fact leaves the police free, as Hart notes, to coerce selected
others, including minority groups as well as suspected criminals.

Margaret Levi argues that citizens' sharing the vision of their government enables government to draft them for military service in
wartime and to get them more readily to pay their taxes (Levi 1997).[2]
These are among the relatively rare policy realms in which voluntary
compliance by individual citizens is virtually necessary. In many
other areas compliance can simplify the tasks of government but is
not so crucial. More generally, if trust in government is conceptually
and epistemologically impossible for most citizens in large modern
societies, it simply cannot be true that modern governments are unable to work without such trust. Whatever might be the importance
of citizens' trust for the functioning government, *it is surely more important that government be trustworthy than that it be trusted.*

To give an account of trust in government on analogy with trust in
individuals requires two classes of argument. First, we must give an
account of the trustworthiness of government agents. Second, we must
account for the knowledge citizens are likely to have of such trustworthiness. In the second account, the central problem is the translation of
individual-to-individual relationships to individual-to-group or individ-
ual-to-institution relationships. What is called trust in government may
in fact be something short of trust as we experience it in interpersonal
relations. This is confidence, or what we might call quasi trust. It is based
on reasons for believing government agents to be trustworthy, reasons
that do not involve direct relationships with the quasi trusting citizen.
These elements ground this chapter's discussion of the current claims of
declining trust in government (at least in the United States), the possibility of general distrust of government (even absent any possibility of
general trust of government), and an instance of such general distrust in
the problem of endemic distrust of government.

Governmental Trustworthiness

In vernacular usage, the term trust is readily applied to many institutions and institutional actors, such as banks, nations, and political

leaders. As observers of politics we often speak in analogies that may be fallacies of composition, as noted in chapter 4. For example, one might try to explain peaceful Anglo-American relations by saying that England and the United States trust each other. However, this would be a loose claim that we might be hard pressed to articulate beyond its seeming metaphor. Many psychological and normative accounts of individual behavior are difficult to generalize to institutional behavior. If trust cannot be applied to institutions, it is of limited interest in political theory and international relations.

If our notion of trust comes from understandings of individual behavior and character, the term is likely to be entirely out of place in application to a nation, group, or institution. There may be ways to interpret the notion to apply it to such actors, but it is not likely to be prima facie applicable without interpretation. It is now a commonplace understanding that interest is not readily generalized from individual to group or national levels. It should not surprise us to find that trust, which is commonly at issue just because interests are at stake, is not readily generalizable, either. In principle at least, the encapsulated-interest conception of trust can be generalized to fit institutions, although in practice it might not generally fit because the knowledge and the iterated interaction conditions cannot be met.

As a matter of simple descriptive fact, it appears that many institutions can be reliably expected to fulfill their missions. It would be odd if this were merely a regularity or a hard law of nature. I can predict an organization's reliability from a lot of data, but I have no reason to think the organization especially takes my interests somehow into consideration. If we cannot meet the latter condition, we can only say we have a regularity from which we induce a tendency, as we infer future expectations about many things from the mere fact that they have been true up until now. In discussions of government we often do not even have such inductive evidence, and the question of government reliability is often resolved by fiat. It is merely assumed that the officials in an organization act, for example, from the desire to accomplish some organizational goal of service (as argued by Paul Quirk [1990]).

Against this resolution by fiat, it would be odd if we found as a rule that individuals in organizational contexts have motivations for action that are systematically different from their usual motivations. They typically do have different incentives—that is how organizations work, by giving role holders incentives, positive and negative, for and against various actions and by coordinating people acting from varied incentives. If individual trustworthiness correlates strongly with interest in individual-to-individual relations, it seems likely that it must do so as well in intraorganizational relations that are, in various moments, individual-to-individual relations. If so, then the answer to the question of whether role holders in an organization are trustworthy will tend to correlate with whether it is in their interests to do what they are expected or trusted to do.

In rough outline, the most plausible theory of intraorganizational trustworthiness is one that takes James Madison's analysis down to the level of individual officials. Defending the U.S. Constitution in *The Federalist Papers*, Madison (1961 [1788], 322) writes that "in framing a government which is to be administered by men over men, the great difficulty lies in this: you must first enable the government to control the governed; and in the next place oblige it to control itself." His recommendation? "Ambition must be made to counter ambition." How? If I violate the norms determined by our bureaucratic mission, you and others are likely to find it in your interest to oppose me (Hardin 1988a, 526–27). Sometimes the enticements to malfeasance are so great that they infect almost everyone in a relevant agency, as we often hear of whole governmental structures, as in Italy, or entire police units, as in the United States, that succumb to bribery or even direct involvement in profitable relations with the Mafia or illegal drug traders. Often, however, even in such extreme cases, someone will have a strong career interest in bringing them to account. Strong moral commitment beyond interest may help and may be common, but it may also lead officials into taking the law into their own hands, and we cannot generally expect such commitments to prevail.

Citizen Trust of Government

If there were trust in government, most or even all of it would be one-way trust. Elected officials might be involved in mutual trust with their constituents, especially if the constituencies are small, as in the republican cities of Renaissance Italy. In principle at least, a unique appeal of democratic government is that, because elected officials can be held accountable, such government creates the possibility for mutual trust between citizens and governors, which makes much less sense in a nondemocratic government. Either one-way or mutual trust might seem to license the officials to act on behalf of their constituents without having constantly to canvass their views or to seek their approval. (However, even officials who are not elected, whole agencies of government, and the government itself might earn quasi trust, which is one-way.)

Hart's conclusion that government requires the willing obedience of most citizens if it is to control others seems to be false. In Nazi-ruled Czechoslovakia, obedience out of fear of severe reprisal seems likely to have been virtually the whole story for a large segment of the population. Not many non-Fascist Slavs in Czechoslovakia can have been willingly obedient, in Hart's sense, to their Nazi regime. As is true of most who address this issue, Hart seems to have had no grasp of the power of coordination—rather than normative commitments—in sustaining social order even among those who dislike the order (see further Hardin 1985). The Czechoslovak case, while extreme, is not as rare as one might wish. Spanish rule of southern Italy, medieval rule of randomly conquered regions, various Chinese empires, and many colonial governments have had little more than the acquiescence of large parts of the relevant population. Similarly, for many partial rules, such as white rule over African Americans in the United States and the apartheid government of South Africa, acquiescence of many was the most that could be claimed. Acquiescence is even arguably the main story for modern democratic governments, such as that of the contemporary United States (Hardin 1999d, chapter 4).

One might make an argument for trust in government that is analogous to Hart's argument for obedience to government: Only because enough people do trust can government work well despite the lack of trust or even the active distrust of others. Again, however, not many non-Fascist Slavs in Czechoslovakia can have trusted their Nazi regime.

My concern here is with benign cases in which trust is more nearly plausible than in Nazi Czechoslovakia and in which its plausibility is to be analyzed. The case of Czechoslovakia shows that the claim that government requires citizen trust is false. A claim that is worthy of investigation is whether a government that depends on extensive reciprocal participation by citizens requires trust to work well. Largely for empirical reasons, I argue that even such a claim cannot be sustained—or, rather, it cannot be sustained if what we mean by trust when we speak of trust in government is conceptually the same as what we mean when we speak of trust in another individual. Often, all that is needed for government to work is for citizens not actively to distrust it.[3]

As argued in chapters 1 and 3, trust is a fundamentally cognitive notion. To trust or to distrust others is to have some presumption of knowledge about them. For the vast majority of people in the world, including those whom we are likely to encounter, we know essentially nothing about their specific motivations toward us. That is also true of most of the people in our government: We do not know enough to trust them. If we are confident of their behavior in some context, that is because we generalize inductively from the behaviors of many of their peers or because we infer from the organizational incentives they face that they are more than likely to be trustworthy in that context.

To bring trust of government into political theory requires a micro-level account of how government works at the macro level. This must largely be an account of rational expectations of what government and its agents are likely to do. In the encapsulated-interest account, I must know that the agents or the institution act on my behalf because they wish to maintain their relationships with me. That is generally not possible for government and its officials.

A somewhat less demanding account of trust could allow us to unpack our trust of an institution in two ways. First, we could be confident that every individual in the organization, each in the relevant ways, would do what each must do if the organization is to fulfill our trust. Second, we could be confident that the design of the roles and their related incentives will get role holders to do what they must do if the organization is to fulfill our trust. In this case, the individual role holders might be broadly interchangeable, and we need know few if any of them.

Neither of these visions is plausible for citizen trust of modern governmental institutions. Virtually no one can know enough of the large number of individual role holders to claim to be confident of judging that these role holders have interests or the relevant moral commitments to do what would serve their clients' interests. In addition, few people can have an articulate understanding of the structures of various agencies and the roles within them or of the government overall to be confident of the incentives or other motivations that foster trustworthiness among role holders. Hence as a matter of actual practice, it is utterly implausible that trust in any strong sense underlies most citizens' views and expectations of government.

Quasi Trust

As you can be trustworthy even though I do not know it and therefore might not trust you, so too an institution can be trustworthy even though its individual clients do not know it—even, perhaps, could not know it. In lieu of the knowledge that would make me judge a government official or agency to be trustworthy, I might have expectations that are rational merely in the sense that they extrapolate from current and past actions, as might be adequate for a sociological account of credible, inductive expectations. Merely institutionalizing government and the implementation of policies should lead to greater stability of citizens' expectations. The vernacular claim of trust in government seems to be little more than such stable expectations.

In actual life we might often not trust an organization but might merely depend on its apparent predictability by induction from its past behavior. Then we have merely an expectations account of the organization's behavior. Such inductive knowledge in some contexts seems compelling, and it is central to our lives in manifold contexts in which we do not have adequate theoretical understanding to make explanatory sense of our experience. As suggested earlier, let us call this quasi trust. It is grounded in inductive extrapolation from past behavior or reputation.

Expectations about human behavior are much less reliable than many of the most common inductive expectations about nature. Indeed, their unreliability is the central driving force of most great literature. In a cute moment, one might say that one of the strongest expectations we must have of people in the long run is that they will defy our expectations. (On a recent flight, a pilot told us, "We are now experiencing the unexpected turbulence I mentioned earlier.") On the other hand, though there is no analog of high-powered scientific understanding to reinforce our expectations of human behavior, there is a consideration that is arguably far more widely understood than is such scientific understanding. We base many of our expectations of people's actions on beliefs about human psychology. Among the most compelling and generalizable of psychological traits is that people commonly are strongly motivated by their interests. Hence for many people, trust—expectations grounded in encapsulated interest—may be more widely motivated than are beliefs about physical relationships that are grounded in nothing more than induction.

Of a large part of the population perhaps we can claim no more than that they have inductive expectations about government, not that they have grounds for trust as encapsulated interest or as grounded in the moral commitments of government agents. That an agency or its role holders are trustworthy might matter to some people, but to most there is nothing beyond expectations. People who merely have inductive expectations cannot be said to trust government in any but the trivial vernacular sense that they "trust" the world to continue more or less as it is. Inductive expectations that government will be capricious might be sufficient to ground distrust, but for most people there might be neither trust nor distrust of a reliable government or agency.

The trustworthiness of government might matter enormously to some citizens, but it might count only by default for many others. If John Locke's understanding of government is that it must be grounded in trust to be legitimate (see Dunn 1984), then no major government of modern times is likely to be legitimate for more than passing moments. For example, the government of the Czech Republic in its early days or the governments of England and the United States during World War II might have been legitimate in this demanding sense in the eyes of most citizens, but the government of the

United States since World War II cannot have counted as legitimate in Locke's sense. Evidently, however, government need not be legitimate in Locke's sense to survive and even to manage a nation through major difficulties and into prosperity. It may suffice that government not be generally and deeply distrusted. If some core of the populace genuinely does have confidence in a government and not too many of the rest of the populace deeply distrust it, then it is likely to have done extremely well by historical standards for governments of large states.

In the end, trust may still be crucial to the success of government. Those most attentive to government will also be those most likely to know enough about governmental actions and structures to know whether at least parts of the government and some of its agents are trustworthy. If they are also the people most likely to oppose government effectively in response to its failings, then the possibility of trustworthiness and the epistemological possibility of trust could be fundamentally important to the stability of government. The significance of their role in support of government might be ramified by the implicit support of those who act from mere expectations without articulate knowledge of the trustworthiness of government. The expectations of the latter group might be based in large part on the expectations of others, just as most of us know many of the things we know only in the sense that we gather that others think those things are true. Our crippled epistemology is little more than mimicry.

On Russell Neuman's (1986, 3–4) account, those who know enough to be able to judge much of the government trustworthy might constitute only about 5 percent of the American electorate. Orlando Patterson (1999, 185) says that this small group, who are attentive and active, "accounts for the vibrancy and integrity of the democratic system in America." If so, a few activists go a long way toward making democracy be responsive.

For most of us, however, reliance on government and other important institutions in our lives does not turn on our being able to trust them or their agents as we might be able to trust the people we deal with on various matters. One might know little about one's bank and yet feel relatively confident that it will handle one's money reasonably honestly. We accept the use of such institutions because they are virtually necessary, or at least very helpful, to us and because we begin to have a fairly high degree of confidence that they will perform better for us than any extant alternative would. Indeed, banks are an instance of an organization that we might even think we understand well enough to be confident that its individual agents will perform their jobs in our interest as expected. They are so thoroughly and richly monitored in all their actions that systematic cheating is difficult, although it must sometimes happen. Similarly, as corrupt in various ways as a police force might be, police forces in general seem to improve life for us by enforcing order better than could be done without them.

To be confident of such an institution, we need not understand its design and incentive system well enough to claim we trust it in the sense of understanding how its incentive structures produce correct actions by its agents. We also need not know those agents in an ongoing relationship that could give us the bases for trust in them. To be confident of it, we need only inductively generalize from what we think to be the facts of its behavior or even only from the apparent results of its behavior, as we inductively generalize that the winter will be cold.

Declining Trust in Government

How far wrong might some other accounts go in focusing on trust rather than trustworthiness? Consider the largest recent body of speculative thought on trust in government. The causal fact that trustworthiness commonly begets trust allows and perhaps encourages fretting about the ostensible decline in trust in government in some contemporary societies, especially in contemporary America. If the decline is real, it must be a decline in perceived trustworthiness. Of course, it might rather be a decline in faith or some stance that is labeled trust in the vernacular.

Declining faith in religion has historically followed increased understanding of the nature of the world. Declining faith in government, its agents, and various others may similarly be the result of increased understanding or, more likely, increased knowledge of the nature of government. For a trivial example, the kinds of information we had about President Bill Clinton went far beyond what was popularly known about any previous president, including some whose actions as president were arguably more scurrilous than Clinton's. The knowledge we have about many governmental actions is also astonishing in comparison with past times. The civil rights movement may well have been so successful largely because of instant television coverage of the brutality and stupidity of many southern officials (Garrow 1978).[4] The White House tapes drove Richard Nixon out of office when mere testimony probably could not have done so.[5] Comparable events in earlier times could not have been so vividly grasped by much of the populace. Even though it was massively manipulated by the military, televised coverage of the Persian Gulf war in 1991 similarly brought it to the sharp attention of people who a generation or so earlier would only curiously have read a bit about it.

Recent students of declining trust sometimes try to discover what is wrong with citizens that they are so increasingly distrustful of government. The conclusions come from survey research responses to often relatively crude questions (see the appendix). Because he defines so-called generalized trust as part of social capital, Putnam frames the question instead as why there has been a decline in such capital.[6] For reasons argued in chapter 3, labeling trust as social capital is misleading and wrong. Putnam's thesis still stands, however, as an argument about declining confidence in government. He looks at many factors but not generally at the evidence on trustworthiness of the officials and others whom the citizens supposedly distrust. (They are mentioned as part of a period effect on those who came of political age during the era of the revelations of governmental duplicities in the Vietnam War, the Watergate scandal, and, one might add, the practices of J. Edgar Hoover's Federal Bureau of Investigation [Putnam 1995b, 674; 2000, chapter 14].)

Putnam (1995b, private correspondence, 26 May 1998), in particular, cites the amount of time people now spend watching television as one cause of their reduced group activity, which—along with rising rates of divorce, structural economic changes, generational effects, and other trends—he speculates, have led to reduced attachment to the political system over the past several decades. Just how important television viewing seems to him is suggested by the title of his paper, "Tuning In, Tuning Out." However, other changes—especially the period effect of changing generations—are clearly also important in the sense that they correlate with reduced civic engagement over recent decades. Putnam's data suggest that the generational effect is about twice the effect of television viewing, although these two are not independent. The television generation accounts for between 10 and 15 percent of the total decline in group participation rates over the period from 1965 to 2000 (Putnam 2000, 284).

Why does television viewing matter? As Putnam (2000, 223) says, "The single most important consequence of the television revolution has been to bring us home." Staying home more, we participate in various groups less, and therefore we trust government less. This has the sound of a functional explanation that is not spelled out articulately, but it does not appear to fit such an explanation. The functional explanation of the maintenance of trustworthiness in Luhmann's work (as discussed in chapter 6) is likely often to fit the claim that participation in groups sustains trustworthiness of the group members toward one another and hence to trust of one another. The arguments of Putnam and others require further that there be some kind of spillover from local group participation and the trust it engenders in those participating with one another to trust in general others, including government. However, the argument might be indirect. Declining civic participation reduces incentives for trustworthiness of government officials, so that citizens, rightly, begin to trust those officials less.

A spillover argument could take at least three forms. The first is that participation in groups gives us talents or abilities that we can then use in other contexts. That is to say, we develop human capital that we can use in various other ways. The second is that participation gives us networks that we might then use for political purposes. Hence we develop social capital—in the form of networks—that can serve us in varied ways (see further Hardin 1999e, especially 177–80). These are surely common results of group interaction. There are, however, alternative ways—other than group participation—for these forms of human and social capital to develop, so that the putative decline in group participation does not necessarily mean that the relevant forms of human and social capital are in decline in our time (Hardin 2000b).

The third form of spillover argument is essentially about the creation of a disposition on which people then act even without direct reasoning in particular instances. This is roughly Oliver Williamson's (1993) view, as discussed in chapter 3, that trust is not generally calculative. There is calculation or at least solid reasoning somewhere in the past but not in this moment when I am dealing with you. This raises the question of whether there is calculation when I first meet someone or whether my disposition is applied generally to virtually any and everyone, including those newly met and those never to be met again. To assess whether the dispositional (or spillover) thesis is correct would require psychological data that go beyond the correlations between measures over time of trust in government and participation in group activities. This is a fundamentally important issue on which we have inadequate knowledge.

The decline in supposed trust of government might be merely a decline in the disposition to trust without first giving serious thought to assessing the trustworthiness of the other. Is that a bad thing? Never being willing to take a risk on anyone would likely be a bad thing. However, for a person not to trust unless there is reason for, or until there is evidence of, trustworthiness may not always be a bad thing for that person. Is it bad for others? The claim of Putnam and others is, essentially, that such not-trusting is bad for the larger society. In not trusting you, then, I free ride on the collective benefits of others' trusting. If trust in government is impossible in any sense that is analogous to trust in individuals, this claim has no content. It reduces, perhaps, to the claim that the typical person today is individually less likely to have ungrounded faith in government. To treat this as a worry is to suggest that the world would work better for us if people did have such ungrounded faith. Indeed, a *New York Times* editorial (cited by Rotter 1980, 1) on "the age of suspicion" in the late 1970s supposes that there are political costs of distrust of government, that citizens would be better off trusting more—or, more accurately, having greater faith. Let us try out such a thesis.

If you have ungrounded faith in me, that might benefit me (but not you) by getting you to do things for me out of misplaced trust. If you have ungrounded faith in our government, that would benefit me only if that government happens to serve my interests fairly well and if, as we may assume, your faith in the government helps to license its actions and reduces the chance of its being successfully challenged by you and similarly placed others. Hence in the United States, ungrounded faith by the upper middle class might be okay for that class (because to license the government's continuation of its policies would not harm their interests). However, because the government might actually be thought to do a good job of serving their interests anyway, that class might also have correct, grounded expectations that it will do so. It makes little sense to say that the interests of the large American underclass would be better served by its faith in the government than if it—or its leaders and advocates—pushed government to be more responsive to those interests. Indeed, it is hard to imagine how any group's interests would be served *better* by its having ungrounded faith than having grounded expectations.

One might suppose that the first and last steps of Putnam's argument are right: watching television and declining confidence in government are causally related. The cause, however, might not be Putnam's indirect one of displacement of group activities in favor of time before the television screen, which leads to fewer trusting relationships in group activities, which in turn spills over into less trust in government. The intervening step need not be this claim of spillover but might instead be the claim that citizens, in part because of the visual power of television, now know too much to have confidence in many officials. Television does not tell us as much about politics as our former newspapers did, but it gives us information far more viscerally. Television helped to destroy the credibility of many local politicians in the South during the civil rights era (Garrow 1978), and it helped to destroy the credibility of the war in Vietnam.

Indeed, one need not even think contemporary leaders are less committed to caring for our interests than were earlier leaders, many of whom were venal, avaricious, grievously biased in favor of certain narrow interests, or all of these. One need only have the sense, which may be widely shared, that the world is much harder to manage than was thought earlier. The fact that we now actually can understand more of the world raises the bar on how much we might expect government, professionals, and more or less everyone ought to do. Competence may not have increased in tandem with understanding, however, so that we now see people in roles of many and varied kinds fail to achieve what we demand of them. Our trust or faith declines because our expectations rise and we increasingly judge our leaders incompetent. It is striking that, in retrospect, Harry Truman is seen as a paragon of competence. This is not because people have forgotten how limited he was—rather, we now know others are at least as limited but, being perhaps less self-aware than Truman, expect to be judged competent.[7] William Butler Yeats (1956, 184–85) spoke as a profoundly committed conservative when he wrote that "the centre cannot hold." Even liberals today might add that little or nothing else holds, either. The economic progress that not long ago seemed like a nearly unmitigated good now seems sour to many—especially when it is happening to people other than themselves.

To see the decline in faith in government as a result of, in a sense, the decline of citizens is to treat it as a problem of trusting when it should more cogently be seen as a problem of trustworthiness. The differences in what we must explain in these very different visions of the problem are categorical. We would need data on psychological dispositions toward trust and an account of how these work for the Putnam thesis. On the other hand, we would need data on evidence people have to trust or not trust government officials—or to have or not have faith in them—for the thesis that trust is primarily dependent on trustworthiness.

Recall the view cited in the previous section: that having only 5 percent of the citizenry alert and committed to politics is all it takes to make things work. If this is even roughly true, then the survey evidence on declining trust, confidence, or faith in government across the general population is of little interest. What we need to know if we are to assess the prospects for government in this era is how the 5 percent who are alert and active in politics rate government. Finally, it is interesting to note that the currently popular thesis that rampant distrust is a recent result of various kinds of contemporary social breakdown might be belied by Robert Merton's (1946) treatment of the use of Kate Smith to instill trust (or confidence in the role of government) in a generally cynical, distrustful society (as discussed in chapter 4). Rampant distrust was a problem in the supposedly united America that was fighting the just, unifying war at the end of the war-bond drive in 1943. Although there may be no compellingly comparable data from the 1930s and the war years to compare with the data of the past four decades in the United States, Merton's study suggests that the supposed declines of our time are merely an interlude in a long series of swings in optimism about the society and its government. His interview subjects contrasted Smith's integrity with the "pretenses, deception, and dissembling which they observe in their daily experience" (Merton 1946, 142). Where is Kate Smith now when we need her?

Distrust in Government

Ordinarily, I am likely to distrust you if I believe your interests strongly conflict with mine. (My distrust might make no difference for any action of mine, however, because I might have no interaction with you.) Often, this is the position we are in with respect to government officials. We can imagine that their interests are not clearly ours. Trust and distrust of government and its agents may therefore be asymmetric. We may have knowledge and theory to distrust when it would be hard to have knowledge or theory to trust. From a Humean or Madisonian view of the corrupting influence of having power with the discretion to use it, one can theoretically distrust government officials in principle as sometimes likely to use their offices for personal benefit in ways that conflict with the public interest or any citizen's individual interest. It is not so sensible to argue for a converse general principle that such officials are likely to share my interests and therefore to serve them.

Alexis de Tocqueville (1966 [1835, 1840], 244) gives democracy a backhanded compliment in his insight that "not what is done by a democratic government, but what is done under a democratic government by private agency, is really great."[8] His comment is in fact too generous to mere democracy. It is more narrowly liberal democracy and limited government under such democracy that have this quality. An economist can say that government should leave economic matters of certain kinds—what job or profession to pursue, who should have rights of producing and selling, what to produce—to individuals to determine through their success or failure in the market. A government that wishes to tackle these things is apt to invest far less wisdom in them than are individuals and firms acting on their own incentives if allowed to act freely. Among the reasons for a government's incapacity here is the likelihood that its officials will be too concerned with the particular interests of themselves, their families, and their friends, as under the restrictive system of mercantilism. That is to say, officials cannot be trusted on these matters and, indeed, should commonly be distrusted. This is, of course, a theoretical claim, but it can be supported with many actual cases, including the difficulties of the Communist world before 1989 and the malaise of the English economy under mercantilism that stimulated Adam Smith's economic writings.

Seldom in history has anyone gone so far toward establishing institutional trust as did Soviet president Mikhail Gorbachev, head of a system that, throughout its seven decades, had exhibited extraordinary variance. He made some previously possible Soviet threats virtually impossible by putting institutional barriers in their way. For example, in inviting the reformation of the Eastern European regimes and in dismantling the Iron Curtain, he greatly reduced the possibility of a sudden Soviet conventional attack on Western Europe. By withdrawing troops and certain materiel he made it virtually impossible to launch a secret attack without first visibly warning of attack during the necessary restoration of troops and equipment to the European theater. The obstacles he created consist of institutional structures that can impede individual audacity. Such institutional arrangements are appealing partly because they stabilize our expectations. Institutional behavior can regress toward the mean to average out the variance of individual behavior.

Yet it would be wrong to say that Gorbachev actually succeeded in generating trust in government in the Soviet Union or its successor states. All he did was greatly diminish grounds for distrust in certain contexts, by both Soviet citizens and the West. He did so by disabling the Soviet government. It was the deliberately designed weakness of the early U.S. national government under the Constitution of 1787 that similarly disabled it from making policies that would have created massive distrust in that government (Hardin 1999d, chapter 6). Severe distrust might well have led to actions that would have undermined the government in its early years.

Distrust comes easily, virtually by inference from a simple theory of general human incentives; trust requires too rich an understanding of the other's specific incentives for it to come so easily. Sometimes, however, our expectations may be grounded not in any theory or explanation of why they are justified but simply in experience. For example, political confidence of certain limited kinds may be easier in Russia and the successor states of the Soviet Union now than it was a generation ago, so that younger Russians debate political issues and criticize officials far more openly than anyone did in the Soviet Union a generation ago. At the same time, many of the older generation may still be reticent in trusting others with their opinions. Many of those who are open and many who are reticent might have no real understanding of why openness is less troubling to today's regime; they need merely know from experience that they and vast numbers of others seem to get away with it now or that it was once extremely risky to be open.

Even as the young openly criticize their government today, however, they presumably distrust it in more substantial ways because they grasp that it sacrifices their interests to serve the interests of certain well-placed people. This distrust is often very likely founded in a crude but sufficient theoretical grasp of the humans who inhabit their world and the world of Russian fiction, from whom generalization is easy.

Without much experience of government action toward me, my "distrust" of government might be little more than the sense that people with no connection to me are not likely to take my interests to heart and might even abuse them. At first hearing, this might sound unduly cynical. This expectation is not restricted to government agents, however; it is far more general, because it fits virtually all of us. For example, suppose you hear or come to expect that a company in which you hold stock is in trouble and that its stock price is about to fall. You are likely to sell your stock so that not you but someone else takes the loss. If you are likely to seek benefit at cost to unknown others in this context, you might therefore expect others to do the same in various other contexts.

Consider a more extreme grounding for distrust in government. For an easy case, consider an individual who has been abused by government in the past, as were the subjects of the notorious Tuskegee experiments designed to watch the progress of syphilis in untreated black southern prisoners, or the subjects of supposedly harmless exposure to radiation in various experiments by U.S. government agencies to find out what effects such exposure might have (for the latter, see D'Antonio 1997, 41–42). Such an individual has good personal reason to be wary of distant government officials, indeed to distrust them in a relatively unspecific and vague way that might have no counterpart in trust. As I generally should expect most people to act from their incentive to free ride on various collective actions, therefore acting against my interests, I might similarly expect government officials to act in their interests and against mine in many contexts, especially when there are issues of which I am not even aware. British citizens have recently discovered that their political leadership looked too carefully after the interests of the cattle industry and ignored the spread of bovine spongiform encephalitis (mad cow disease). French citizens—especially the relatives of hemophiliacs—learned that their leaders were so intent on a French solution to the problem of testing blood for human immunodeficiency virus (HIV) infection that they let thousands of hemophiliacs and other users of blood get infected rather than use an American test. Scores of such abuses could be cited. Seemingly ordinary public officials are capable of cavalierly murderous policies.

This is the asymmetrical conclusion. I need not think it very likely that any official would be as brutally unconcerned with my interests as the Tuskegee and radiation experimenters seemingly were with respect to their experimental subjects. I need merely think it quite likely that officials will occasionally—perhaps only rarely—find it in their interests to violate mine, and that they will do so. For example, they often have an interest in covering up errors of judgment even when exposure of such errors is necessary to correct them. Therefore, on the encapsulated-interest account, I can sensibly distrust them even though I could not have any chance of being able to know enough to trust them—even in the event that they might be trustworthy toward me, as most of them might in fact be. Logical limits that block the possibility of trusting perversely enable us to distrust. I may believe that government generally benefits me, and I might be right in that belief; but that is merely an inductive generalization grounded in the vague sense that I am better off than I would be without government or the less vague sense that certain policies are actually in my interest. My weak distrust is different. It is grounded in a real understanding of the likely incentives that government officials sometimes face, including the perverse incentive of professional deformation to protect their own agencies. That understanding is not merely an inductive generalization but is rather a logical inference from normal human interests.

This dispiriting conclusion might be exacerbated by an unfortunate characteristic of many government policies, including many of the best understood and most important policies on economic benefits. If the populace is distributed along some rough continuum of preferences with respect to some policy arena, then any specific policy that is adopted will be very near the positions of only a fraction of the populace. Among those who are at all aware of policies, then, most people might think that they fare relatively poorly from any given policy. Hence they might not even reach the inductive generalization that an actual government does serve their interests at all well. They might conclude, rather, that it typically trades off their interests for the interests of others.

In sum, it makes far readier sense to distrust government than to trust it. The kinds of understanding necessary for trusting government are almost logically ruled out for typical citizens, while the kinds necessary for distrusting it are commonplace and resonant with ordinary life experience. Even the best of governments, Madison supposed, should be distrusted. To counter his view, one would have to invent or discover a remarkably benign race of humans with more stalwart commitments to the interests of others than to their own. We can sometimes count on parents and lovers to be so stalwart with respect to the small number of their loved ones; we would be foolish to count on most of our governors to be that stalwart with respect to the vast collection of citizens.

Madison's response to this overwhelming problem of contrary incentives was to design governmental institutions that would be too weak to overwhelm the public and to build in many devices for internal opposition between agencies and agents of government. Although the government he designed has evolved into the most powerful government ever seen, it is still hamstrung by internal forces against its controlling citizens in many ways. We may almost all agree in principle on, for example, the protection of civil liberties, but we know that we might be tempted by our own interests, personal mores, or religious values to override our abstract principled beliefs in particular instances. We therefore want to tie our hands in advance against such abuses—but even more, of course, we want to tie the hands of others in advance. Any account of trust in government as based on the truster's assessment of the trusted's incentive to be trustworthy is likely to be specious. Yet we can easily give an account of distrust in government as based on the distrusted's incentive to be untrustworthy at least occasionally, sometimes in major ways.

Endemic Distrust

When distrust in government is endemic, as in the Eastern European and Soviet worlds at the end of the 1980s, there may be no better move than to weaken government substantially (Hardin 1999d, chapters 5 and 6). Elimination of agencies and powerful bureaus and bureaucrats will eliminate the objects of distrust. "Strong" leadership is precisely what is not wanted when strong leaders have been the problem. Weak leaders unable to intervene capriciously are what is wanted to make the society develop successful trusting relationships. As it happens, the only economic system that works without leadership is the market—although the internet may prove to be another. However, even the market requires stable law enforcement in certain realms if firms are to be trusted, either by workers, customers, or other firms.

Still, creating trustworthy institutional supports for legal and economic relations may be difficult even when the institutions are created de novo. The staff of any new organization or of any massively reformed organization is likely to come from the staff of prior organizations. If one created a new agency in New York City to handle some problem in a new and innovative way but hired staff from the extant pool of seemingly qualified people, one might discover that the new agency almost immediately fell into the usual New York malaise of forcing supplicants to invest in wasteful hassling to get routine, reasonable things done. To create a genuinely new agency, it might be better to recruit staff from Texas, Wyoming, and scattered other places.

This potentially grievous problem stands in the way of simply changing policies in Russia and expecting to get the desired results. The distrust of the Russian state agencies that oversaw the economy during its woeful years includes, rightly, distrust of many of the officers of those agencies. To give them proper incentives for behaving constructively might require massive organizational redesign. As is commonly true, they seem to have come to view their interests as tied to the interests of their organization rather than to the interests of their clientele. This can happen simply because it is within the organization that they are rewarded, so that it is their organization and not their clientele who give them their incentives for action or inaction. This problem is exacerbated when there is the credible threat that some of these institutions will be abolished. Hence I cannot trust the agents—because I believe their interests do not encapsulate mine. This may primarily be a theoretical conclusion, but any experience of dealing with some organizations would reinforce belief in the theory.

At the most extreme change in government, as after a major social revolution, the problem of establishing stable expectations may make reducing distrust nearly impossible for a while.[9] Tocqueville (1955 [1856], 176) notes the seeming paradox that typically a revolution intended to improve things initially makes things worse. Many might have faith in the new regime because they think it represents their interests, and they might therefore say they trust the regime. They might continue to have such faith even after arduous years of failure, as in the Stalinist years in the Soviet Union, when the virtual deification of Stalin was evidently effective in many parts of the population. This would not be grounded trust, although it might be an unusual case of what some philosophers call trust as blind faith. It is hard to see how such trust can be good except by blind fortune.

It may be nearly impossible to avoid endemic distrust in much of politics without simultaneously avoiding clear positions on issues. Perhaps the most striking difference between leaders of many nongovernmental organizations—such as business firms—and elected officials is that the former often must live up to relatively clear expectations while the latter often can attempt to make expectations vague and the judgment of achievements therefore pliable.[10] In politics, it is often a drastic mistake to be specific, because for many issues most people must necessarily have preferences that fall some distance away from any proposed policy. Much of the appeal to voters is therefore directed at their identifications, not at the programs they might like to see implemented.

There are, of course, many issues for which politicians do not face such a problem because the distribution of preferences will not be normal. For example, preferences on abortion policy and gun control in the contemporary United States are partly bimodal, with fairly sharply defined pro and con positions. In the face of the absolutist stance of some opponents of any abortion for any reason, the arguments of such writers as the lawyers Ronald Dworkin (1993) and Laurence Tribe (1990) that the two sides are not so far apart are prima facie unconvincing (see further Davis 1993). Some candidates attempt to straddle this divide by being vague about how they would handle abortion policy or by passing the issue off to an alternative decision arena (such as the courts or a possible constitutional amendment).

For issues that have a more or less normal distribution of preferences, on the other hand, staking oneself to a precise position is tantamount to putting distance between oneself and most voters. The task of gaining the trust of constituents, then, is complicated by the virtual certainty that effectiveness in office will correlate strongly with disappointing or even offending large numbers of constituents on particular issues. Dwight Eisenhower had the nearly unique advantage of being elected by a populace ignorant of any of his views (if he had any), and he did a fairly good job of maintaining such vagueness through eight years in office. Ronald Reagan, the best president the American right has ever had, was reviled by much of that right soon after he entered office. Franklin Roosevelt campaigned as a fiscal conservative and then soon abandoned the policy as president. Thomas Jefferson, among the most committed of democrats, bought Louisiana from the French without constitutional authority or congressional approval.

Concluding Remarks

Low voter turnouts in many nations, including, notoriously, the United States, are commonly taken as evidence that government has failed to elicit support. Prima facie, an equally or even more plausible conclusion may be that such turnouts are evidence that government has not engendered grievous distrust and opposition. Silence cannot unambiguously prove the case for or against government. If the crippled epistemology of mimicry underpins our expectations of government, then the limited commitment of most people to try to change or affect government makes epistemologically good sense.

In speaking of government, John Dunn (1988, 90) supposes we should choose Bernard Barber's (1983) trust in *capacity*, rather than trust in good *intentions*, in large-scale politics. (Throughout this book, I assume that both elements must be met for trust, although, as noted at the outset, I have not constantly addressed the potential problems of lack of capacity.) This "trust in capacity" is a substantially different meaning from the usual sense of "trust" in interpersonal relations, where it includes concern with both competence and intentions. Does the restriction of our focus to capacity nevertheless make sense?

It seems true that, when people say they trust government or the president or some other officeholder, they typically mean something different from what they mean when they say they trust a friend. Maybe what they mean is merely that the government or officeholder has the capacity to do the job well. Perhaps it includes an element of the intentions of the trusted, but only an inductive sense of these and not a sense that the government or its officials specifically care about any citizen's interests. If trust reduces merely to this inductive expectation, however, it loses its usual positive valence. In this relatively hollow expectations sense, I can trust an official to act against my interests or to follow policies I oppose.

If capacity is the measure of trust, we might have to say we trusted Richard Nixon more than most presidents, but that seems to be a quite unlikely claim in the vernacular. Perhaps Europeans, who were not subject to Nixon's tax audits, FBI investigations, and election shenanigans, could give most weight to his capacities in attempting to reduce the scale of international conflict in at least his China policies. Many Americans would not so easily have slighted the political abuses, which seemed to be driven not by concern with his better policies but by personal paranoia.

In a poll reported in *Business Week* (17 May 1999, 8), people responded that, when looking for advice in assessing some product to be purchased, they most trust *Consumer Reports,* a friend's recommendation, a news article (not an ad), and a magazine article, in that order. This is presumably what trust in government often means in the survey literature. "I trust" for some of these responses means no more than that I can rely on government or I can expect it to act in decent ways. "I trust" *Consumer Reports* does not mean what "I trust" my close friend means. It reduces to the French, "j'ai confiance," I have confidence. Presumably this primarily means confidence in the capacity of these agencies to judge products, although the failure of advertisements to make the list of useful judgments suggests that at least part of the response turns on the likely motivations of the various sources.

Perhaps much of the reason people moralize the notion of trust is that they wish to restrict it to cases in which their expectations are in their favor. In the vernacular, to say I trust an official, such as the president, may mean that I expect that official to behave in certain ways that will serve my interests or that will fulfill my policy hopes.

Hence we probably should not adopt Dunn's redefinition of trust for politics as merely about competence. Rather, we should generally speak not of trust in government but only of confidence in it, as Luhmann (1988, 102) argues.[11]

In sum, government and its agents might be genuinely trustworthy in many cases, but most citizens cannot be in a position to know that they are. Hence most citizens cannot be said to trust government in any of the standard senses in which individuals can trust one another. This follows for simple epistemological reasons. Most of us most of the time cannot know enough to trust government (or other large institutional) agents or agencies to judge their fit with any of the standard conceptions of trust. These conceptions are that trustworthiness is a matter of character or brute dispositions, of moral commitment, or of encapsulated interest. An institution can be filled with people who are trustworthy on some of these conceptions, but few potential clients or subjects of an institution can know this to be true. At best, most of the time, we can inductively suppose that an organization that has been performing well in some sense is likely to continue to do so unless its conditions are altered.

Chapter 8

Trust and Society

W E ARE concerned with trust and trustworthiness because they enable us to cooperate for mutual benefit. *Cooperation is the prior and central concern.* There are manifold instances of cooperation that need not and quite likely do not involve trust. Trust is merely one reason for confidence in taking cooperative risks, and trustworthiness is merely one reason such risks can pay off. In the large contemporary literature on trust, the clear point of wanting more trust is that trust eases the way to cooperative social relations (Luhmann 1980; Putnam 1993; Fukuyama 1995; and many others). Similarly, much of recent experimental work on trust is an outgrowth of earlier identical or nearly identical experiments that focused on cooperation. Cooperative relationships constitute a broader and more inclusive category than trusting relationships—generally a much larger category. At the end of the day, therefore, when trust has run out, we still need to explain most cooperation in other ways. A large part of the explanation of such cooperation in the face of obstacles to trust rests in the social structures of norms and institutions that can be explained as devices to get us around such obstacles.

On every account of trust based on assessments of trustworthiness, we obviously face epistemological and time constraints that prevent us from having strong trusting relationships with more than a limited number of people. The trustworthiness can be morally motivated, the result of encapsulated interest, or a matter of character or disposition. The constraint of time is clear enough if we must have ongoing relations with others in order to build trust in them. The epistemological constraints even cut against the possibility that we can trust large numbers of people through their reputations. In addition, in some contexts of dealing with groups rather than merely dyadically with individuals, the logic of encapsulated interest must be violated even if we have essentially ongoing relationships. Hence there are two ways in which we can come up against essentially numerical limits on trusting. First, unlike a medieval villager, whose world was tiny, we cannot trust more than a relatively small fraction of the individuals in our worlds. Second, we cannot trust large groups of individuals as such. We might be able to trust most or even all of the members of a collectivity when we engage with them dyadically, but we often cannot count on them as members of a group to encapsulate the interests of others in the group in cooperating in any collective purpose.

Does social order grow out of trust? It might prosper better with widespread trust and trustworthiness, but it does not follow that it must initially be grounded in such trust. Consider the velvet revolutions in Eastern Europe in 1989. Masses coordinated behind the expression of hostility to the prior regimes (see further Sztompka 1996). Distrust must have been endemic in, for example, East Germany at that time, with a large fraction of the population implicated in the STASI (secret police) oversight of citizens at all levels. It was partly distrust that stimulated the quest for a new order. On Piotr Sztompka's (1999, 160–90) account, the new order soon produced higher levels of trust in Poland after 1990. It would be odd to suppose that the Polish quest was grounded in trust. Many moves signaled the commitment to joint action against the dying Communist regime, and these enabled people to think that the risks of their opposition would not be disastrous. The last days of the regimes in Poland, Czechoslovakia, East Germany, and Romania saw mass actions in major public squares in which, by coordinating with so many, all were substantially protected against violent reprisals from the regimes. There were some individuals who had charismatic appeal for leadership of new regimes. Hence there may have been some degree of confidence in the behavior of many others, but it seems unlikely that the dramatic actions for change were founded on trust.

Can we successfully live together without trust? Put somewhat differently, is trust necessary for maintaining social order? One might presume to answer this question by putting societies in a two-by-two matrix of the possible combinations of high and low trust on one side and high and low social order on the other. Suppose there were no cases of low trust and high social order.[1] Unfortunately, this fact would not settle the issue because social order provides the background conditions that facilitate trust by creating the conditions for stable ongoing relationships and backing them with law to block the risk of massive losses from wrongly trusting someone. That is, social order produces the conditions for trust and therefore must commonly produce trust. Moreover, as argued in chapter 1, levels of trust are likely to vary across different domains, and therefore, one might suppose, social order could also vary.

The questions to be addressed in this chapter are whether trust relationships are necessary for much of social order and, when they are not feasible, how we achieve cooperation. Certain limits are implicit in the nature of trust relationships that depend on cognitive assessments of the trustworthiness of others. Once these limits are taken into account, there are various ways in which cooperation can be achieved in groups, in the economy, and in nongovernmental institutional settings. These particular social structures seem to be responses to the possibilities and limits on organizing our cooperative relationships as trust relationships. Much of social structure can be explained as a response to obstacles to resolving problems of cooperation and coordination through simple individual-to-individual trust. Indeed, Hobbes' political theory addresses the need for government to back cooperative life when trust relationships without such coercive backing would be inadequate to the task. In contexts in which individual-to-individual trust commonly fails, we find institutional and cultural arrangements that make life work more or less well in lieu of trust. These devices often work by securing trustworthiness on the part of those with whom we must deal, even though epistemological and time constraints may keep us from knowing enough to assess their trustworthiness or to trust them.

Cooperation in Dyads

Earlier chapters have given accounts of the working of trust in many contexts, most of them involving individual trust of other individuals. For trust as encapsulated interest, trust relationships have a naturally disciplining quality. If you prove not to be trustworthy, I stop dealing with you if possible. Often, however, we cannot simply refuse to deal with those who are untrustworthy unless we are willing to forgo important opportunities for mutual benefit that would be possible if only we could secure the cooperation of many who are seemingly untrustworthy. The biggest and most pervasive problem for us in trusting others is not the malign problem of dealing with cheaters but the relatively neutral problem of often having to deal with people with whom we cannot expect to have ongoing relationships in which to ground incentives for trustworthiness.

Consider the limits on how many individuals one can trust. Even before getting to trust, someone who already has several friends may not think the possible benefits of investing in developing a friendship with yet another person is worth the risk. This problem may explain at least part of the phenomenon of clique and friendship-group formation. It might also be part of the explanation of familism in contexts in which families are relatively large, that is, large enough to exhaust a substantial part of the resources any member might have for investing in rich relationships. It may also be part of the explanation of ethnic exclusion. Members of cliques may concentrate their investments in exchange relations in a small number of intensive relationships and may shun others merely to avoid the difficulties of dealing with those with whom they do not have intensive relationships. Similarly, groups might actively develop exclusionary devices to keep their membership comfortably associated only with those with whom they have rich enough relationships to have developed trust (Hardin 1995, chapters 4 and 6). Trust relationships may often therefore be cliquish.

Both of these phenomena—clique formation and familism—turn on the epistemological limits on developing more than a modest number of close relationships. Limits on investments of time are especially important and obvious. For example, the members of a subsistence farming family might wind up in conflict with other families primarily because they simply have no time for them while they are heavily engaged in daily life and toil with one another.[2] Lacking rich relationships with others beyond their cliques or their families, they are not even in a position to develop trusting relationships with those others because they do not have the ongoing exchange relationships in which to embed interests in trustworthiness or even relationships rich enough to gain knowledge of the trustworthiness of those others. Hence it is the rational and relational structure of trust that blocks trusting more universally.

In the substantial literature on the subject, generalized trust is loosely seen as unspecific trust in generalized others, including strangers (Rotter 1980).[3] From various experimental studies and surveys, it is supposed by many social scientists that Americans have higher levels of generalized trust than do people in many other societies (see, for example, Fukuyama 1995; Yamagishi and Yamagishi 1994). In the United States and some other cases, there is supposed to be declining trust in government (as discussed in chapter 7) as well as declining trust more generally in other people. In some nations, trust in government is not declining, but trust in others is (see several contributions to Pharr and Putnam 2000). Let us focus here on the problem of declining trust in our fellow citizens and associates, which is evidently independent of declining trust in government.

What is in fact needed if we want successful cooperative relations is trustworthiness, which is likely to beget trust from those who learn of our trustworthiness and recognize its utility in reputational and trial-and-error experience. Many writers claim that generalized trust—that is, individual trust of one another among citizens—has great value for society, even that it is necessary for society to function or to develop economically. There is an explicit or implicit claim for the necessity of trust in many current claims that American and some other democratic societies face a crisis of declining trust. Claims of necessity that are causal rather than conceptual are among the strongest claims one can make in the social sciences and among the most difficult to make compelling. Nevertheless, the claim of the necessity of generalized or widespread trust for social order is strikingly commonplace, as though it were beyond much serious doubt.

Recent discussions of the crisis of declining (generalized) trust in society are grounded in contemporary survey data. Recall the criticisms of conclusions from such data in chapter 3. Such data do not firmly establish any claim about levels of generalized trust because they are confounded with the encapsulated-interest account of trust, and it is not clear that they tap generalized trust. People are asked to respond to survey questions such as "Do you trust most people?" and "Are people generally trustworthy?" (See the appendix for questions that are commonly asked.) Unfortunately, such questions are insufficiently articulated to distinguish trust as encapsulated interest from generalized trust. In actual fact, I trust most of the people I deal with at least in those matters over which I have dealings with them. Had I not eventually trusted them, I would have stopped dealing with them as much as possible.

Do I trust the vastly larger number of people with whom I have no dealings in those matters? No—but this is not a harsh answer. Most of these are people I do not even know and have no reason either to trust or to distrust. Unfortunately, if we begin to articulate our questions precisely enough to get at such discriminating differences, we virtually have to explain what we are seeking to those we survey (or those whom we put through experiments). We thereby give them theoretical understandings they did not have, and we elicit answers or experimental responses to those understandings rather than to their normal experiences.[4]

If we compare across nations, we find lower levels of reported generalized trust in some societies than in the United States. What questions are people in the United States answering when they say they trust most people? What questions are those in certain other societies answering when they say they do not trust most people? Evidently, we are answering different questions, perhaps because we are differentially alert to the problem of dealing with those with whom we do not have ongoing relationships or perhaps because our background institutional structures differ in the scope of the interactions they protect. That is to say, we frame the questions differently. Even within the same nation, when the range of "most people" is unspecified, people may be answering quite different questions. (These issues are relevant also to claims that trust in government is declining, as discussed in chapter 7, but here the focus is on individual trust of other individuals.)

Consider, as well, variations over time in the responses to such questions within a single culture. Again, it is supposed that levels of generalized trust are in decline in many Western societies, especially in the United States. Such longitudinal claims are apt to be confounded with various other trends that might make the apparent trend in trust an artifact. For example, the level and extent of interactions a typical person has in the United States in the 1990s might be substantially greater than those a similar person had in the 1950s. On average, then, the later person would be less trusting of the whole—larger—class of those with whom he or she deals than the earlier person would have been. But the two might be equally trusting of any particular class of people, such as close friends, associates at work, relatives, neighbors, and so forth. Indeed, the 1990s person might substantially trust more people in various matters than the earlier person would have while still distrusting or lacking trust in more people in his or her dealings than the earlier person would have. To assess whether there is a meaningful decline in trust, one would need to have responses over the decades to questions asking people how much they trust their close associates, random strangers, and so forth. Questions that do not control for context are too hopelessly underarticulated to yield the grand thesis that individual-level trust is in decline.

Has the scale of our interactions changed over the past four decades? The discussions of Robert Putnam (1995a, 1995b, 2000) and many others of the impact of television, divorce, and other changes on the privatization of American life suggest that we interact less today than our peers did fifty years ago. A similarly widespread thesis, however, asserts that increasing urbanization has produced more extensive interactions with people as compared with earlier small-town life. The truth of the latter thesis seems especially evident to the vast number of people who have moved from small to larger communities or who have prospered in ways their parents never knew. This number probably includes many, maybe even most, of the academic and other researchers who claim that generalized trust is in decline. The trend from small-scale organization of society and social relations in medieval times to the large-scale complexities of modern industrial states continues (see Leijonhufvud 1995).

Even if we establish that there has been a meaningful decline in levels of optimism that others are trustworthy, controlling for types of others, we still have, unfortunately, data on only a short-term trend. As they stand, such data at best demonstrate episodic decline rather than secular decline (see further Patterson 1999). For example, one might suppose that, had similar surveys been done in the United States in the 1930s, the 1890s, the 1850s and 1860s, and the late 1830s, similarly declining levels of supposedly general trust would have been found. General declines in well-being, the loss of grounds for expected stable economic and other relationships, and perhaps the general faltering of institutional backings of trustworthiness during those interludes must rightly have suggested to people that, under prevailing conditions, they could trust many others less, especially on the encapsulated-interest model of trust, which requires stable ongoing relationships. We do not know from available survey data, which exist for only a few decades, whether there is a secular trend in trust or distrust. Those particular decades suffered from many episodic crises that might have undercut optimism about the trustworthiness of others, and the effects of these crises might last the lifetime of a particular generation. For many families of my generation, even intrafamilial trust was shattered by conflicts over the ugly politics of Vietnam. It would be perversely ahistorical to suppose there were not even greater losses of optimism in earlier times. Yet we seem to have survived into a richer social life and a radically more productive economic life than our predecessors knew—despite all passages through periods of significantly lower levels of trust.

Return to the creation of social order, as in the Eastern European transitions of 1989, or the sustenance of such order, as in most ongoing states. There might be instances in which fairly widespread trust has facilitated the move to civil society. We might suppose that widespread individual-level trust is facilitated by civil society and that trust, in turn, supports social order. Trust as encapsulated-interest rules out the possibility or coherence not only of generalized trust but also of widespread trust by any individual. If there is widespread trust, it is therefore of the form that lots of people trust other particular people. That is to say, there are pockets of trusting relationships, and possibly almost everyone is included in such pockets. Alternatively, it may be that a typical individual is involved in various relatively small networks in which each trusts the others with respect to some range of issues.

Current writings seem to go much further than this in their claims. For example, Shmuel Eisenstadt and Luis Roniger (1984, 16–17) write of "the necessity for and the ubiquity of trust in human relations and the impossibility of building continuing social relations without some element of trust." This short sentence includes three extravagant terms: necessity, ubiquity, and impossibility. One can sensibly question the claim for each of these terms here. For example, one might note that society without trust is very nearly impossible, but in a sense very different from that apparently intended by Eisenstadt and

Roniger. That is to say, if we do build stable, continuing relations with others, we will commonly have the conditions, including the relevant incentives, for trustworthiness and trust. It would therefore be virtually, although not logically, impossible to escape the development of some trust.[5]

The claim by many scholars that generalized trust is necessary for social order is surely wrong on one count and undemonstrated and perhaps beyond demonstration on another. First, it is merely widespread, not generalized, trust that even *might* be necessary. Second, although there might be a causal arrow from social order to trusting, and as well a causal arrow from trusting to enhanced social order, it may be beyond demonstration whether there is any necessary link. Furthermore, both for initiation of social order and for mere maintenance of social order, widespread trust seems not to be necessary, as is suggested by quite diverse cases, such as Fredrik Barth's accounts of the Omani and Swat Pathan social orders (discussed in chapter 4), social orders (including Nazi-ruled Czechoslovakia) that have been maintained nearly by pure force, and the transitions from endemic distrust to social order in Eastern Europe from 1989 forward.

Generalized trust is, at best, like trust in government in the following sense: We are merely confident that most of those with whom we might interact will be at least moderately trustworthy. It is not truly generalized but has scope constraints. Those who rely on generalized trust for explanations of various things must grant that their claims depend on context. Hence they are saying, for example, that middle-class Americans are likely to be trustworthy with respect to certain kinds of things, so that other middle-class Americans can relatively safely rely on them.

Cooperation in Groups

Much of our ordinary cooperative activity is embedded in groups of which we are members. Groups are themselves the focus of cooperation for collective purposes, and they can help to induce cooperative behavior by their members even in essentially dyadic relationships. In the former case, when we need collective action, we might wonder whether our groups can be trusted to cooperate in accomplishing our purpose. In the latter case, we often find that our groups oversee our individual actions and induce us to be cooperative even though we could not say that the group and its members trust us. The way small communities induce their members to behave in certain cooperative or coordinative ways is through sanctions for the violation of communal norms, among the most important of which is a norm of cooperativeness within the group.

Collective Action

Can a collectivity be trustworthy on the encapsulated-interest account? Consider two very different strategically defined classes of groups: groups mobilized by coordination and groups mobilized for collective action (see further Hardin 1991a). Suppose a group is coordinated behind a leader, as happens with charismatic leaders, in response to what the leader wants it to do, as in the case of the seventeenth-century Sabbatai Sevi, "the mystical Messiah," who led a messianic movement in central Europe. Coordinators can commonly count on such a leader because they will withdraw support if the leader violates their mission, making it generally in the leader's interest to attempt to fulfill their expectations. Of course, the leader's interest in fulfilling that expectation can be trumped by changed incentives or preferences. So long as the leader has an interest in pursuing the goals behind which the followers are coordinated, however, he or she can be trusted and derives power from the coordination of the followers. It is limited power in the sense that it cannot be used for just any purpose. Rather, it can be used only for the group's purposes or mission (Hardin 1995, chapter 3). Coordination power therefore fits very well with the three-part relational account of trust. The followers follow only insofar as the leader pursues a particular purpose that the followers share. If the leader attempts to change direction, the committed followers may quickly drop off, as in the extreme case of the Sabbatai Sevi, who lost his charisma when he submitted to conversion to Islam (Scholem 1973). Examples of such trustworthy leaders include certain political leaders of more-or-less single-issue parties, such as religious and right-wing Poujadist parties.

In standard contexts of collective action that takes the form of a large-number prisoner's dilemma exchange, however, the group cannot be trustworthy. The members of the group might well share some set of interests as, for example, the people of Los Angeles and Houston virtually all share an interest in reduced pollution in their cities. If all of them would stop barbecuing over open flames in their backyards, pollution would be significantly reduced. The interest of any given individual in these cities, however, is typically to renege on acting for the collective benefit, to free ride on the efforts of others, while barbecuing as usual. According to the logic of collective action, your own interest, as in this example, is to free ride on the efforts of others even with respect to your own personal interest in the product of group effort (Olson 1965; Hardin 1982a). *Eo ipso*, your interest is not likely to encapsulate mine with respect to that joint product if it does not even include your own. There might be people who would bear costs on behalf of others that they would not bear on behalf of themselves, but we cannot rely on many people to do so, and therefore collective actions often fail. In sum, we commonly cannot trust large groups of individuals as such. We might be able to trust many or most of the members of a collectivity in individual-to-individual interactions, but we cannot count on them as members of a group to encapsulate the interests of others in the group.

To elaborate on a point briefly made in chapter 7, the difficulties of trusting a collectivity are not the whole story of the problem of trusting institutions, but they are an important part of it. I cannot trust a collectivity to act for my interests because their members are not likely to encapsulate my interests in their own. As in the preceding example, their own trumping interest individually is to barbecue, not to contribute to reducing our pollution—but the latter is my interest with respect to their actions. An institution or organization is in part a collection of people. If all of them are to act in my interest, it will not be because they are acting against the logic of collective action but rather because the institution has been structured to give them the relevant incentives. That leaves me, of course, with a severe epistemological problem of knowing enough about the organizational structure and incentive system to have reason to believe the people in the organization are acting in my interest. I will often be left with nothing more than crude inductive generalization from its apparent past success (as in the case of the institution of government, as discussed in chapter 7).

Note a peculiar asymmetry in the possibilities for trust and distrust in such collectivities. The worst implication of the grand transition from a small-scale to a very large-scale, impersonal society might eventually, because of power differences and general cynicism, be to produce fairly generalized distrust, which can make sense in a way that generalized trust does not. Generalized distrust would not, however, block the possibilities for trust as encapsulated interest in ongoing relationships.

Our personal welfare often depends on group, and not merely individual, action, but we commonly cannot trust the group to act for us. In the logic of collective action, small groups are often expected to succeed even though very large groups cannot. The principal reason for their success is that the dyadic relationships between each pair of group members play a large role in motivating cooperative action. Hence trust relationships can enable us to cooperate beyond the dyadic level to some extent even though such relationships and their effects must run out for interactions within very larger groups. Groups can also motivate individual actions that serve the interests of individuals and not the whole group. Let us turn to this phenomenon, which involves the communal enforcement of norms of cooperativeness.

Norms of Cooperativeness

When we have the thick relationships of a small, close community, we may find that our interactions are governed by norms of cooperativeness that are collective rather than dyadic. I behave well toward you because the community will sanction me if I do not. In such a case, the norms of cooperativeness may be sufficiently effective that we do not so readily develop dyadic trust relationships over many things, because those things are governed by the communal norms (Cook and Hardin 2000).

Consider a compelling example of a communal norm of cooperativeness, in particular of hospitality, that virtually precludes any need for trust as encapsulated interest (or of trust under any other conception). In Shizuko Go's *Requiem*, a painfully beautiful novel about the destruction of a vast web of social relationships in Japan through wartime deaths in the last months of World War II, the heroine Setsuko is entertained by an older woman whom she has never met before and is unlikely ever to see again. She recalls "the familiar precept of perfect hospitality: 'We meet but once'" (Go 1985, 107). There is strategic subtlety in this bit of popular wisdom. If I know we meet but once, my hospitality is not an initial move in a potential trust or exchange relationship. It does not encapsulate your interest in reciprocity over the long run. It is purely a gift or an expression of my hospitable character.[6] That precept is striking in the most ordinary circumstances, but it seems almost dreadful in the context of Setsuko's recollection of it. The precept was, she notes, "literally true of everything that happened now."

The hospitable older woman whom she meets but once has a son whom Setsuko wishes to visit. Since the woman loves her son and wishes him well, interest should incline her to be nice to Setsuko on her singular visit. At the same time, independently of her interest, she may also be normatively motivated to kindness. One could construct arguments for the rationality of developing strong normative commitments: for example, following a norm saves on the burden of making decisions anew in many contexts. Alternatively, one might be able to give a rational reconstruction of the rise of such a norm, in which case the individual's behavior might simply be normative outright. Setsuko's older woman has been taught to be kind in certain circumstances of hospitality, and she might behave that way more or less independently of broad incentives to vary her degree of kindness. She has simply made a virtue of hospitality. She might also have made a virtue of acting as though she trusts people. In both cases, she would presumably conclude that particular people whom she has tried and found repeatedly wanting are not worthy of hospitality or trust. Still, her initial stance is one of virtue rather than of interest.[7]

If you and I are part of a fairly rich web of interactions in a relatively small, close-knit community, we might imagine that we would therefore grow up to be relatively trustworthy. Although the data do not yield definitive conclusions, some studies suggest that small, close communities are governed more by norms than by trust relationships (Amato 1993; Fischer 1982; see also Cook and Hardin 2000). In urban contexts, people find their ways into multiple networks for varied purposes, such as work, recreation, close friendship, and so forth. In one of these networks, they are likely to develop ongoing relationships that enable them to develop trust in one another with respect to the particular issues around which that network has formed. If I violate your trust with respect to the issues at stake in our network, your sanction is simply to withdraw from further interactions with me, and if my reputation gets around, I might even be dropped from the entire network. I would then have to find other people with whom to deal on the relevant issues.

In small communities, instead, general norms of cooperativeness govern many behaviors. Anthropologists and sociologists sometimes call this generalized reciprocity. These norms are enforced at the group or communal level and not in reciprocal one-on-one relationships. For example, if one of us has a serious illness or death in the family or some other crisis, others help in various ways according to their own particular capacities. I might help you but then we might never be in positions in which you should, according to our norm, help me. Hence the norm is not reciprocal but is general—it is "universal" within our community.

Moreover, the sanction against you for violating our communal norm need not have anything specifically to do with the nature of your violation. We do not simply withhold help from you—you might not need help for a long time or ever. Instead, we shun you, perhaps mildly, but potentially so severely as to make continued life in our community difficult or untenable for you. We do not merely exclude you from a network, we exclude you from everything. If we were to describe relations in the small, close community as networks, we would have to say that they are a single multiplex network that covers virtually all matters of any concern to us and that includes virtually every member of the community.

Incidentally, the claim of Adam Seligman (1997) and Niklas Luhmann (1980) that trust is a modern phenomenon may be correct if turned into a claim that it arises in relatively large communities in which we must rely on particularized networks and need not arise in small communities in which norms of cooperativeness handle the problems that trust relationships might have handled. The transition from smaller communities to relatively urban communities has proceeded further in many societies than in others, and national differences in the vocabulary of trust may correlate with the differential development.

Although members of a small community might never develop a sense of reciprocal trust such as that in the encapsulated-interest account, they could all or almost all develop trustworthy behavior. These members would then be somewhat like the infant whose parents are supportive and whose experiences are benign, so that the child develops optimistic expectations of the trustworthiness of people and is therefore relatively ready to take the risks associated with cooperating with people. When a member of such a community enters a broader society without the protection of the sanctions of the communal norm of cooperativeness, this optimism should lead to attempts to cooperate with others and therefore mastery of assessing trustworthiness.

It would, however, be difficult merely to transport the local norm of cooperativeness to another community or to an urban context. Indeed, such a norm would not be workable in an urban community except in an enclave. People in such an enclave might readily live in both the urban and the communal worlds, with norms in the communal world and networks of trust relationships in the urban world. Having the community as a background might even enable some people to take greater risks in the larger world and therefore to discover good trust relationships there.

Of course, the person who is trustworthy while in the ambit of the community and its norms and sanctions might be completely untrustworthy outside that community—where its norms do not reach. It is especially problematic for trustworthiness as moral or other commitment if these are group specific. Ethnic and even merely neighborhood conflict is commonly exacerbated by the attitude of a group's members that nonmembers are proper subjects for exploitation and abuse. Indeed, they sometimes think it actively a good thing to abuse certain outsiders. Hence small communal groups can be hostile to developing reciprocal trust relations across group lines. Norms themselves are not necessarily either good or bad; norms of exclusion are often vile (Hardin 1995, chapters 4 and 6).

An ideal compromise world might be one in which we have relatively thick relations with some core group or groups and then far-flung networks of relationships with respect to many and varied particular things. With quasi thick relations, we might better be able to translate the trustworthiness that we develop within a relatively close group or neighborhood to other contexts that are more limited in their range of interactions. The fact that we actually do share interests in the quasi thick group makes it possible for us to fit our actions within it to the encapsulated-interest model. We can then try this incentive structure on other relationships, especially if we start with low stakes and build to higher stakes only over a long run of interactions with another person.

Suburban contexts may generally be a hybrid between the close communal norm system and the multiple, possibly non-overlapping networks of urban life. Such communities have grown up in North America and some other societies largely at the expense of close, often rural communities, which are in steady decline. The growth of hybrid communities, such as suburbs, may bode well for the richness of potential and actual trust relationships. In a neighborhood there might still be collective sanctioning of some kinds of miscreant behavior, while, however, much of life and much of our need for other relationships is outside such a norm-governed community. A coincidental benefit of such a hybrid system is that it is much less prone to the exclusionary hostilities of close, small, more nearly total communities. Many urban enclave communities may also have a similarly hybrid structure of norms of cooperation within the community and networks of trust relationships outside it.

Cooperation in the Economy

One of the most important arenas of social life outside ordinary one-on-one individual relations and relations with the state is the economy. Any economy, including a complex market economy, may work in part through trust relationships, and it may also enable us to achieve things we could not achieve merely through such relationships. It is the genius of the market to organize exchange in ways that commonly do not require high levels of trust. Its workings recall Barak's response when asked whether he trusted Arafat (quoted in chapter 1). His answer was that trust was not at issue because each sought to push the interests of his own people. Similarly, in the market, I do not trust Ford or Microsoft, but I do rely on them to follow their own interests in being disciplined by market incentives, perhaps with a bit of help from public regulatory agencies. In their cases, unlike the case of Arafat and Barak, I can suppose these firms grasp that their interest is fulfilled best if they fulfill the interests of their customers. Such incentives are not always adequate, as is suggested by the known design flaws of Ford's large suburban utility vehicles. Still, successful corporations commonly face external discipline from their customers to produce goods that serve the mutual advantage of themselves and their customers.

Under typical circumstances in large markets, I can have stable expectations of fairly good results from my entering ordinary exchanges. My "trust" in the market may be like my trust in simple facts of nature—it is merely confidence from induction. I will correct specific details of my confidence when any dealer out there violates it, but I will otherwise treat each dealer as benign, at least in the sense of not malign. If I share Adam Smith's view that most dealers are likely to share my interests (because they must serve my interests to serve their own), I may even think of them as actively benign. I can do this because dealers are typically in competition with other dealers and they must live by their reputations and by the development of ongoing customer bases. (Strangely, it took creativity on the part of merchants finally to learn Smith's lesson and to begin to treat customers with care in order to invite more sales [Mueller 1999, 80]). The public good of tending to act cooperatively even in commercial relations, which many writers label somewhat grandly as generalized trust, then, need not require a moral foundation. It is little more than a manifestation of the self-interest of all or most of us if we take a slightly longer view. There are risks in such cooperativeness, but in a benign society these are likely to be outweighed by the benefits.[8]

I wish to discuss three major issues of the role of trust in an economy: first, the development of economic relations where they have been hampered; second, the development of those relations in a socialist, centrally planned economy, which one might suppose hampers economic relations; and third, the general atmosphere of apparent trustworthiness or of benign expectations in a working market economy. All of these issues evidently involve institutional problems in securing trust or, alternatively, in eliminating the need for it. As already noted, institutions play a role in underwriting even interpersonal trust. As Hume (1978 [1739–40], 3.2.8, 546) says of contracts, if they "had only their own proper obligation, without the separate sanction of government, they wou'd have but little efficacy in [all large and civilized] societies. This separates the boundaries of our public and private duties, and shews that the latter are more dependant on the former, than the former on the latter." Hobbes may have exaggerated the extent to which powerful institutional sanctions are required for grounding trust and promises, but he was not radically mistaken.

First consider the problems of trust in the development of economic relations. This topic is addressed in a massive literature that includes, illustratively, works already cited here or in the discussions that follow by Kenneth Arrow, Edward Banfield, Albert Breton and

Ronald Wintrobe, Francis Fukuyama, Ernest Gellner, Niklas Luhmann, Douglass North, and others. Most of that literature focuses on modern market economies, and much of it on the nascent development of market relations in earlier times or currently in some places. Some of it focuses on historical developments of exchange relations in, for example, the medieval and earlier contexts of international disorder and weak legal institutions, in which one might have expected international trade to founder (North 1990; Knight 1992; Greif 1993; Greif, Milgrom, and Weingast 1994; Milgrom, North, and Weingast 1990).

Anthony Pagden (1988, 127) supposes that the conditions of Neapolitan society under Spanish rule until the eighteenth century suggest answers to larger questions about the necessary conditions for economic growth and social development in the early modern world. After the revolt of 1647, the Habsburgs deliberately worked to destroy trust relations in order merely to maintain control (until Naples passed to Austria under Bourbon rule in 1738). Three Neapolitan political economists of the eighteenth century, Paolo Mattia Doria, Antonio Genovesi, and Gaetano Filangeri, attempted to explain how a working economy could be created on the ruins of the distrusting Spanish order.

Doria and Genovesi suppose that trust is the basis of the well-ordered republic (Pagden 1988, 129). The Italian words are not exact equivalents of the English "trust," but we might suppose Doria's sense is roughly that of the encapsulated-interest account presented in chapter 1, because for him trust is the motive to behave toward members of the society at large in much the same way that one behaves toward members of one's own kin group, with whom, of course, one has ongoing reciprocal exchange relations (Pagden 1988, 138). This secular ethic of classical republicanism performs the role of Max Weber's (1951, 237) Protestantism: it shatters "the fetters of the kin."[9] Hence it runs against the view of community in Ibn Khaldun in his defense, discussed later in this chapter, of anarchic tribal Muslim communities in North Africa, communities that depend centrally on kin relations (Gellner 1988). Breaking dependence on kin relations opens up the opportunity for much greater economic activity and therefore economic progress—this is roughly Fukuyama's (1995) argument about the difficulties of economic development in China and the greater success of Japan (as seen shortly before 1995—how fickle the times are).

Filangeri supposes that confidence is the soul of commerce and that the credit it can generate should be regarded as a second species of money. (Pagden 1988, 130). Doria argues that trade can flourish only under two conditions, "liberty and security in contracts, and this can only occur when trust and justice rule" (Pagden 1988, 137). Again, these institutional devices enable us to rely on others far beyond our kin. It has been so taken for granted that contract enables cooperative dealings, even absent trust, that a recent literature has grown up to say that much of apparent contractual dealing is in fact regulated by informal devices (see, for example, Macauley 1963; Ellickson 1991; Rousseau 1995) and even that legal regulation hampers some contractual possibilities (Bohnet, Frey, and Huck 2001). Hence many contracts and, even more, many details of contracts are often handled through trust and trustworthiness.

Second, turn briefly to problems of trust in a socialist economy. If the theses of Fukuyama (1995) and Seligman (1997) are correct, one might therefore suppose that the chief problems of Eastern Europe and the Soviet Union before 1989 were the lack of trust in many relationships, especially in relationships with the government and its agents. On this view, centralization of the economy might have worked had there only been more trust. For example, we can imagine that a much more benign central government, such as that of Sweden, would have attempted to enhance production and productivity with greater sensitivity to its citizen workers, so that its agents would not have provoked such distrust and enmity as Soviet commissars did.

Alternatively, one might suppose that centralization was a problem in addition to low levels of trust or even that centralization tended to produce distrust or to reduce trust. It probably did lead to distrust through the need to monitor production. For example, the government set quantitative quotas, and the natural way to meet these was often to stint on quality. In a market, this would merely mean that the poorer producer would have poorer sales. In a centralized economy, the qualitatively poor producer could only be rebuked or fined, and this would be done by a recognizable personal agent of the government, not by the invisible hand and the noninvidious forces of the market. If a producer's reputation with potential buyers is of great interest, the producer has reason to produce higher-quality goods even though there might be no easily specified contractual definition of quality. Hence, as in the literature on extracontractual aspects of business dealings (for example, Macauley 1963; Bohnet, Frey, and Huck 2001), producers and buyers would be in a partially cooperative relationship rather than the nearly adversarial relationship of the Soviet economy.

In the current transition to a market economy, the nations of the former Soviet Union are hampered by the lack of institutional and personal experience with enforceable contracts and also by the sadly rich experience with adversarial dealings, with their single "buyer" of the past. Even if a workable regime of enforceable market contracts is introduced, it may be difficult for older Russians ever to overcome their adversarial stance and to begin to think positively about the quality of their work. The difficult part of the transition to a regime of contract is the transition to loose contracts whose finer terms are not legally enforceable. Part of what makes such terms compelling to someone fulfilling the contract is expectations of long-term iterated interactions and reputational effects. In the early years of a transition, no one can have great expectations of the stability and longevity of contracting partners. Hence there is a strong incentive to focus on short-term profits rather than long-term benefits of building reputation, thus undercutting the transition.

Ernest Gellner (1988, 156) claims that politically a socialist government "needs to atomize society; economically it needs autonomous institutions." In the second part of this claim, he evidently supposes that an economy must be organized somewhat entrepreneurially, which is to say somewhat as a market. Yet if the first part of his claim is true, this need founders on the state's efforts to undermine trust relationships in atomizing society. On Gellner's view, then, socialist government is inherently self-contradictory. Gellner's claim might be right, although the drive to atomize society in the Soviet era was substantially opportunistic rather than inherent. That is, giving government power to regulate prices—and the economy more generally— gives it power to do many other things as well, such as suppressing the writings and political activities of more or less everyone and the symphonies and operas of Dmitri Shostakovich just because their dissonance offended the Great Musician. Any lousy official can abuse such power, and a Stalin at the top can abuse it grossly even though there need be no reason associated with the economic purposes of centralization to use the power in such ways. As was reputedly remarked by Montesquieu, one would have to have an arrogant view of the rectitude of one's own beliefs to justify killing others merely for having different beliefs. It seems inconceivable that the effusion of the arts in the Soviet Union in the 1920s and the work of poets, composers, and others thereafter needed to be suppressed if the Soviet experiment was to succeed.

Finally, consider our willingness to be open to new others by tentatively treating them as though we could trust them, even if only in small ways. Such willingness or confidence underlies a commonplace claim that even the market and other more or less purely exchange relations depend on a general level of honesty—and hence confidence that others will not cheat us. Some economists consider this general level of honesty a public good that is voluntarily provided by individuals through their piecemeal actions (Arrow 1974; Hirsch 1978, 78–79). Kenneth Arrow (1974) supposes that normal economic relations require a background or atmosphere of normative commitments to be honest, to keep promises, and so forth (but see Mueller [1999] on how norms of good business practice arose commercially). In a similar sense, we might suppose that social relations of many kinds require or at least are simplified by a background of trustworthiness, although this might be more nearly rationally than normatively motivated. If our expectations are stabilized at a high enough level of cooperativeness, we may finally be able to treat much of the behavior we expect to encounter as a relatively benign force of nature, just as microeconomic theorists of the market essentially do.

This general background or atmosphere of trustworthiness makes not only the market but also social life more generally go much better than it would without such an atmosphere. Hence life in a harsh ghetto or in a society that has broken down into violence and rabid self-seeking, as in Somalia at the end of the twentieth century, is hampered by the prudent lack of trust and by the disastrous lack of institutions to enable joint enterprises to proceed even without much trust. Introducing trust in such a context would be pointless. What is required for a constructive atmosphere is trustworthiness, which cannot easily be established by individuals across a whole society that has destroyed it. Again, before trustworthiness can be established there must first be institutional safeguards against the potential for disastrous consequences of dealing with others so that people can begin to take the risk of cooperating in ways that, if successful, would lead to trust relationships.

Cooperation in Institutional Settings

In two arenas—science and the professions of law, medicine, and others—trustworthiness is commonly reinforced by the natural or institutionalized incentive structures of those arenas. Both depend heavily on reputational effects but in different ways. In addition, institutionalized self-sanctioning arguably works to keep scientists and professional practitioners reliable to some extent. As well, sanctioning by external institutions may be on the rise in science and some of the professions.

Some of the earliest and most extensive work on trust has focused on the professions (see especially Barber 1983), and I do not discuss the professions at length here. Without debating whether trust is really the issue, we can presumably all agree that expectations of reliable behavior by professionals whose clients or patients we are is centrally important. This was an early insight of some doctors and lawyers, who introduced associations of qualified practitioners and codes of professional responsibility (Berlant 1975; see Gorlin 1999 for various codes). There is some doubt that these professional codes and institutional oversight have been very effective—in part, simply because they are seldom invoked to sanction either lawyers or doctors. For example, dreadful medical errors are evidently fairly common, and yet those who make such errors often continue in practice (Alpert 2000; Jennifer Steinhauer, "So, the Brain Tumor's on the Left, Right?" *New York Times*, 1 April 2001).[10] Increasingly, the oversight of medical professionals is being taken over by government. The behavior of legal professionals is substantially regulated by market reputation, so that the simple market discipline of competition may be far more important than is sanctioning by bar associations.

Now consider science and scientists, on whose motivations there has not been extensive research—scientists themselves often argue that their motivation is simply to seek the truth (see further Hardin 1999b).[11] This is too romantic and ethereal a rationale for most real scientists. An individual scientist who wants support for her research and promotion for her achievements depends on a reputation for good work, work that can often be checked by others who would be happy to second-guess and correct her findings if they seem to be wrong. There is an internal competition in the enterprise of science that forces all to adhere to certain practices, such as reporting data truthfully. This competition works for truth even when the personal motivation of a scientist is not the pure search for truth. Of course, under duress, the norms of good practice may be overridden, and a scientist might fabricate data. Indeed, if the background norm is one of relatively trustworthy people in particular roles, the untrustworthy can take parasitic advantage of that background expectation.

In a society in which the background standards are those of the con artist, stances toward others will generally be defensive, and wariness might block most cooperative dealings, as in contexts of pervasive distrust and untrustworthiness. In a much more cooperative society, which is likely to be either a very close society or one with relatively good institutional structures to protect various dealings, the typically correct stance will be one of openness rather than wariness. Science has traditionally seemed to be such a society. Scientists generally seem to think that fraud is rare in science, but there are few data to establish that claim. The U.S. Office of Research Integrity recently established a grant program to investigate the prevalence of fraud, and some preliminary estimates are troubling. Although documented cases are rare, Nicholas Steneck of the University of Michigan, Ann Arbor, has drawn up a list of estimates according to which many scientists claim to know of cases of fraud (Marshall 2000). The office found that about half of 150 cases investigated (apparently most of them by universities) between 1993 and 1997 resulted in misconduct findings (Kaiser 1999).

Still, the competitive structure of science, with the possibility of having one's results dismissed by others, is evidently a bracing discipline. A collection of ten papers on plant development by a group of plant scientists at a Max Planck Institute in Cologne has been shown to be based on irreproducible results (Balter 1999). Scores of papers by a German team of leukemia researchers have been found to include falsifications and suspected data manipulation (Hagmann 2000). The latter papers were questioned in part because the reported data were often too good to be true.[12] In both cases, careers have been ended as a consequence of the misrepresentations. Also in both cases, it was evidently other scientists who raised questions about the published research. Hence the commonplace image of science as a self-disciplining enterprise seems credible, although the German government heightened the scrutiny. Therefore, as Dennis Flanagan (1992), the former editor of *Scientific American*, has said, abuse may be typically a matter of pathology.

Researchers now worry that the growing possibility for great wealth from discoveries, especially but not only in genetic science, may reduce the openness of their enterprise (see, for example, Zandonella 2001). Moreover, the general commercialization of biological findings increasingly puts scientists in conflicts of interest between doing good science and making huge sums of money. In a recent case, a young man, Jesse Gelsinger, died during an experimental test of a new method of gene therapy. The University of Pennsylvania and one of the clinicians involved in the test held stakes in a gene-therapy company ("Controversy of the Year: Biomedical Ethics on the Front Burner," *Science*, 22 December 2000, 2225). Reports on such cases might eventually damage the reputation of scientists enough that educated publics might begin to doubt the reliability of science, scientists, and agencies that have access to biological information of various kinds and that stand to benefit from the use of such information.[13] As in many other areas of life, the crux of the matter for popular confidence in science may turn out to be conflict of interest on the part of scientists.

Trust and Social Structure

The Hobbesian problem of dreadful disorder arises from the assumption that anarchy, the absence of enforcement of order, leads to distrust and social disintegration. Ibn Khaldun, a fourteenth-century Arab historian, supposes that it is precisely anarchy that engenders

trust or social cohesion (Gellner 1988, 143). His argument is somewhat circular. In anarchy there are, by definition, no institutional
structures for regulating cooperative interactions. Hence if there is uncoerced cooperation, it must typically require trust. That there is trust
in instances of anarchic order therefore need not entail that such conditions engender trust, because trust might commonly be constitutive
of such order in anarchic conditions more than it is the product of
order. That is to say, the causal argument goes the opposite way. If
anarchy works at all well for people, that is because there is trust to
organize cooperation. Still, trust is not a necessary element of anarchic
order, as is suggested by the example of the Swat Pathan (discussed
in chapter 4) and by the possibility that small communities can be
governed by norms rather than by trust relationships.

Hobbes supposes that in the state of nature distrust would be so
rampant that individuals would turn on other individuals. What is
more likely, and what is consistent with the vast literature on anarchy
and on acephalous anthropological societies, is that there would be
small-community organization. Individuals within small communities
would thereby have some protections that would make productive
life possible. The small societies might, however, engage in hostilities
with one another. Experimental work on Japanese and American societies suggests that reliance on a group builds trust relationships
within the group but blocks or at least hinders the development of
trust relationships more broadly (Yamagishi, Cook, and Watabe 1998).
As Gellner (1988, 147) argues, in segmentary, pastoral society, there is
only one means of protecting oneself against sudden onslaught from
others: to gang up in a group.

Khaldun says that urban life is incompatible with trust and cohesion. His concern is with the transition from traditional, anarchic
Muslim societies in North Africa to urban societies. The very fact that
these societies are urban means that urban lineages accept governmental authority (Gellner 1988, 147). Urban organization and economic
specialization separate individuals from their relatives and immerse
them in a larger, less knowable society. Hence they cannot be anarchic
and, on Khaldun's mistaken argument, it immediately follows that
trust is at risk. In Khaldun's vision, the city is made up of specialists;
and metaphorically speaking, a specialist has no cousins. In a tribal
culture the specialist is despised. Every excellence is a form of specialization, and specialization precludes full citizenship. The unspecialized
human being constitutes the moral norm. (Recall the peasant Chinese
dictum that we should cut down the taller poppies, those that stand
out and are not part of the ordinary mass—as though the standout
violates some esthetic principle.) The unspecialized can lose themselves in a solidary unit and gladly accept collective responsibility.

Against Khaldun's thesis we might suppose we would rather live in a society with the advantages of division of labor and scale than in one so small that there would be little division of labor (except perhaps the painfully traditional divisions by gender). Khaldun's moral thesis is that we would be better off in a small, close-knit community. That is a staggeringly complex and contestable normative claim, one that is partially shared by communitarian theorists of our time in the West. None of those communitarian theorists would be able to live in a society such as Khaldun extolled. Nor could Khaldun, as an impressive social theorist, have fitted into that society—he would, on his own account, have been excluded by his own excellence. Interestingly, however, the usual concern of communitarians is not with the richer relationships of trust in community but rather with the origin of values in communal practice and knowledge (Hardin 1995, chapter 7).[14]

Against the appeals of Khaldun's argument even on its own terms of communal engenderment of trust, and parallel to the trend toward division of labor, is a trend toward the reduction of the extremes of distrust that lead to violence in such small-scale societies as medieval Iceland and the traditional Muslim societies that concern Khaldun. We can thank institutions for this change. Legal institutions replace the feud and the system of personal vengeance with police protections and replace the need for restrictive systems of barter with general exchange grounded in enforceable contracts and money. Other institutions organize our cooperation in various contexts in which spontaneous cooperation is unlikely to succeed. Through the help of some of those institutions we can cooperate without the sometimes suffocating hand of small-community norms to control us. Although Gellner makes Khaldun's analysis one of trust, it seems likely that the actual communities Khaldun extols were more pervasively organized by such norms. In contexts in which trust did not work earlier, owing to pervasive distrust over certain matters, and in which norms also would not work today, because we are no longer embedded in restrictive communities, it is often of no concern that they fail to lead us to cooperate, because with our institutional devices we have far less need to rely on trust relationships and norms in order to engage in joint enterprises.

Khaldun dislikes specialization because it sets individuals apart from the uniform community. Part of the specialization he rejects is in the task of handling difficult interpersonal exchanges and other enterprises. For such matters, we may be glad that no one of us relies on our cousins for managing those relationships. When your cousins now do play a strong role in mediating our relations, I have reason for distrust. This is, of course, the point of Max Weber's thesis (1981,

228) on the rise of the modern business corporation and the invention of the idea of corporate capital of fourteenth century Florence: the resources and accounts of the individual get separated from those of the firm. It was also the original point of rules against nepotism that are now increasingly in abeyance when the relative who might work for a firm is not a brother or male cousin but a woman, especially a spouse.

In our more complex, open, mobile, and relatively impersonal society, Breton and Wintrobe (1982, 80) note that large investments in trust in a small number of intensive relationships are unusual. What we see instead are many contacts that are less intense. Breton and Wintrobe are concerned with something roughly like commercial relationships, because we might still see substantial investments in trust and trustworthiness in close, intensive relationships with family and friends even in such a society as the United States. Indeed, Breton and Wintrobe themselves have had an admirably long and close collaborative academic relationship. The differences in the two patterns are, again, virtually a matter of arithmetic logic, because the development of intensive relationships requires substantial investments of time. If I must have relations with large numbers of people, I cannot have intensive relations with many of them.

The change from traditional to modern industrial societies in this respect is radical. Axel Leijonhufvud (1995) compares the life of a Frenchman, Bodo, a tenth-century serf of the abbey of St.-Germain-des-Prés, to that of a French professional living in Paris today. We can know much about Bodo because good records of his life were kept. At that time, St.-Germain was well outside Paris, but today it is near the center of the city, where Leijonhufvud's contemporary professional lives and works. Almost all of Bodo's consumption in his lifetime was derived either from his own efforts or from the efforts of about eighty people, all of whom he knew well on a nearly daily basis. The bit of his consumption that did not come from his small community would have been salt, which would have come from the sea, and which would have passed through several, perhaps many, hands along the way. His modern counterpart consumes things that have inputs from millions of people around the globe, most of whom the Frenchman will never know. There may be no one outside his family whom the professional knows as well as Bodo knew many of his fellow villagers.

Economic, political, and social progress bring new groups and classes into the center of society, making changes in culture and values much easier. A seeming concern of Khaldun and other communitarians is to block such changes. They argue de facto for a society in which current dispensations as of some moment are turned into fairly rigidly determined positional goods with strong constraints on change. The implications of such a view are that we either are stuck relatively fast or are finally overwhelmed by changes that come from outside our community. Khaldun would presumably have preferred Bodo's world to contemporary Paris, but there was no way to secure that world against overwhelming change.

Finally, note that for a real-world society in which there must be substantial variance on most social, intentional, cognitive, and other such measures, average levels of anything may be far less important than actual distributions, especially if individuals and societies have ways of selecting on the relevant dimension to found social structures on differences in trustworthiness. So, for example, if we are in a society that is hierarchically organized for various purposes, it may often be more important that the most competent or trustworthy people be in certain hierarchical roles than that people of average competence or trustworthiness be in those roles. Even in a strictly egalitarian context it may be more important that there be some highly trustworthy individuals in the system than that everyone be close to the average in trustworthiness. For example, in a market one exceptionally trustworthy dealer may force others to be more trustworthy in order to stay in competition, as John Mueller (1999, 79–80) argues for the case of John Wanamaker and the modern department store. On the other hand, in certain contexts, in a society in which personal relationships are generally not deviously exploitative, one can take a lot for granted on first meeting a new associate. Con artists, sexual exploiters, and many others have a field of play only because the background standards and expectations of behavior are relatively high.

Concluding Remarks

In the academic literature, there are four main theories or models of trust that are actually brought to bear in empirical claims and research. Three of these are based on the kinds of reasons for judging the trustworthiness of the potentially trusted, and we could as sensibly say that these are three different theories of trustworthiness as that they are theories of trust. These kinds of reasons are encapsulated interest, moral commitment, and commitment from character. Two of these—moral commitment and character—are dispositional reasons, and the other—encapsulated interest—is a reason from interests. The fundamentally important common feature of these three theories or models of trust is that they require cognitive assessments of the trustworthiness of the potentially trusted. The fourth theory is purely dispositional trust that is not grounded in the assessment of the trustworthiness of the trusted and therefore is not at all a theory of trustworthiness. The one frequently assumed model of trust to which most of the discussions of this book do not apply is trust as purely dispositional and unrelated to anything to do with the trusted.

Most of the discussion of a disposition to trust (for example, Rotter 1980) could easily be read as supposing that people can be relatively optimistic about others generally, perhaps for reasons of early experience, as discussed in chapter 5. If this is the meaning of trust as dispositional, then it is not generally a theory of trust but merely an explanation of why some take risks more readily than others do or why some read the risks as less serious than others do. Hence the dispositional view is about marginal variations in trusting in the face of whatever evidence of trustworthiness is available. The view that trust is purely a disposition and that it is therefore unrelated in any specific instance to the object of the trust (trusting B to do X) is surely irrelevant to the experience of trust for most of us most of the time—and perhaps no one genuinely holds such a view, which in any case would not be a general theory of trust. Perhaps the largest body of current work on trust as a disposition is on generalized trust. Trust as purely dispositional would be noncognitive and not relational. Genuinely generalized trust must be dispositional and neither cognitive nor relational in the sense that it is not based on cognitive assessments of or relationships with others.

As noted in chapter 1, most people, when asked whom they trust, speak immediately of people with whom they have ongoing relationships. For them and for the encapsulated-interest view, trust is relational. My trust of you grows out of my relationship with you; it is not independent of that relationship (or of reputational proxies for such a relationship). Some other models of trust may also be relational if in order to judge someone to be trustworthy out of moral commitment or character one needs knowledge that is available only in relationships or through reputations from relationships with others. One might imagine, however, having other sources of knowledge that would not depend on having a relationship with the trusted person.

A core part of sociology is work on ongoing relationships that involve iterated interactions, as in the vast literature on iterated prisoner's dilemma and large-number prisoner's dilemmas or collective actions (some psychologists and sociologists prefer to call these social dilemmas). That is to say, motivations generated within relationships are at the heart of our understanding of social and interpersonal interactions. Indeed, it is ongoing relationships that make it meaningful for us to speak of society rather than merely of an aggregation of individuals. A misfortune of much empirical work on trust through survey research and experimental games is that it generally misses any relational aspect of the choices and commitments of the subjects, although surveys and games could be designed to capture relational elements of the interactions.

As discussed in chapter 3, there are many conceptions of trust, including the four mentioned here. Several of these have been proposed in a sense theoretically but have not been applied in empirical studies, and few if any conclusions about social structure and broader relationships have been inferred from them. They are strictly conceptual. Concepts are neither true nor false, but they are typically theory laden, and the associated theories can be true or false. Trust is a term that is associated, explicitly or implicitly, with several quite different theories. These theories commonly include psychological claims. People seem to differ enough psychologically that some of them fit almost any theory of trust grounded in the relevant psychological claims. The conception of trust as encapsulated interest implies many theoretical claims, such as those presented in the last four chapters of this book.

The differences in various accounts of trust are mostly grounded in an account of trustworthiness, although this latter account is often at best implicit. The standard views of trustworthiness seem likely each to be true of some people in some contexts. I trust some people because I know they have a stake in our ongoing relationships, others because I know they are morally committed to fulfilling my trust with respect to certain things, and others still because I think their character dictates their trustworthiness. A few have an especially strong stake in our ongoing relationships because they are close friends, and a very few because they love me.

In chapter 6, I discuss falling in love and into friendship as ways in which trust comes quickly, virtually before any interaction. What often happens, however, is that people grow into a richer relationship of friendship or at least cooperativeness with respect to some range of matters. At that point, trust may often be overdetermined because trustworthiness is overdetermined. You may be trustworthy out of interest, morality, and friendship. You may even develop a simple disposition to be trustworthy to me, and you might develop a disposition to trust me. (Such dispositions toward particular persons could be shattered by misunderstanding or bad faith.) For example, we can start purely from financial interests, as we might with a local merchant, and then we can develop a relationship that goes beyond market concerns even while it remains grounded in such concerns. We might have a natural proclivity for attributing our motivations to moral considerations, but it would be easy to see in such a case that the actual relationship began from concern with interests on both sides.

Trust typically arises at the level of, and is grounded in, relatively small-scale interactions. It is not restricted to merely dyadic relation-ships, but it cannot be grounded in interactions involving very large numbers of people. It is generally a cognitive notion, and it faces epis-temological and temporal limits on just how many relationships one person can master. Because most of us live in large-scale societies, we need devices other than trusting and trustworthiness to make many of our more or less cooperative activities go well. Typically, we can overcome the scale limits of direct trusting by relying on social con-structions such as intermediary guarantors and reputations, although even these devices are commonly limited. To go much further, we must have strong institutional and especially legal backing that displaces the need for trust and reliance on others' doubtful trustworthiness. Unfor-tunately, such backing cannot be made to work efficiently—or, in some contexts, even at all.

It may still be true that trust and trustworthiness are fundamen-tally important in making large-scale activities and, especially, large social institutions function. To show how they do this, however, re-quires substantial unpacking of the relationships within those institu-tions to understand how trust plays a role at the micro level. Trust is inherently a micro-level phenomenon. It is individuals who trust, and it is individuals who, under institutional and other constraints, are trustworthy to some, perhaps limited, extent in particular contexts. Trust and trustworthiness may permeate the social structure, but they do so bit by bit. And much of that structure is a response to the difficulties of relying on trust and trustworthiness to motivate cooper-ation.

Appendix:
Survey Questions on Trust

THE GENERAL Social Survey, which is conducted by the National Opinion Research Center, has tapped attitudes on trust for several decades. These are the survey questions that are commonly interpreted as measuring generalized trust:

1. Do you think most people would try to take advantage of you, or would they try to be fair?

2. Would you say that most of the time people try to be helpful, or that they are mostly looking out for themselves?

3. Generally speaking, would you say that most people can be trusted, or that you can't be too careful dealing with people?

One might argue that the first two of these questions are not really about trust but about the elemental decency of "most people," not about their actual—trusting or nontrusting—relationship to anyone in particular.

One might also say that the one question that is clearly about trust seems to refer only to a two-part relation because it does not specify the matters on which one might trust most people. Here, of course, the vagueness of the instrument, which may be necessitated in part by the nature of survey research, is at fault in that it does not give respondents much leeway. Sensible respondents must read this question as not being about substantial issues, such as whether one could trust another to donate a kidney or to repay a large, unsecured personal loan, or even much less substantial issues. Hence although it is unspecified, the range of matters on which "most people can be trusted" is not likely to be unrestricted. It would be of interest to attempt to unpack what people think they are saying when they answer such questions. So far, however, survey work on trust has not done this. To date, the methodologies used to analyze such data have been radically more sophisticated than the designs of the questionnaires and, arguably, than the answers to them.

The most commonly used measure of trust in government in the United States is the set of responses to four questions regularly asked in the National Elections Studies biennial surveys. Similar surveys are taken in many other nations, although none over as long a period as the National Elections Studies surveys. The questions are as follows:

1. How much of the time do you think you can trust the government in Washington to do what is right—just about always, most of the time, or only some of the time?

2. Would you say the government is pretty much run by a few big interests looking out for themselves or that it is run for the benefit of all the people?

3. Do you think that people in the government waste a lot of money we pay in taxes, waste some of it, or don't waste very much of it?

4. Do you think that quite a few of the people running the government are crooked, not very many are, or do you think hardly any of them are crooked?

Again, only one of these questions—the first—actually uses the term trust. The third question might elicit a judgment of policies more than of trust. The second and fourth questions address motivations that might bear on the trustworthiness of officials. As is true also for the General Social Survey questions, answers to these questions tend to be strongly correlated, so that it is sensible to claim that they are tapping something coherent even though it is arguably bold to assert that they tap a sense of trust in any particular conception of trust. Reputedly, when they were first added to the National Elections Studies battery, these questions were intended to tap political cynicism, not trust.

On the complications of reading such surveys, see Putnam (2000, 415–24).

Notes

Preface

1. Adam Seligman (1997, 13–15) claims that trust as we know it is a strictly modern concept because it arises out of strictly modern conditions. This is a perhaps Platonic stipulation in its own right. Niklas Luhmann (1988, 96) makes a similar claim: "Trust comes with the discovery or reconceptualization of life as involving risk in early modern times."

Chapter 1

1. Some philosophers suppose we should distinguish our trust of another individual from our expectations about that individual's behavior in particular respects (Baier 1986; Hertzberg 1988).

2. The basic form could be extended in various ways. For example, A might trust B to do Y for C, but one could simply take "Y for C" as a complex version of "X" in the three-part pattern.

3. Henceforth, I merely say "to do X" and assume that X has a potentially wide domain.

4. Donald Davidson (1986, 200) writes that behavioralism is objectionable if it maintains "that mental concepts can be explicitly defined in terms of the behavioral concepts."

5. In many conferences sponsored by the Russell Sage Foundation, participants have objected to the claim that trust is cognitive because they want to say that it is behavioral. See also Sztompka 1999.

6. Annette Baier (1986) is concerned with the trusted's motivation toward the truster, but it is unclear whether she would equate that to the incentive of the trusted to fulfill the trust.

7. Aristotle (*Eudemian Ethics* 8.2.123b.12–16) notes that "there is no stable friendship [philia] without trust [pistis], and there is no trust without time." We may suppose that the point of time in this claim is to have opportunity for enough interactions—including interactions into the future—on which to ground trust. According to Paul Bullen (personal

communication, 26 February 1998), Aristotle uses the word "philia" to cover more than just what we would call friendship. It can include any harmonious relationship, even impersonal ones based purely on self-interest. Depending on the context, "pistis" can mean belief, confidence, and rhetorical proof, as well as trust. If pistis is trust for Aristotle, then evidently it is a cognitive term.

8. Baier (1986, 251) thinks the prisoner's dilemma is overemphasized in discussions of moral philosophy and that this is especially a mistake for discussion of trust. However, she has an unduly formal view of the prisoner's dilemma as inherently fitted to contracts and fixed payoffs. It is because many relations have the prisoner's dilemma structure that trust is at issue in them. Moreover, the prisoner's dilemma need not represent anything vaguely approaching equality of the parties. Baier says trust is quite different from promise keeping "in part because of the very indefiniteness of what we are counting on [the other] to do or not to do." She holds that contracts are at one extreme of trust, infant trust at the other extreme. "Trust in fellow contractors is a limit case of trust, in which fewer risks are taken, for the sake of lesser goods." She does not spell out why there are fewer risks or lesser goods. In fact, of course, some contracts govern dealings that stand to wreck lives if fulfillment fails.

9. For more extensive discussion of promising in its strategic variety, see Hardin (1988b, 41–44, 59–65).

10. It is sometimes supposed, on the contrary, that promising is typically used to regulate relations with strangers. Baier (1986, 246) says that exchange of promises typically requires "one to rely on strangers over a period of time." Unless my worldly experience is extraordinary, this view is prima facie false. Promises to genuine strangers are rare, not least perhaps because a stranger would not trust one's promise (see further Good 1988). Schelling (1989) canvasses peculiar devices for securing compliance with promises in such difficult contexts as those between strangers. Establishing reliability in such contexts requires strong measures, such as subjecting oneself to risk of real, often unrelated, harm if one fails to comply with one's promise. When we have to rely on strangers in important matters, we commonly prefer to bind them through contracts under law.

11. For more extensive discussion see Hardin (1982a, chapter 9). The conclusion of the backward induction argument has become a virtual dogma despite the fact that many, perhaps most, discussants think it perverse. Its appeal as a dogma may simply be that it is cute and perversely contrary to common sense. See further Hardin (1992; in press b, chapter 2).

12. This section summarizes an argument presented in Hardin (2001).

Chapter 2

1. Luhmann (1980, 64) also says that trust is a kind of capital. Although trustworthiness might be seen as a form of capital, as reputation is, it is

hard even to imagine what it means for trust to be a form of capital. See further chapter 3.

2. It is possible that trustworthiness is affected by the perception of being trusted. If we reward people beyond what they might seem to deserve, they might therefore attempt to live up to the reward by performing at a high level. Similarly, when we think people will perform well, they often do (see further Peel 1998; Braithwaite 1998; Blackburn 1998; Daunton 1998).

3. The translation here, by Andrew Porter, was intended for performance as well as for conveying meaning, and it is perhaps inadequate to reveal the nature of Alberich's "passionate fevers." The German makes clear that what is at issue is a lascivious rutting fire. Many of Wagner's characters, some of them among the most loathsome and treacherous in all of opera, are obsessed with trust. Like Lohengrin, they demand it without evidence that they merit it; like Wotan, they are unworthy of it.

4. Alberich does not say "forever" in the German, although one might sensibly suppose that serious curses are meant to be forever. To assert, "I curse you, but I'll embrace you again tomorrow," could only be said with comic intent. Moreover, Wotan, in his confessional soliloquy to Brünnhilde in *The Valkyrie* (2.2), mourns that, because he was always overcome by the longing for love, he had never been able to act so forcefully as to renounce it, as the "cringing" gnome Alberich had done (Wagner 1977, 106–7). This hardly makes sense if Alberich's curse was not meant to last. Here and elsewhere, we could be bogged down for pages trying to interpret Wagner. Nothing turns on that for the present argument, and we may leave that task to J. R. R. Tolkien and others who have the gift for it. An apparent acolyte of the god Wagner wrote me a charmingly arrogant letter to say that reading my article, "Trustworthiness" (Hardin 1996) any further after I had so badly misread Wagner was clearly pointless because, as any philosopher must know, nothing of value could follow from a mistaken premise.

5. "Liebe Lust" in the Rhine maiden Woglinde's German.

6. One might suppose that the first of these branches is incoherent almost by inspection of the nature of our lives, in which action of moral significance is most often interaction. Social life is relational, not individual. I cannot cause outcomes by my actions but must rely on our joint causation of outcomes as merely a partial function of my own actions. To focus on rules for behavior or the individual's action taken separately from others' actions therefore grossly oversimplifies the nature of our problem (see further Hardin in press b, chapter 6; Hardin 1988b, 68–70). For example, such deontological rule following is fundamentally irrelevant to most public policy. Indeed, when it is intruded into public policy, it is often harmful to the purposes of the policy, as Jonathan Baron (1998) argues forcefully. He notes that we should not be surprised when policies produce suboptimal outcomes, such as organ shortages and even world poverty, when the policies result from reliance on deontological

rules that ignore consequences. It is hard even to conceive of many public policies as other than consequentialist in their purpose, and it would
be astonishing if some limited set of moral rules should always be congruent with achieving those purposes. Any view of the wrongheaded-
ness of deontological moral theory in many public policies, however,
should be irrelevant to the assessment here of its plausible undergirding
of a moral disposition for trustworthiness.

7. Gauthier (1986) and also McClennen (1990) suppose that we adopt a
    cooperative disposition in order to fit our interests in achieving mutual
    cooperation.

8. For an analogous argument on the utilitarian grounds for promise keep-
    ing, see Hardin (1988b, 61–62).

9. In Hobbes' own words, "Nor is it possible for any person to be bound to
    himselfe; because he that can bind, can release; and therefore he that is
    bound to himselfe onely, is not bound."

10. For many such examples, see George Ainslie (1992), Jon Elster (1979, 36–
    111), and Thomas Schelling (1984, 57–112).

11. We could include discussion of social norms here, but they are complex
    enough to merit separate treatment because they often include elements
    of strictly internal motivations. They are therefore a mixed category that
    cuts across internal and external motivations.

12. Such conventions are often reinforced by more formal institutional con-
    straints, including law. Such reinforcement is not typically necessary, but
    it is likely to be a natural move. It can derive from the common but
    specious supposition that what is ought to be—and therefore ought to
    be legally or otherwise enforced. Alternatively, it can happen because
    those who back a convention or norm can get it reinforced by law.

13. In such a context norms can be forcefully coercive (see Hardin 1995,
    chapter 4).

14. See the discussion of endgame motivations in contract-by-convention
    resolutions of iterated prisoner's dilemma in Hardin (1982a, 200–5).

15. See, for example, "Prenuptial Pacts Rise, Prenuptial Trust Fails," *New
    York Times*, 19 November 1986. This is a less revolutionary change than
    one might think. In many times and places, national and familial inter-
    ests have dominated some marriages, and powerful institutions have
    stood behind those interests. The principal change in contemporary con-
    ditions may be that far larger fractions of marriages put substantial eco-
    nomic interests at stake. Schwartz argues that, once satisfaction of per-
    sonal interests "becomes the goal of friendship and marriage, it destroys
    these activities as distinct, organized, and coherent" (Schwartz 1986,
    269). Unless he means "the *only* goal" or these terms are defined in odd
    ways, this is utterly implausible. Marriages must often have strong, even
    predominant elements of satisfaction of personal (and other) interests.
    Are they then destroyed as "distinct, organized, and coherent" activities?

16.   For one attempt at explaining internalization, see Scott (1971).

17.   On such norms and their power, see Hardin (1995, chapter 4).

18.   Universalistic norms that do work are, as noted, often enforced within dyads. If I lie to you, it is likely to be in your interest to sanction me, and you may do so. Many norms work in seemingly large-number contexts, such as norms for professional integrity, honesty in scientific research, confidentiality in many contexts, and fairness in institutional roles (such as dealing with welfare clients or grading students). These typically are backed by institutional sanctioning power, so that they do not depend merely on spontaneous sanction from within the relationship, as communal norms or dyadic norms do. They fall somewhere between spontaneously enforced norms and institutional regulations.

19.   In Indiana, a woman who was accused of driving the wrong way in order to commit suicide and to take her children with her was charged with murder. Given the nature of the driving convention, few people would disagree that hers was a moral and criminal action if the accusation is correct ("Woman Convicted of 7 Murders in Wrong-Way Accident," *USA Today*, 11 May 2001).

Chapter 3

1.   This is true of many fundamentally important terms in any scientific realm.

2.   The declaration "Trust me" might have a quite different role in the vernacular. If I am doing something for you and you seem to doubt my competence, I might say, "Trust me," meaning that you should not be so doubtful of my abilities.

3.   One might be obligated to act in certain ways contrary to one's degree of trust. This is presumably what Held means here.

4.   Baier (1985, 61) says trusting someone is always a risk "given the partial opaqueness to us of the reasoning and motivation of those we trust and with whom we cooperate." There is an "expected gain which comes from a climate of trust"—hence, in trusting we give up security for greater security. But, again, it is not trusting that is risky, it is acting on trust that is risky. Trusting is merely a bit of knowledge, and, of course, knowledge is fallible. Fallible trust can seem to give us grounds for acting when the acting will turn out to be harmful to our interests.

5.   See, for example, the General Social Survey questions that are commonly used to measure so-called generalized trust (see the appendix). Only one of the three questions actually uses the term trust.

6.   This is the rationale in Gary Becker's (1971) analysis of discrimination in hiring.

7.   Such an argument already appears in William Wollaston's *Religion of Nature Delineated* (1722), cited in Dunn 1984, 289–90.

8. We could presumably give a psychological account of the development of greater or lesser optimism (see further chapter 5), although we might suppose that genetic dispositions differ independently of developmental experiences.

9. His argument is of a kind that often crops up in criticisms of analyses of strategic interactions. He says it "is not clear how any rationally defensible form of trust would even differ, conceptually, from knowledge or power [because] either I can compute the risk that what you say will be incorrect or I cannot." If I can compute it, I simply act from expectations of your behavior (Becker 1996, 47, 49). A central element in my trusting another, however, is the presumption not merely that she will do what she says but that she will do it for reasons of her own interest—for example, in maintaining her relationship with me—in fulfilling my trust. I should therefore think strategically, because my outcome is a function of both my actions and her actions taken together. Hence, I have to think through or guess at her motivations. This is not a matter of computing the odds in an interaction with nature, and it is not determinate.

10. Becker supposes that an abused child who clings to an abusing parent, or an abused spouse who clings to the abuser, trusts the abuser—hence noncognitively trusts. I am not qualified to discuss the psychological literature on such relationships, but this seems unlikely. Rather, the child or the abused spouse has no better place to go. The citizens abused by Papa Doc did not reveal noncognitive trust by the mere fact of staying on in Haiti.

11. John Locke (1955 [1689], 52) supposes that atheists cannot consistently be trusted because they do not fear ultimate retribution from God. On his account, then, trust is essentially a matter of rational expectations grounded in the rationality of the trusted. See further the discussion by John Dunn (1984, 286–88).

12. In chapter 8 I relate an incident from Shizuko Go's (1985) *Requiem*. Setsuko, the novel's heroine, is impressed by the kindness of an older woman, a stranger she is unlikely ever to see again. The older woman may have been only normatively motivated. If so, then her kindness to Setsuko was not necessarily based on grounds. In this case, however, it would be odd to say of the particular people to whom she was gracious that she trusted them to reciprocate. Her graciousness was almost entirely an expression of herself, without objective correlates, not specifically directed at particular people—although it perhaps had a strong class bias. If "trust" is selectively directed at only certain other people but not based on grounds for selecting which others, then it must be capricious—unrelated to its objects and not a consistent expression of character. Such "trust"—which should be characterized as acting as though one trusts—seems neither sensible nor meritorious.

13. Variants of a view of trust as grounded in scant expectations have often been proposed at various Russell Sage Foundation workshops on trust.

14. Virginia Held (1968, 157) has proposed an intermediate position. She supposes that "trust is most required exactly when we least know whether a person will or will not do an action." This statement is ambiguous, and it may not imply a definition of trust. Suppose she means it partially as a definition. It is true that where there is no room for choice on the part of another, trust cannot be at issue. Yet it can be at issue when I am quite confident of your choice of action. In a particular context, it makes sense to say I trust most the person I think most likely to act in a certain way, and I trust least the person I think least likely to act that way.

15. Karamazov's lieutenant colonel has a very strange morality and sense of honor. He can act illegally and irresponsibly toward the army and the nation in which he is an officer. Yet he expects Trifonov to act in a trustworthy way with respect to him in their criminal dealings. Morality and trust often do not correlate well.

16. Mansbridge (1999) calls such actions "altruistic trust."

17. Such considerations could not, of course, commend acting as though one trusted those others in many other matters in which their actual untrustworthiness might have grim consequences. For example, acting in these ways in such cases need not trump such other considerations as responsibility to one's child.

18. "Etwas" means "something," not "someone." These passages are quoted in English in Hertzberg (1988, 308).

19. Elster's claim clearly makes sense for altruism because I can genuinely have your interests at heart independently of any causal connection back to my own interests. Most of us are probably altruistic to some extent, even if not to a great extent. It is not clear, however, what is analogous about trust in Elster's view. Elster's concern is with altruism, and he does not spell out the analogous nature of trust implied in his brief aside, which may really be about trustworthiness.

20. In a classic study of military performance, Samuel Stouffer and colleagues (1949, 142–49) argue that great familiarity among members of a small combat unit often leads to great courage under fire because the members of the unit are loyal to one another rather than merely to the larger national purpose. In this case, all members incorporate the interests of the others in their own to some extent (see further chapter 6).

21. In an informal poll of taxi drivers, I found their main concerns to be about who will give the biggest tips. Women, blacks, and the very young are reputedly poor tippers. White men in suits are good tippers, and well-dressed older men escorting younger women are among the best. In some cities, the drivers also seem to be concerned with whether their fare might want to go to a part of the city from which no return fare could be expected. For example, anyone with a suitcase trying to hail a taxi in the southern end of Manhattan might be feared to want to go to Newark Airport, where New York City taxis are not allowed to solicit

riders for the return trip. Despite some history of attacks on taxi and livery drivers, not one of the drivers I queried expressed any concern about whether their fares would be untrustworthy in any way. Drivers of all races and ethnicities seemed to have similar views.

22. Gambetta (1988, 217) has a similar view.

23. The word trust, in prominently large letters, is featured in current advertising campaigns by Fortunoff, a jewelry merchant, Invitrogen, a maker of biological cell cultures, and Mercedes Benz. In a Fortunoff ad, trust is supposedly exemplified by a bride receiving a ring; in an Invitrogen ad, by a trapeze artist who flies through the air expecting to be caught by a partner; in a Mercedes ad, by a lion tamer who has the temerity to kiss his lion on the nose

24. Part of the discussion here is taken from Hardin (1999e).

25. It is a standing joke that among the academics most adept at augmenting their salaries and reducing their duties are theorists who insist that human behavior is not substantially self-interested.

26. This paragraph is drawn from a longer discussion of issues in law and norms (Hardin 2000a).

Chapter 4

1. Thresholds for behavior may be important and asymmetric here. We may tip from trust to distrust only when big enough news comes in. Additionally, it may be generally harder to tip from distrust to trust. See further Luhmann (1980, 73, 79).

2. See further chapter 5. See also general findings reported in Holmes (1991, 63). One might suppose from Holmes' account that the studies seem to turn the learning model discussed in chapter 5 into a psychological disposition that is theoretically unmotivated. Also, see Toshio Yamagishi's (1998, 2000) account of trust as a form of social intelligence.

3. Virginia Woolf (1938, 109) comments on the thoughts of a family listening to the paterfamilias expound on politics: "All of them bending themselves to listen thought: 'Pray heaven that the inside of my mind may not be exposed,' for each thought, 'The others are feeling this. They are outraged and indignant with the government about the fishermen. Whereas, I feel nothing at all.'" See further David Nyberg (1993).

4. See *Animal Legal Defense Fund, Inc. v. Shalala,* 104 F.3d 424, 431 (D.C. Cir. 1997) (holding that the Research Council of the National Academy of Sciences was "utilized" by the Department of Health and Human Services within the meaning of the term as used in the Federal Advisory Committee Act and thus is subject to its provisions).

5. As Nagel (1998, 6) says, "If I don't tell you everything I think and feel about you, that is not a case of deception, since you don't expect me to do so and would probably be appalled if I did."

6. What follows is from Barth's discussion at the New York University–Russell Sage Foundation conference on trust held at New York University on February 25 and 26, 1995.

7. Oman opened to tourists only in the mid-1990s, and it now seems, on one account, to be a remarkably hospitable society. Presumably the change is largely owing to a relatively benign ruler, Sultan Qabus bin Said (Judith Miller, "Exotic Oman Opens Its Doors," *New York Times,* 8 February 1998).

8. This discussion is adapted from Cook and Hardin (2000).

9. This era and especially the isolated status of Lisle suggest an extreme version of paranoid cognition. See further K. M. Colby (1981) and Roderick Kramer (1994, 1998).

10. Elkin related the visit in a private conversation in Bellagio, Italy, in May 1988, at the Rockefeller Center.

11. Hobbes was, of course, bothered by religious fundamentalists because different fundamentalist sects were ravaging England in the attempt coercively to impose their own religious beliefs on everyone.

12. As Gambetta (1988, 172–73) notes, the Mafia might help someone sell fraudulently. This implicitly would make clear that without Mafia protection distrust of one's fellows is rational and would therefore undercut competition that would benefit almost everyone.

13. Other factors further burden Sicilian society. For example, economic backwardness produces little opportunity for advancement. A standard way to advance is to prevail over others in one's own society—hence, advancement is a positional good (Gambetta 1988, 163).

14. See, for example, the argument of John Hart Ely (1980) in favor of constitutional oversight by a court. Also see Mark Warren (1999).

15. Locke (1988 [1690], §171: 381) holds that society turns power over to its governors, "whom society hath set over it self, with this express or tacit Trust, That it shall be imployed for their good, and the preservation of their Property."

16. Howard Margolis (1982) proposes a model of altruism in which the individual has two different sets of desires: self-interested or selfish and other-directed or altruistic. We then balance between these, indulging more in altruism for a while and then in selfishness.

17. Virtually the whole of political philosophy is relevant to this issue, and the political and economic philosophers of the Scottish Enlightenment, such as Hume and Smith, in particular, were almost entirely concerned with it.

Chapter 5

1. Julian Rotter (1980, 1–2) speaks of a "generalized expectancy."

2. In context, this seems to be a claim about the trustworthiness of those we might trust. See further chapter 2. As Partha Dasgupta (1988, 51) says, trust is important because "its presence or absence can have a strong bearing on what we choose to do and in many cases what we *can* do" (see also Akerlof 1970; Arrow 1974).

3. This is the claim of Baier (1986) in her account of infant trust. See discussion in chapter 3, in the section titled "Trust As Ungrounded Faith."

4. Although there is dispute about such a claim, the incidence of severe post-traumatic stress disorder (PTSD) may be extremely high among those abused at very young ages. A recent Dutch study found that 62 percent of women who were victims of childhood incest suffered from PTSD. A control group of women with "ordinary negative life events" in childhood suffered no PTSD (Albach and Everaerd 1992). The disorder, first well studied in soldiers with grim combat experiences, now seems possibly to afflict abused children. A central problem of effective therapy is establishing trust with patients who do not readily trust ("Post-traumatic Stress: Part 2" 1991).

5. The contrary view is assumed or argued by many writers. See, for example, Dunn (1988, 73, 80), Luhmann (1980, 19).

6. Carter's remarks at the Russell Sage Foundation, New York, 24 September 1992, during a brief account of an Atlanta project to reach the very poor.

7. Perhaps this is the sense of Luhmann's (1980, 4) claim that distrust is self-reinforcing: It does not generate enough information for the distruster to correct his or her view of possibilities.

8. This may be another ethological constraint on development.

9. This is a common theme in the trust literature, especially the social psychological literature; for example, see Robert Swinth (1967). Some experimental tests suggest that as-if testing is less important than one might think (Swinth 1967, 343).

10. Coleman (1990, 180–85) discusses various intermediary effects.

11. Despite their nearly definitional ring, the findings in Rotter's experiments may have provided evidence about the validity and generality of his scale.

12. The worst payoffs are the (1, 4) and (4, 1) payoffs in the prisoner's dilemma of game 2 in chapter 1. The first of these is worst for the column player, and the second is worst for the row player. These represent the outcome of one player's taking the other's holdings without anything in trade—hence theft rather than exchange.

Chapter 6

1. In competition with a relatively large set of alternative strategies, tit-for-tat cooperators survive quite well (Axelrod 1984).

2. In addition, Frank (1988, 18), agreeing with Pascal, notes that behavior influences character: "few people can maintain a predisposition to behave honestly while at the same time frequently engaging in transparently opportunistic behavior." My experience suggests that this claim is false because people can be opportunistic on some matters and honest on others.

3. In chapter 2, I discuss this issue in the context of a consideration of dispositions.

4. A similar incitement may have made Emma see Knightley's value. Mrs. Weston insists to Emma that Knightley has strong affection for Jane Fairfax: "I say that he is so very much occupied by the idea of *not* being in love with her, that I should not wonder if it were to end in his being so at last" (Austen 1985 [1816], 290).

5. On the force of the social convention on one's own credibility in marital relations and related problems, see Hardin (1982a, 213).

6. Elster adds two other considerations that seem unnecessary (see further Hardin 1995, 82–86; Merton 1968, 104–9; Stinchcombe 1968, 80–101).

7. The title of this paper (Hardin 1980) should perhaps say "functional explanation" rather than "functionalist explanation," because the latter suggests the blind assumption that whatever is good for a society must have happened and whatever behaviors a society develops must be good for it.

8. For several other cases, see Hardin (1980) and Hardin (1995, 82–85 [the norm of group identity], 93 [the dueling norm], and 132 [the norm of *omertà* in the Mafia and of public order more generally]).

Chapter 7

1. Hart says, in what is for him an unusual sociological claim, that without the voluntary cooperation of many, "the coercive power of law and government cannot be established."

2. This work is, surprisingly, one of the few substantial efforts to document that citizens' views make much difference in how well government functions. Levi speaks of quasi-voluntary compliance.

3. In general, it is important to note that one may neither trust nor distrust another or a government with respect to some issue. As noted in chapter 4, this is contrary to the vernacular sense of not trusting. A person who says, "I do not trust him," very likely means that he or she actively *distrusts* him. However, we are often ignorant of another's intentions or likely behavior, and therefore we are in a state of neither trust nor distrust toward that other.

4. The words "stupidity" and "brutality" were used by the *Alabama Journal* at the time to characterize the actions of Alabama state troopers who broke up a march in Marion, Alabama (quoted in Chong 1991, 26).

5. Indeed, a centerpiece in his downfall was the notoriously missing twenty minutes of a White House tape.

6. I discuss logical problems in the notion of generalized trust (individual trust of virtually all other individuals) in chapter 3 and putative relationships between generalized trust and social order in chapter 8. Generalized trust is not generally of concern in the problem of declining trust in government unless there is a general decline in trust in individuals that spills over into declining trust in government—but this is not a thesis central to the debates on declining trust in government.

7. I once stood on line at the stand of a German street vendor who dispensed wurst, sandwiches, drinks, and many other things with seemingly choreographed efficiency of movement that was remarkably graceful. When complimented by the person before me, the vendor replied, no doubt truthfully, "I know my limits."

8. The translation here is quoted in Mill 1997 (171). See further discussion in Hardin (1999d, 66–68).

9. For a rich account of the vicissitudes of trust during the Polish transition in the 1990s, see Piotr Sztompka (1999, 160–90).

10. The difference is not stark. For example, in the so-called cola wars, Pepsi engaged not in defining its product but in identifying its potential consumers, the Pepsi generation. This move began in the 1940s. By now, in a trick of marketing, virtually every living American is in "the" Pepsi generation. See Alexander Schuessler (2000, chapter 5) and Richard Tedlow (1990).

11. Luhmann (1980, 22, 30) earlier wrote of "system-trust," which must transcend interpersonal (thick) relations.

Chapter 8

1. Fredrik Barth's (1981) Omani society would be in this cell. See discussion in chapter 4.

2. These are the conditions in Banfield's (1958) account of life in the fictionally named village of Montegrano in southern Italy.

3. For analytical criticism of the concept of generalized trust, see chapter 3.

4. This is a claim that should be testable experimentally. To my knowledge it has not been subjected to any tests, although one might draw inferences from some experiments surveyed by John Ledyard (1995).

5. There is still, however, the nagging possibility of Fredrik Barth's trustless societies of Oman and Swat, as discussed in chapter 4.

6. For an odd twist on the older woman's hospitality, note the statement of Heathcliff, an exceedingly inhospitable man, to Lockwood, the ostensible teller of Emily Brontë's novel, *Wuthering Heights*. Heathcliff asks Lockwood, who has happened by for a final time, to "sit down and take your dinner with us—a guest that is safe from repeating his visit, can generally be made welcome" (Brontë 1981 [1847], 304).

7.   There are other possibilities. You might extend hospitality or act as though you trust me in order to demonstrate to me that you have faith in my morality or character or to give me an opportunity to live up to your hopes even though I may have no incentive to reciprocate your action. Alternatively, you may act according to a rule of reciprocity, doing unto others what they do unto you, even when it is not strictly in your interest to do so. Hence you may be trustworthy toward me because I am trustworthy toward you or because you may not wish to be the kind of person who acts toward another as though out of distrust that is not based on solid evidence. Such motivations are apt to lead to disappointment in many contexts, but they might be statistically justified in certain milieus. In particular, they might be justified in contexts in which there are rich possibilities of further interactions. In such contexts, however, interest is likely to conspire with your hopes in getting me to reciprocate.

Coleman (1990, 177–80) implicitly includes the trusted's incentives when he notes that a reciprocal trusting relationship, as in mutual trust in the iterated prisoner's dilemma, is mutually reinforcing for each truster. Why? Because each person now has additional incentive to be trustworthy. I trust you because it is in your interest to do what I trust you to do so long as you want me to do what you trust me to do. If there is some residue beyond rational expectations in one-way trust, there is less role for that residue in this straight, likely self-interested, exchange.

8.   I was once cheated by a small shop owner in downtown Chicago, who sold me a watch battery that was already dead, although it had recovered just enough to make my watch run for long enough to let me think the battery was okay. That shop owner's success was parasitic on the larger system of shops and stores that were more trustworthy, because my behavior in his shop was merely a generalization of my normal behavior in shops, most of which in my experience had been trustworthy. In a particular shop that I might have used in my own neighborhood, I would not have needed to bother to check whether the shopkeeper opened a sealed package to take out a new battery. That shopkeeper depended on reputation for business by repeat customers. In the downtown shop, I should have kept a more diligent eye on the shopkeeper because his business depended on casual traffic and not on repeat business or reputation.

9.   Weber argued that "the great achievement of the ethical religions, above all the ethical and asceticist sects of Protestantism . . ., [was] to shatter the fetters of the kin" and that, therefore, China did not develop a modern economy on its own.

10.   A modest percentage of even sometimes fatal medical errors is likely to be unavoidable in even the best-run hospital with all of the organizational complexity involved in care. One doctor supposes that "inept physicians and nurses" are likely to be a relatively minor factor (Sherwin B. Nuland, "The Hazards of Hospitalization," *Wall Street Journal*, 2 December 1999).

11. As Charles Peirce (1935, 3) expresses this commonplace view, "The scientific man is above all things desirous of learning the truth and, in order to do so, ardently desires to have his present provisional beliefs (and all his beliefs are merely provisional) swept away, and will work hard to accomplish that object."

12. This was also true of the eighteenth-century data of Gregor Mendel on the inheritance of color among his peas. Mendel was essentially right in his views of inheritance, but he lacked insight of the full genetic structure of the process, in which the occasional plant might inherit two recessive genes and therefore might be the "wrong" color for its parents. A scientist today, facing such an anomaly as Mendel thought he faced, might be delighted at the implication that theory must be wrong and that the anomaly would itself be of great and original interest to fellow scientists.

13. Partly because of conflicts motivated by religious views and partly because of concern over the value to insurers of genetic information on individuals, this is already happening. See the report on a recent survey in the United Kingdom ("Survey Shows Public Concern over Biology," *Nature*, 8 March 2001, 138–39).

14. As discussed in chapter 7, it is the vision of Robert Putnam (1993) that the existence of smaller associations in a society is conducive to political participation and, one might suppose, to trust in government.

References

Aguilar, John L. 1984. "Trust and Exchange: Expressive and Instrumental Dimensions of Reciprocity in a Peasant Community." *Ethos* 12: 3–29.

Ainslie, George. 1992. *Picoeconomics*. Cambridge: Cambridge University Press.

Akerlof, George. 1970. "The Market for 'Lemons': Qualitative Uncertainty and the Market Mechanism." *Quarterly Journal of Economics* 84: 488–500.

Albach, Francine, and Walter Everaerd. 1992. "Posttraumatic Stress Symptoms in Victims of Childhood Incest." *Psychotherapy and Psychosomatics* 57: 143–52.

Alpert, Mark. 2000. "Physician Heal Thyself." *Scientific American* (May): 32–34.

Amato, Paul R. 1993. "Urban-Rural Differences in Helping Friends and Family Members." *Social Psychology Quarterly* 56 (December): 249–62.

Arrow, Kenneth J. 1972. "Gifts and Exchanges." *Philosophy and Public Affairs* 1: 343–62.

———. 1974. *The Limits of Organization*. New York: Norton.

Atiyah, P. S. 1979. *The Rise and Fall of Freedom of Contract*. Oxford: Oxford University Press.

———. 1981. *Promises, Morals, and Law*. Oxford: Oxford University Press.

Austen, Jane. 1985. *Emma*. 1816. London: Penguin.

Axelrod, Robert. 1984. *The Evolution of Cooperation*. New York: Basic Books.

Bacharach, Michael, and Diego Gambetta. 2001. "Trust in Signs." In *Trust in Society*, edited by Karen S. Cook. New York: Russell Sage Foundation.

Baier, Annette. 1985. "What Do Women Want in a Moral Theory?" *Nous* 19: 53–64.

———. 1986. "Trust and Antitrust." *Ethics* 96: 231–60.

Bailey, F. G. 1988. "The Creation of Trust." In *Humbuggery and Manipulation*, by F. G. Bailey. Ithaca, N.Y.: Cornell University Press.

Balter, Michael. 1999. "Data in Key Papers Cannot Be Reproduced." *Science*, 26 March: 1987–89.

Banfield, Edward C. 1958. *The Moral Basis of a Backward Society*. New York: Free Press.

Barber, Bernard. 1983. *The Logic and Limits of Trust*. New Brunswick: Rutgers University Press.

Baron, Jonathan. 1998. *Judgment Misguided: Intuition and Error in Public Decision Making*. New York: Oxford University Press.

Barth, Fredrik. 1981. *Features of Person and Society in Swat: Collected Essays on Pathans.* Volume 2 of *Selected Essays of Fredrik Barth,* edited by Adam Kuper. London: Routledge and Kegan Paul.

Bateson, Patrick. 1988. "The Biological Evolution of Cooperation and Trust." In *Trust: Making and Breaking Cooperative Relations,* edited by Diego Gambetta. Oxford: Blackwell.

Becker, Gary. 1971. *The Economics of Discrimination.* 2d ed. Chicago: University of Chicago Press.

Becker, Lawrence C. 1996. "Trust as Noncognitive Security About Motives." *Ethics* 107(October): 43–61.

Berlant, Jeffrey. 1975. *Profession and Monopoly.* Berkeley: University of California Press.

Blackburn, Simon. 1998. "Trust, Cooperation, and Human Psychology." In *Trust and Governance,* edited by Valerie Braithwaite and Margaret Levi. New York: Russell Sage Foundation.

Blok, Anton. 1974. *The Mafia of a Sicilian Village, 1860–1960: A Study of Violent Peasant Entrepreneurs.* New York: Harper and Row.

Bloom, Allan. 1987. *The Closing of the American Mind.* New York: Simon & Schuster.

Bohnet, Iris, Bruno S. Frey, and Steffen Huck. 2001. "More Order with Less Law: On Contract Enforcement, Trust, and Crowding." *American Political Science Review* 95: 131–44.

Bok, Sissela. 1978. *Lying: Moral Choice in Public and Private Life.* New York: Pantheon.

Boyer, Peter J. 1997. "American Guanxi." *New Yorker,* 14 April, 48–61.

Braithwaite, John. 1998. "Institutionalizing Trust, Enculturating Distrust." In *Trust and Governance,* edited by Valerie Braithwaite and Margaret Levi. New York: Russell Sage Foundation.

Brehm, John, and Wendy Rahn. 1997. "Individual-Level Evidence for the Causes and Consequences of Social Capital." *American Journal of Political Science* 41: 999–1023.

Bretherton, Inge. 1992. "The Origins of Attachment Theory: John Bowlby and Mary Ainsworth." *Developmental Psychology* 28: 759–75.

Breton, Albert, and Ronald Wintrobe. 1982. *The Logic of Bureaucratic Conduct: An Economic Analysis of Competition, Exchange, and Efficiency in Private and Public Organizations.* Cambridge: Cambridge University Press.

Brontë, Emily. 1981 [1847]. *Wuthering Heights.* Edited by Ian Jack. Oxford: Oxford University Press World's Classics.

Buber, Martin. 1951. *Two Types of Faith.* Translated by Norman P. Goldberg. London: Routledge and Kegan Paul.

Byrne, Muriel St. Clare, ed. 1983. *The Lisle Letters: An Abridgement.* Chicago: University of Chicago Press.

Chandler, Raymond. 1955. *The Little Sister.* 1949. Harmondsworth, England: Penguin.

Chong, Dennis. 1991. *Collective Action and the Civil Rights Movement.* Chicago: University of Chicago Press.

Colby, K. M. 1981. "Modeling a Paranoid Mind." *Behavioral and Brain Sciences* 4: 515–60.

Coleman, James S. 1990. *Foundations of Social Theory.* Cambridge, Mass.: Harvard University Press.

Cook, Karen S., and Russell Hardin. 2000. "Networks, Norms, and Trustworthiness." In *Social Norms*, edited by Karl-Dieter Opp and Michael Hechter. New York: Russell Sage Foundation.

D'Antonio, Michael. 1997. "Atomic Guinea Pigs." *New York Times Magazine*, 31 August: 38–43.

Dasgupta, Partha. 1988. "Trust as a Commodity." In *Trust: Making and Breaking Cooperative Relations*, edited by Diego Gambetta. Oxford: Blackwell.

Daunton, Martin. 1998. "Trusting Leviathan: British Fiscal Administration from the Napoleonic Wars to the Second World War." In *Trust and Governance*, edited by Valerie Braithwaite and Margaret Levi. New York: Russell Sage Foundation.

Davidson, Donald. 1986. "Judging Interpersonal Interests." In *Foundations of Social Choice Theory*, edited by Jon Elster and Aanund Hylland. Cambridge: Cambridge University Press.

Davis, Nancy (Ann). 1993. "The Abortion Debate: The Search for Common Ground, Part 2." *Ethics* 103(July): 731–78.

Dawson, John P. 1980. *Gifts and Promises: Continental and American Law Compared.* New Haven: Yale University Press.

Dostoyevsky, Fyodor. 1982 [1880]. *The Brothers Karamazov.* Translated by David Magarshack. London: Penguin.

Dunn, John. 1984. "The Concept of 'Trust' in the Politics of John Locke." In *Philosophy in History*, edited by Richard Rorty, J. B. Schneewind, and Quentin Skinner. Cambridge: Cambridge University Press.

———. 1988. "Trust and Political Agency." In *Trust: Making and Breaking Cooperative Relations*, edited by Diego Gambetta. Oxford: Blackwell.

Dworkin, Ronald. 1993. *Life's Dominion: An Argument About Abortion, Euthanasia, and Individual Freedom.* New York: Knopf.

Dylan, Bob. 1995. *Lyrics, 1962–1985.* New York: Knopf.

Eisenstadt, Shmuel N., and Luis Roniger. 1984. *Patrons, Clients, and Friends.* Cambridge: Cambridge University Press.

Elkin, Stanley. 1996. *A Bad Man.* 1965. New York: Avon.

Ellickson, Robert C. 1991. *Order Without Law: How Neighbors Settle Disputes.* Cambridge, Mass.: Harvard University Press.

Elster, Jon. 1979. *Ulysses and the Sirens: Studies in Rationality and Irrationality.* Cambridge: Cambridge University Press.

———. 2000. "Arguing and Bargaining in Two Constituent Assemblies." *University of Pennsylvania Journal of Constitutional Law* 2: 345–421.

Ely, John Hart. 1980. *Democracy and Distrust: A Theory of Judicial Review.* Cambridge, Mass.: Harvard University Press.

Erikson, Erik H. 1963. *Childhood and Society.* 2d ed. New York: Norton.

Fischer, Claude S. 1982. *To Dwell Among Friends: Personal Networks in Town and City.* Chicago: University of Chicago Press.

Flanagan, Dennis. 1992. "Fraud in Science: A Media Event." Remarks addressed to the Midwest Consortium on International Security Studies, Wingspread Conference, "The Moral Role of Scientists." Racine, Wisconsin (October 9–11).

Frank, Robert. 1988. *Passions Within Reason: The Strategic Role of the Emotions.* New York: Norton.

Fried, Charles. 1981. *Contract as Promise*. Cambridge, Mass.: Harvard University Press.

Fukuyama, Francis. 1995. *Trust: The Social Virtues and the Creation of Prosperity*. New York: Free Press.

Gambetta, Diego, ed. 1988. *Trust: Making and Breaking Cooperative Relations*. Oxford: Blackwell.

Garrow, David J. 1978. *Protest at Selma*. New Haven: Yale University Press.

Gauthier, David. 1986. *Morals by Agreement*. Oxford: Oxford University Press.

Gellner, Ernest. 1988. "Trust, Cohesion, and the Social Order." In *Trust: Making and Breaking Cooperative Relations*, edited by Diego Gambetta. Oxford: Blackwell.

Go, Shizuko. 1985. *Requiem*. Tokyo: Kodansha.

Goldberg, Jeffrey. 2001. "Arafat's Gift: The Return of Ariel Sharon." *New Yorker*, 29 January: 52–67.

Good, David. 1988. "Individuals, Interpersonal Relations, and Trust." In *Trust: Making and Breaking Cooperative Relations*, edited by Diego Gambetta. Oxford: Blackwell.

Gorlin, Rena A. 1999. *Codes of Professional Responsibility: Ethics Standards in Business, Health, and Law*. 4th ed. Washington: Bureau of National Affairs.

Govier, Trudy. 1997. *Social Trust and Human Communities*. Montreal: McGill-Queens University Press.

Greif, Avner. 1993. "Contract Enforceability and Economic Institutions in Early Trade: The Maghribi Traders' Coalition." *American Economic Review* 83(June): 525–48.

Greif, Avner, Paul Milgrom, and Barry R. Weingast. 1994. "Coordination, Commitment, and Enforcement: The Case of the Merchant Guild." *Journal of Political Economy* 102: 745–76.

Hagmann, Michael. 2000. "Panel Finds Scores of Suspect Papers in German Fraud Probe." *Science*, 23 June: 2106–7.

Hardin, Russell. 1980. "Rationality, Irrationality, and Functionalist Explanation." *Social Science Information* 19(September): 755–72.

———. 1982a. *Collective Action*. Baltimore: Johns Hopkins University Press for Resources for the Future.

———. 1982b. "Exchange Theory on Strategic Bases." *Social Science Information* 2:251–72.

———. 1985. "Sanction and Obligation" *Monist* 68: 403–18.

———. 1988a. "Constitutional Political Economy: Agreement on Rules." *British Journal of Political Science* 18: 513–30.

———. 1988b. *Morality Within the Limits of Reason*. Chicago: University of Chicago Press.

———. 1991a. "Acting Together, Contributing Together." *Rationality and Society* 3: 365–80.

———. 1991b. "Hobbesian Political Order." *Political Theory* 19: 156–80.

———. 1992. "Determinacy and Rational Choice." In *Rational Interaction: Essays in Honor of John C. Harsanyi*, edited by Reinhard Selten. Berlin: Springer-Verlag.

———. 1995. *One for All: The Logic of Group Conflict*. Princeton, N.J.: Princeton University Press.

———. 1996. "Trustworthiness." *Ethics* 107(October): 26–42.

———. 1999a. "Do We Want Trust in Government?" In *Democracy and Trust*, edited by Mark Warren. Cambridge: Cambridge University Press.

———. 1999b. "Ethics in Big Science." In *The Proceedings of the Twentieth World Congress of Philosophy*, edited by Klaus Brinkmann. Vol. 1. Bowling Green, Ohio: Philosophy Documentation Center.

———. 1999c. "Intending to Win at Chess." Paper presented at the conference, Rationality and Intentions, University of Amsterdam, 15–16 October.

———. 1999d. *Liberalism, Constitutionalism, and Democracy*. Oxford: Oxford University Press.

———. 1999e. "Social Capital." In *Competition and Cooperation: Conversations with Nobelists About Economics and Political Science*, edited by James Alt, Margaret Levi, and Elinor Ostrom. New York: Russell Sage Foundation.

———. 2000a. "Law and Social Norms in the Large." *University of Virginia Law Review* 86: 1821–37.

———. 2000b. "The Public Trust." In *Disaffected Democracies: What's Troubling the Trilateral Democracies*, edited by Susan J. Pharr and Robert D. Putnam. Princeton, N.J.: Princeton University Press.

———. 2001. "The Normative Core of Rational Choice Theory." In *The Economic World View: Studies in the Ontology of Economics*, edited by Uskali Maki. Cambridge: Cambridge University Press.

———. In press a. "Gaming Trust." In *Trust and Reciprocity: Interdisciplinary Lessons from Experimental Research*, edited by Elinor Ostrom and James Walker. New York: Russell Sage Foundation.

———. In press b. *Indeterminacy and Society*. Princeton, N.J.: Princeton University Press.

Hart, H. L. A. 1961. *The Concept of Law*. Oxford: Oxford University Press.

Heimer, Carol. 2001. "Solving the Problem of Trust." In *Trust in Society*, edited by Karen S. Cook. New York: Russell Sage Foundation.

Held, Virginia. 1968. "On the Meaning of Trust." *Ethics* 78(January): 156–59.

———. 1984. *Rights and Goods: Justifying Social Action*. New York: Free Press.

Hertzberg, Lars. 1988. "On the Attitude of Trust." *Inquiry* 31: 307–22.

Hirsch, Fred. 1978. *Social Limits to Growth*. Cambridge, Mass.: Harvard University Press.

Hobbes, Thomas. 1968 [1651]. *Leviathan*. Harmondsworth, England: Penguin.

Holan, Frank. 1997. Letter to the editor. *New Yorker*, 19 May, 10.

Holloway, Marguerite, and Paul Wallich. 1992. "A Risk Worth Taking." *Scientific American*, November: 126.

Holmes, John G. 1991. "Trust and the Appraisal Process in Close Relationships." In *Advances in Personal Relationships*, edited by Warren H. Jones and Daniel Perlman. Vol. 2. London: Jessica Kingsley.

Homans, George Caspar. 1974. *Social Behavior: Its Elementary Forms*. Revised ed. New York: Harcourt Brace Jovanovich.

Horsburgh, H. J. N. 1960. "The Ethics of Trust." *Philosophical Quarterly* 10: 343–54.

Hume, David. 1978 [1739–40]. *A Treatise of Human Nature*. Edited by L. A. Selby-Bigge and P. H. Nidditch. Oxford: Oxford University Press.

———. 1985. *Essays Moral, Political, and Literary*. Edited by Eugene Miller. Indianapolis: Liberty.

Ishiguro, Kazuo. 1990. *The Remains of the Day*. New York: Vintage.

Jones, Edward E. 1979. "The Rocky Road from Acts to Dispositions." *American Psychologist* 34: 107–17.

Jones, Karen. 1996. "Trust as an Affective Attitude." *Ethics* 107: 4–25.

Kaiser, Jocelyn. 1999. "ORI Report Tracks Gun-Shy Feds." *Science,* 7 May: 901.

Kant, Immanuel. 1909. "On a Supposed Right to Tell Lies from Benevolent Motives." 1797. In *Kant's "Critique of Practical Reason" and Other Works on the Theory of Ethics,* edited and translated by Thomas Kingsmill Abbott. 6th ed. London: Longman's.

Knight, Jack. 1992. *Institutions and Social Conflict.* Cambridge: Cambridge University Press.

Kramer, Roderick M. 1994. "The Sinister Attribution Error: Paranoid Cognition and Collective Distrust in Organizations." *Motivation and Emotion* 18(2): 199–230.

———. 1998. "Paranoid Cognition in Social Systems: Thinking and Acting in the Shadow of Doubt." *Personality and Social Psychology Review* 2: 251–75.

Kreps, David. 1990. "Corporate Structure and Economic Theory." In *Perspectives on Positive Political Economy,* edited by James Alt and Kenneth Shepsle. Cambridge: Cambridge University Press.

Lawler, Andrew. 1997. "Government Bows Out of Academy Case." *Science,* 3 October: 28.

Ledyard, John O. 1995. "Public Goods: A Survey of Experimental Research." In *Handbook of Experimental Economics,* edited by Al Roth and John Kagel. Princeton, N.J.: Princeton University Press.

Leijonhufvud, Axel. 1995. "The Individual, the Market, and the Industrial Division of Labor." In *L'Individuo e il mercato,* edited by Carlo Mongardini. Rome: Bulzoi.

Levi, Margaret. 1997. *Consent, Dissent, and Patriotism.* New York: Cambridge University Press.

Lin, Ann Chih. 2000. *Reform in the Making: The Implementation of Social Policy in Prison.* Princeton, N.J.: Princeton University Press.

Locke, John. 1955 [1689]. *A Letter Concerning Toleration.* 2d ed. Indianapolis: Bobbs-Merrill.

———. 1988 [1690]. *Two Treatises of Government.* Edited by Peter Laslett. Student edition. Cambridge: Cambridge University Press.

Luhmann, Niklas. 1980. *Trust: A Mechanism for the Reduction of Social Complexity,* in *Trust and Power.* New York: Wiley.

———. 1988. "Familiarity, Confidence, Trust: Problems and Alternatives." In *Trust: Making and Breaking Cooperative Relations,* edited by Diego Gambetta. Oxford: Blackwell.

Macauley, Stewart. 1963. "Non-Contractual Relations in Business: A Preliminary Study." *American Sociological Review* 28(February): 55–67.

Macneil, Ian R. 1980. *The New Social Contract: An Inquiry into Modern Contractual Relations.* New Haven: Yale University Press.

Madison, James. 1961 [1788]. *Federalist,* no. 51. In *The Federalist Papers,* edited by Clinton Rossiter. New York: New American Library.

Mansbridge, Jane J. 1999. "Altruistic Trust." In *Democracy and Trust,* edited by Mark Warren. Cambridge: Cambridge University Press.

Margolis, Howard. 1982. *Selfishness, Altruism, and Rationality: A Theory of Social Choice.* Cambridge: Cambridge University Press.

Marshall, Eliot. 2000. "How Prevalent Is Fraud? That's a Million-Dollar Question." *Science,* 1 December, 1662–63.

McCabe, Kevin, and Vernon Smith. In press. "How Game Structure Affects Reciprocity and Trust." In *Trust and Reciprocity: Interdisciplinary Lessons from Experimental Research,* edited by Elinor Ostrom and James Walker. New York: Russell Sage Foundation.

McClennen, Edward. 1990. *Rationality and Dynamic Choice: Foundational Explorations.* Cambridge: Cambridge University Press.

McKean, Roland N. 1975. "Economics of Trust, Altruism, and Corporate Responsibility." In *Altruism, Morality, and Economic Theory,* edited by Edmund S. Phelps. New York: Russell Sage Foundation.

Melville, Herman. 1984. "Bartelby, the Scrivener." In *Melville: Pierre, Israel Potter, The Piazza Tales, The Confidence-Man, Uncollected Prose, Billy Budd,* edited by Harrison Hayford. New York: Library of America.

Merton, Robert K. 1946. *Mass Persuasion: The Social Psychology of a War Bond Drive.* New York: Harper and Row.

———. 1968. *Social Theory and Social Structure.* 1949. Enlarged ed. New York: Free Press.

Meyerson, Debra, Karl E. Weick, and Roderick M. Kramer. 1996. "Swift Trust and Temporary Groups." In *Trust in Organizations: Frontiers of Theory and Research,* edited by Roderick M. Kramer and Tom R. Tyler. Thousand Oaks, Calif.: Sage.

Milgrom, Paul, Douglass North, and Barry Weingast. 1990. "The Role of Institutions in the Revival of Trade: The Law Merchant, Private Judges, and the Champagne Fairs." *Economics and Politics* 2: 1–23.

Mill, John Stuart. 1977. "De Tocqueville on Democracy in America, Part 2." In *Essays on Politics and Society,* edited by J. M. Robson, volume 18 of *Collected Works of John Stuart Mill.* Toronto: University of Toronto Press.

Mueller, John. 1999. *Capitalism, Democracy, and Ralph's Pretty Good Grocery.* Princeton, N.J.: Princeton University Press.

Murasaki, Shikibu. 1976. *The Tale of Genji.* 11th century. Translated by Edward G. Seidensticker. New York: Knopf.

———. 1982. *Murasaki Shikibu: Her Diary and Poetic Memoirs.* Translated by Richard Bowring. 11th century. Princeton, N.J.: Princeton University Press.

Nagel, Thomas. 1998. "Concealment and Exposure." *Philosophy and Public Affairs* 27: 3–30.

Neuman, W. Russell. 1986. *The Paradox of Mass Politics: Knowledge and Opinion in the American Electorate.* Cambridge, Mass.: Harvard University Press.

Nisbett, Richard, and Dov Cohen. 1996. *Culture of Honor.* Boulder: Westview.

North, Douglass. 1990. *Institutions, Institutional Change, and Economic Performance.* Cambridge: Cambridge University Press.

Nyberg, David. 1993. *The Varnished Truth: Truth Telling and Deceiving in Ordinary Life.* Chicago: University of Chicago Press.

Olson, Mancur, Jr. 1965. *The Logic of Collective Action.* Cambridge, Mass.: Harvard University Press.

Pagden, Anthony. 1988. "The Destruction of Trust and Its Economic Consequences in the Case of Eighteenth-Century Naples." In *Trust: Making and Breaking Cooperative Relations*, edited by Diego Gambetta. Oxford: Blackwell.

Pateman, Carole. 1988. *The Sexual Contract*. Stanford, Calif.: Stanford University Press.

Patterson, Orlando. 1999. "Liberty Against the Democratic State: On the Historical and Contemporary Sources of American Distrust." In *Democracy and Trust*, edited by Mark Warren. Cambridge: Cambridge University Press.

Peel, Mark. 1998. "Trusting Disadvantaged Citizens." In *Trust and Governance*, edited by Valerie Braithwaite and Margaret Levi. New York: Russell Sage Foundation.

Peirce, Charles. 1935. *Scientific Metaphysics*. Volume 6 of *Collected Papers of Charles Sanders Peirce*, edited by Charles Hartshorne and Paul Weiss. Cambridge, Mass.: Harvard University Press.

Pharr, Susan J., and Robert D. Putnam, eds. 2000. *Disaffected Democracies: What's Troubling the Trilateral Democracies*. Princeton, N.J.: Princeton University Press

Portes, Alejandro, and Julia Sensenbrenner. 1993. "Embeddedness and Immigration: Notes on the Social Determinants of Economic Action." *American Journal of Sociology* 98(May): 1320–50.

"Post-traumatic Stress: Part 2." 1991. *Harvard Mental Health Letter* 7(9): 1–4.

Putnam, Robert D. 1993. *Making Democracy Work: Civic Traditions in Modern Italy*. Princeton, N.J.: Princeton University Press.

———. 1995a. "Bowling Alone: America's Declining Social Capital." *Journal of Democracy* 6(January): 65–78.

———. 1995b. "Tuning In, Tuning Out: The Strange Disappearance of Social Capital in America." *PS: Political Science and Politics* (27): 664–83.

———. 2000. *Bowling Alone: The Collapse and Revival of American Community*. New York: Simon & Schuster.

Quirk, Paul. 1990. "Deregulation and the Politics of Ideas in Congress." In *Beyond Self-Interest*, edited by Jane J. Mansbridge. Chicago: University of Chicago Press.

Rawls, John. 1971. *A Theory of Justice*. 2d ed. Cambridge, Mass.: Harvard University Press.

Rempel, J. K. 1987. *Trust and Attributions in Close Relationships*. Ph.D. diss., University of Waterloo, Ontario.

Rotter, Julian B. 1980. "Interpersonal Trust, Trustworthiness, and Gullibility." *American Psychologist* 35: 1–7.

Rousseau, Denise M. 1995. *Psychological Contracts in Organizations: Understanding Written and Unwritten Agreements*. Thousand Oaks, Calif.: Sage.

Scanzoni, John. 1979. "Social Exchange and Behavioral Interdependence." In *Social Exchange in Developing Relationships*, edited by R. L. Burgess and T. L. Huston. New York: Academic.

Schelling, Thomas C. 1960. *The Strategy of Conflict*. Cambridge, Mass.: Harvard University Press.

———. 1984. *Choice and Consequence: Perspectives of an Errant Economist*. Cambridge, Mass.: Harvard University Press.

———. 1989. "Promises." *Negotiation Journal* 5: 113–18.

Scholem, Gershom. 1973. *The Sabbatai Sevi*. Princeton, N.J.: Princeton University Press.

Schuessler, Alexander A. 2000. *A Logic of Expressive Choice*. Princeton, N.J.: Princeton University Press.

Schwartz, Barry. 1986. *The Battle for Human Nature*. New York: Norton.

Scott, James C. 1976. *The Moral Economy of the Peasant: Rebellion and Subsistence in Southeast Asia*. New Haven: Yale University Press.

Scott, John Finley. 1971. *Internalization of Norms: A Sociological Theory of Moral Commitment*. Englewood Cliffs, N.J.: Prentice-Hall.

Seligman, Adam B. 1997. *The Problem of Trust*. Princeton, N.J.: Princeton University Press.

Shklar, Judith N. 1984. "The Ambiguities of Betrayal." In *Ordinary Vices*. Cambridge, Mass.: Harvard University Press.

Simmel, Georg. 1950. *The Sociology of Georg Simmel*. Edited by Kurt H. Wolff. New York: Free Press.

Skyrms, Brian. 1996. *Evolution of the Social Contract*. Cambridge: Cambridge University Press.

Stewart, Frank Henderson. 1994. *Honor*. Chicago: University of Chicago Press.

Stinchcombe, Arthur L. 1968. *Constructing Social Theories*. New York: Harcourt, Brace.

Stouffer, Samuel A., Arthur M. Lumsdaine, Marion Harper Lumsdaine, Robin M. Williams Jr., M. Brewster Smith, Irving L. Janis, Shirley A. Star, and Leonard S. Cottrell, Jr. 1949. *The American Soldier: Adjusting During Army Life*. Volume 2 of *Studies in Social Psychology in World War II*. Princeton, N.J.: Princeton University Press.

Swinth, Robert L. 1967. "The Establishment of the Trust Relationship." *American Psychologist* 35: 1–7.

Sztompka, Piotr. 1996. "Trust and Emerging Democracy." *International Sociology* 11(March): 37–62.

———. 1999. *Trust: A Sociological Theory*. Cambridge: Cambridge University Press.

Tedlow, Richard S. 1990. *New and Improved: The Story of Mass Marketing in America*. New York: Basic Books.

Tocqueville, Alexis de. 1955 [1856]. *The Old Regime and the French Revolution*. Translated by Stuart Gilbert. Garden City, N.Y.: Doubleday.

———. 1966. *Democracy in America*. 1835 and 1840. Translated by George Lawrence. New York: Harper and Row.

Tolstoy, Leo. 1949. *Anna Karenina*. 1875–77. Translated by Louise and Aylmer Maude. Oxford: Oxford University Press.

Tribe, Laurence H. 1990. *Abortion: The Clash of Absolutes*. New York: Norton.

Wagner, Richard. 1887. *Lohengrin*. Leipzig: Breitkopf and Härtel.

———. 1977. *Das Rheingold*. In *The Ring of the Nibelung*, translated by Andrew Porter. New York: Norton.

Warren, Mark E. 1999. "Democratic Theory and Trust." In *Democracy and Trust*, edited by Mark Warren. Cambridge: Cambridge University Press.

Weber, Max. 1951. *The Religion of China: Confucianism and Taoism*. Glencoe, Ill.: Free Press.

———. 1981. *General Economic History*. Translated by Frank H. Knight. New Brunswick, N.J.: Transaction.

Westacott, George H., and Lawrence K. Williams. 1976. "Interpersonal Trust and Modern Attitudes in Peru." *International Journal of Contemporary Society* 13: 117–37.

Williams, Bernard. 1988. "Formal Structures and Social Reality." In *Trust: Making and Breaking Cooperative Relations*, edited by Diego Gambetta. Oxford: Blackwell.

Williamson, Oliver. 1993. "Calculativeness, Trust, and Economic Organization." *Journal of Law and Economics* 36(April): 453–86.

Wittgenstein, Ludwig. 1969. *On Certainty*. Translated by Denis Paul and G. E. M. Anscombe. New York: Harper and Row.

Woolf, Virginia. 1938. *To the Lighthouse*. London: Everyman's Library.

Yamagishi, Toshio. 1998. *The Structure of Trust: The Evolutionary Game of Mind and Society*. Tokyo: University of Tokyo Press.

———. 2000. "Trust as a Form of Social Intelligence." In *Trust in Society*. New York: Russell Sage Foundation.

Yamagishi, Toshio, Karen Cook, and Motoki Watabe. 1998. "Uncertainty, Trust, and Commitment Formation." *American Journal of Sociology* 104: 165–94.

Yamagishi, Toshio, and Midori Yamagishi. 1994. "Trust and Commitment in the United States and Japan." *Motivation and Emotion* 18: 129–66.

Yeats, William Butler. 1956. "The Second Coming." In *The Collected Poems of W. B. Yeats*. New York: Macmillan.

Yunus, Muhammad. 1998. "Alleviating Poverty Through Technology." *Science* (October): 409–10.

———. 1999. *Banker to the Poor: Micro-Lending and the Battle Against World Poverty*. New York: Public Affairs.

Zandonella, Catherine. 2001. "Is It All Just a Pipe Dream?" *Nature* (April): 734–35.

Index

WITHDRAWN